HYPERTEXT
A Psychological Perspective

ELLIS HORWOOD SERIES IN INTERACTIVE INFORMATION SYSTEMS

General Editor: V. A. J. MALLER, ICL Professor of Computer Systems, Loughborough University of Technology; formerly Technical Director, Thorn EMI Information Technology Ltd
Consulting Editors: Dr JOHN M. M. PINKERTON, Information Technology Consultant, J & H Pinkerton Associates, and formerly Manager of Strategic Requirements, International Computers Limited; and PATRICK HOLLIGAN, Department of Computer Science, Loughborough University of Technology

C. Baber	**SPEECH TECHNOLOGY IN CONTROL ROOM SYSTEMS: A Human Factors Perspective**
E. Balagurusamy & J.A.M. Howe	**EXPERT SYSTEMS FOR MANAGEMENT AND ENGINEERING**
R. Barber	**BONES: An Expert System for Diagnosis with Fault Models**
M. Barrett & A.C. Beerel	**EXPERT SYSTEMS IN BUSINESS: A Practical Approach**
M. Becker, R. Haberfellner & G. Liebetrau	**ELECTRONIC DATA PROCESSING IN PRACTICE: A Handbook for Users**
A.C. Beerel	**EXPERT SYSTEMS: Real World Applications**
D. Berkeley, R. de Hoog & P. Humphreys	**SOFTWARE DEVELOPMENT PROJECT MANAGEMENT: Process and Support**
A.C. Bradley	**OPTICAL STORAGE FOR COMPUTERS: Technology and Applications**
R. Bright	**SMART CARDS: Principles, Practice and Applications**
D. Clarke & U. Magnusson-Murray	**PRACTICAL MACHINE TRANSLATION**
V. Claus & A. Schwill	**ENCYCLOPAEDIA OF INFORMATION TECHNOLOGY**
D. Cleal & N.O. Heaton	**KNOWLEDGE-BASED SYSTEMS: Implications for Human–Computer Interfaces**
C. Clegg *et al.*	**PEOPLE AND COMPUTERS: How to Evaluate your Company's New Technology**
T. Daler, *et al.*	**SECURITY OF INFORMATION AND DATA**
D. Diaper	**KNOWLEDGE ELICITATION: Principles, Techniques and Applications**
D. Diaper	**TASK ANALYSIS FOR HUMAN–COMPUTER INTERACTION**
G.I. Doukidis, F. Land & G. Miller	**KNOWLEDGE-BASED MANAGEMENT SUPPORT SYSTEMS**
C. Ellis	**EXPERT KNOWLEDGE AND EXPLANATION: The Knowledge–Language Interface**
J. Einbu	**A PROGRAM ARCHITECTURE FOR IMPROVED MAINTAINABILITY IN SOFTWARE ENGINEERING**
A. Fourcin, G. Harland, W. Barry & V. Hazan	**SPEECH INPUT AND OUTPUT ASSESSMENT: Multilingual Methods and Standards**
M. Greenwell	**KNOWLEDGE ENGINEERING FOR EXPERT SYSTEMS**
N. Heaton & L.W. MacDonald	**HUMAN FACTORS IN INFORMATION TECHNOLOGY PRODUCT DESIGN AND DEVELOPMENT**
F.R. Hickman *et al.*	**ANALYSIS FOR KNOWLEDGE-BASED SYSTEMS: A Practical Guide to the KADS Methodology**
P. Hills	**INFORMATION MANAGEMENT SYSTEMS: Implications for the Human–Computer Interface**
E. Hollnagel	**THE RELIABILITY OF EXPERT SYSTEMS**
R. Kerry	**INTEGRATING KNOWLEDGE-BASED AND DATABASE MANAGEMENT SYSTEMS**
K. Koskimies & J. Paakki	**AUTOMATING LANGUAGE IMPLEMENTATION**
B. Lazzerini & L. Lopriore	**PROGRAM DEBUGGING ENVIRONMENTS: Design and Utilization**
F. Long	**SOFTWARE ENGINEERING ENVIRONMENTS: Volume 3**
K.L. McGraw	**DESIGNING AND EVALUATING USER INTERFACES FOR KNOWLEDGE-BASED SYSTEMS**
C. McKnight, A. Dillon & J. Richardson	**HYPERTEXT: A Psychological Perspective**
M. McTear & T. Anderson	**UNDERSTANDING KNOWLEDGE ENGINEERING**
W. Meyer	**EXPERT SYSTEMS IN FACTORY MANAGEMENT: Knowledge-based CIM**
A. Mili, N. Boudriga & F. Mili	**TOWARDS STRUCTURED SPECIFYING: Theory, Practice, Applications**
J.M.M. Pinkerton	**UNDERSTANDING INFORMATION TECHNOLOGY: Basic Terminology and Practice**
S. Pollitt	**INFORMATION STORAGE AND RETRIEVAL SYSTEMS: Origin, Development and Applications**
C.J. Price	**KNOWLEDGE ENGINEERING TOOLKITS**
P. Quintas	**SOCIAL DIMENSIONS OF SOFTWARE ENGINEERING**
S. Ravden & G. Johnson	**EVALUATING USABILITY OF HUMAN–COMPUTER INTERFACES: A Practical Method**
S. Savory	**EXPERT SYSTEMS FOR THE PROFESSIONAL**
P.E. Slatter	**BUILDING EXPERT SYSTEMS: Cognitive Emulation**
H.T. Smith, J. Onions & S. Benford	**DISTRIBUTED GROUP COMMUNICATION: The AMIGO Information Model**
H.M. Sneed	**SOFTWARE ENGINEERING MANAGEMENT**
R. Stutely	**ADVANCED DESKTOP PUBLISHING: A Practical Guide to Ventura Version 2 and the Professional Extension**
D. van Laar & R. Flavell	**HUMAN FACTORS IN COLOUR DISPLAYS: Principles for Effective Design**
J.A. Waterworth	**MULTIMEDIA: Technology and Applications**
J.A. Waterworth	**MULTIMEDIA INTERACTION WITH COMPUTERS Human Factors Issues**
J.A. Waterworth & M. Talbot	**SPEECH AND LANGUAGE-BASED COMMUNICATION WITH MACHINES: Towards the Conversational Computer**
R.J. Whiddett	**THE IMPLEMENTATION OF SMALL COMPUTER SYSTEMS**

HYPERTEXT
A Psychological Perspective

Editors:
C. McKNIGHT, A. DILLON, and J. RICHARDSON
HUSAT Research Institute, Loughborough University

ELLIS HORWOOD
NEW YORK   LONDON   TORONTO   SYDNEY   TOKYO   SINGAPORE

First published in 1993 by
ELLIS HORWOOD LIMITED
Market Cross House, Cooper Street,
Chichester, West Sussex, PO19 1EB, England
A division of
Simon & Schuster International Group

Printed and bound in Great Britain
by Bookcraft, Midsomer Norton

British Library Cataloguing in Publication Data

A catalogue record for this book is available from the British Library

ISBN 0–13–441650–3
     0–13–441643–0   Pbk

Library of Congress Cataloging-in-Publication Data

Available from the publisher

Table of Contents

1

Why Psychology?

Cliff McKnight, Andrew Dillon and John Richardson
HUSAT Research Institute, Loughborough University, UK

INTRODUCTION

The design and analysis of hypertext, like many modern fields, represents the coming together of several disciplines. Although the ideas underlying hypertext have been around for many years, the current implementations rely heavily on computer technology. Consequently, many computer scientists have been involved in the rise of hypertext. Without computer scientists such as Peter Brown at the University of Kent, hypertext systems such as Guide would not exist.

Similarly, to the extent that hypertext is an information vehicle it has formed a focus of interest for information scientists. The storage, processing, transmission and retrieval of information is naturally their concern and hypertext offers novel approaches to the 'traditional' computer-based information handling. The journal *Hypermedia* was conceived and brought to life in the Information Science department of Strathclyde University.

The present book, however, concentrates on neither of these important aspects of computer science and information science. Instead, we have chosen to offer a psychological perspective on hypertext for several reasons. Firstly, as psychologists we are most concerned with the human aspects of hypertext use. As even non-psychologists have occasionally noted, psychological problems are often more responsible for the failure of effective system use than technical problems.

Although psychology has always been one of the three major fields with a 'stake' in hypertext, this interest has often been manifested through the applied field of human-computer interaction (HCI) or human factors. The ergonomic approach is too often limited in terms of its theoretical work. By its nature, it is concerned more with practical design problems and their solutions, only pulling in relevant psychological theories when needed.

Another of our motives, therefore, in assembling the present book was to flesh this approach out and illustrate some of the more fundamental psychological considerations underlying hypertext design and use. We have adopted this course not only because we believe that psychology has something to offer hypertext but also that hypertext offers a rich area for the exploration of psychological theory. Indeed, as Patricia Wright points out in Chapter 6, hypertext offers some truly unique opportunities for psychologists.

In talking about the psychology of hypertext we are really referring to the psychology of the human engaging a technology, both as a provider and user of the information it contains. Thus we are looking at the human as reader and writer, educator and learner, information builder and navigator, designer and user, scientist and subject. Put simply, a wide range of human attributes and activities are analysed and discussed whenever we examine an application such as hypertext from a psychological perspective.

Our primary aim, therefore, is to provoke an increased concern with the psychological aspects of hypertext and we have chosen to do this by providing examples of work by prominent psychologists within the field. We did not attempt to force our contributors into a particular mould and hence the chapters conform to no set pattern other than a concern with hypertext from a psychological perspective. However, we believe that — modesty notwithstanding! — all offer something of interest to anyone concerned with the presentation and usage of information.

HYPERTEXT AND PSYCHOLOGY: MAJOR THEMES

Since hypertext is an information vehicle, it is not surprising that many of its applications have been in one of the traditional information providing industries — that of education. Hypertext, with its emphasis on non-linear text, exploration and freedom of access, represents for many people (rightly or wrongly) a 'liberation technology' for pedagogy from the prescriptive behaviourist models of early CAL. Hence, it should also come as no surprise that several of the chapters also centre on educational issues within hypertext design and use. Perhaps what might be surprising to those not aware of the diversity of psychological approaches is the lack of similarity between the various education-related chapters.

Peter Whalley has been involved in the study of information use for many years and is a faculty member of the Institute of Educational Technology at the Open University. He shows what we regard as a healthy scepticism for the many claims made for hypertext, particularly with regard to its potential pedagogical impact. In his chapter Peter succinctly argues for an alternative rhetoric for hypertext — a learner-centred rhetoric, through which he explores the positive rôle which hypertext could play in teaching.

Donald Cunningham, Tom Duffy and Randy Knuth are also concerned with fundamental pedagogical principles. From a constructivist point of view, they consider the limited rôle of the textbook and the potentially much wider opportunities for hypertext as a mediator in the learning process. Their views have implications which extend far beyond the design of educational material to the design of education — and thereby society — itself. In the same way that Seymour Papert felt that the purpose of education needed to change before the true benefit of computer-controlled microworlds could be seen (Papert, 1980), so these authors suggest that measuring the *amount* of learning is not necessarily as desirable as appreciating the *nature* of the new insights and understanding achieved by learners during the educational process. Their verbal protocol data are of particular relevance to our own chapter since they argue that, despite the support for the notion of movement within an information landscape, there is little support for the notion of navigation within the context of hypertext.

If we accept that the increased availability of 'computer-power' has enabled the development of hypertext applications, it is natural that those concerned with the rôle of the computer in education should turn their attention to hypertext. In this respect, Nick Hammond is ideally placed to comment, being the Director of the Computers in Teaching Initiative (CTI) Centre for Psychology at the University of York. Although he reviews relevant cognitive processes, he is particularly concerned with learning situations rather than individual cognitions. In this respect his emphasis on situated action and affordance can be seen as a 'new behaviourism' — as Nick has pointed out elsewhere, we know more about providing appropriate learning *environments* than we do about the cognitive *processes* involved (Hammond, 1989).

Peter Whalley's perspective emphasises the possible limitations of hypertext in learning. For him, current implementations and uses are based on a very limited view of documents and have exploited information retrieval and fragmentation rather than presentation and synthesis. Yet it is the synthesis issues that are likely to be most relevant to education. For him, hypertext should not be seen as the major presentation medium for pedagogical material but a component part of a fuller computer-based document.

This raises interesting points of definition. Can one have a computer-based document that is only part hypertext? If a hypertext contains large sections of non-fragmented text is it really hypertext? Whalley's perspective may be seen to suggest that such issues are not of central concern as we should focus first on developing learner-centred teaching materials before we worry too much about their categorisation. There is value in this, but clear definition is also a hallmark of good science.

The concern for learner-centredness is echoed in the other chapters drawn from the education field and essentially is merely a call for good user-centred design that human factors psychologists such as ourselves routinely make (e.g., McKnight, Dillon and Richardson, 1991). Cunningham, Duffy and Knuth place emphasis on the learning task just as typical ergonomists do, but what distinguishes their approach is their treatment of HCI and learning in constructivist terms. Educational psychology has often been seen as one of the remaining battlegrounds between behaviourist and cognitive approaches to psychology but these authors highlight the entry of a third force that many psychologists may find both familiar and alienating in equal measures.

Constructivism is not new (and its strongest advocates seem to take great pleasure in claiming support from any number of established sources that one might traditionally have seen as belonging in other camps) but it turns many of the assumptions of cognitive psychology upside-down without resorting to the rhetoric of 'black boxes' and 'objective observation' associated with behaviourism. In its dismissal of the validity of ideas about knowledge in the head and information processing, constructivism asks psychologists to think again about how we conceive the human learner. Whether constructivism (as a paradigm) offers explanatory possibilities not available with the mainstream approaches remains to be seen. Indeed many of the points raised by Hammond are similar in spirit to those of Cunningham, Duffy and Knuth but he manages to accommodate these within more established cognitive psychological frameworks. We are not sure there is a right or wrong answer but we would concur that the conflict of ideologies should make us all question our perspective and this must be a good thing for psychology.

A major discussion point in work on electronic documentation is the comparative superiority of hypertext over the established paper medium. The evangelical approach to hypertext has led to many claims of its superiority (see, e.g., Nelson, 1981), but to date many of the experimental comparisons of the media have failed to demonstrate any conclusive benefit. As we have pointed out elsewhere (McKnight, Dillon and Richardson, 1990), different situations call for different solutions and since a single variable explanation of differences is unlikely to be found (Dillon, McKnight and Richardson, 1988), adequate presentation rests more on good user-centred design practice than on slavish adherence to one medium.

Tom Landauer and colleagues at BellCoRe demonstrate such practice vividly in the present book. They took as their goal the development of a computer-delivered text which was at least as usable as the paper version. The SuperBook project was the concrete outcome of this goal and their chapter charts the development of the SuperBook. The concern with relative usability of paper and electronic text is one shared by many, not only in the hypertext field but in the more general field of electronic documentation. The reports of the CORE (Chemistry Online Retrieval Experiment) project in Landauer *et al.*'s chapter should therefore also be of interest to those concerned with the electronic journal.

There are several aspects of their whole approach that we should emphasise here. The first is that they tested repeatedly and refined their design, modifying it from a medium that rated worse than paper to one that matched and even surpassed it on certain tasks. If nothing else, their work must be recognised for contradicting the myth that one or other medium is inherently superior — both support some tasks with some texts better than others. Just because one design is better or worse than others does not mean that an entire medium can be described as superior or inferior. The onus is on researchers and designers to identify those appropriate to one or other medium and the design variables within the medium that influence reader performance and satisfaction.

The second point worth emphasising is the fact that in true user-centred design fashion, empirical data proved essential in refining the design. Despite a century of work on the psychology of reading there is no theory of the reader that designers can employ to develop a usable hypertext document from first principles. This is not a criticism of psychology *per se*, after all, the science base does not exist just so that designers of hypertext can better envisage their products. But it is a clear statement of the needs within design for certain types of information that currently (and maybe always) only user testing can provide. One result of this could be the realisation that applied work in psychology might be a useful source of information for theoretical work.

The chapter by Patricia Wright is an excellent illustration of this potential 'two-way traffic' — not only can psychology inform hypertext design but hypertext can also provide a useful test environment for theories in psychology and point the way forward for the development of such theories. She focuses particularly on theories of reading strategy, an area which, with a few notable exceptions, has failed to receive the consideration it perhaps deserves. Within this perspective, Wright argues that reading and information retrieval tasks in hypertext offer psychology a testing ground for theories which attempt to integrate the more fundamental cognitive processes such as memory, attention and comprehension.

Many authors trace the origins of hypertext back to a paper in 1945 written by Vannevar Bush. In this paper, Bush conceived of an information storage and retrieval system — the 'memex'. In the memex, items were associatively linked in a manner which, to Bush, paralleled the 'association of ideas' characterisation of memory. David Jonassen's chapter extends this approach by suggesting that if we could describe the semantic structure of memory, such a structure would be an ideal way of both representing and containing information in a hypertext. His chapter describes a series of studies aimed at deriving semantic structure and testing its utility in a hypertext environment. Devotees of Bush may be disappointed by the results but they raise important psychological and design implications nevertheless.

Finally, our own chapter considers the concept of navigation in hypertext. The issue is interesting not least because some researchers consider it one of the biggest problems in hypertext usage while others consider it to be a myth. We examine the concept from the perspective of schema theory and show how the various posited mental representations of physical environments offer potential insights into hypertext design. The comparison of physical and information spaces lead us to conclude however that discussion of navigation should be restricted in the hypertext context and never applied without qualification to discussions of semantic space.

Part of the problem Jonassen experiences in mapping between experts' semantic structures and hypertext documents may result from precisely the problem outlined in the final chapter — that of reducing *n*-dimensional semantic relationships to two-dimensional screen representations. Our argument is that such a mapping is superficially seductive but inherently distorting. Great care in use of terminology and design of structures is needed to exploit the linking and organisational power of the medium for purposes of knowledge representation.

Like Wright and Jonassen, we are concerned with using the theoretical constructs of psychology where relevant to help design more usable hypertexts. Furthermore, we emphasise, as Wright and Landauer *et al.* do, the importance of experimental analysis of claims about the medium. It may well be the nature of much of the field of technology design that the human sciences like psychology are left to evaluate the claims of the innovators and designers. In itself this is no bad thing; we are best equipped for formal analysis of the human implications. However, it is to be hoped that psychology can contribute more than this and support the derivation of new applications on the basis of insights and theories thrown up by the science. The SuperBook system explicitly shows this is possible, but all the chapters in the book contain much that we believe could be of use in the conception of the technology.

Although psychology is very broad and in many ways a fragmented discipline, what characterises the vast majority of it is a concern with people. We hope that the chapters in this book will provide some insights into a particular area of human activity, not only for psychologists but for others interested in people using hypertext.

REFERENCES

Bush, V. (1945) As we may think. *Atlantic Monthly*, 176/1, July, 101–108.

Dillon, A., McKnight, C. and Richardson, J. (1988) Reading from paper versus reading from screens. *The Computer Journal*, 31(5), 457–464.

Hammond, N. (1989) Hypermedia and learning: who guides whom? In H. Maurer (ed.) *Computer Assisted Learning*. Berlin: Springer-Verlag.

McKnight, C., Dillon, A. and Richardson, J. (1990) A comparison of linear and hypertext formats in information retrieval. In R. McAleese and C. Green (eds.) *Hypertext: State of the Art*. Oxford: Intellect.

McKnight, C., Dillon, A. and Richardson, J. (1991) *Hypertext in Context*. Cambridge: Cambridge University Press.

Nelson, T. H. (1981) *Literary Machines*. Available from the author, 8480 Fredericksburg #138, San Antonio, TX 78229, USA.

Papert, S. (1980) *Mindstorms: Children, Computers and Powerful Ideas*. Brighton: Harvester Press.

2

An Alternative Rhetoric for Hypertext

Peter Whalley
Institute of Educational Technology, The Open University, UK

OVERVIEW

A technology that will revolutionise teaching, a useful tool for education, or 'over hyped and over here'? Discussion concerning the uses and merits of *hypertext* and *hypermedia* has often tended to create more heat than light. The aim of this chapter is to examine some of the theoretical and practical problems associated with the use of hypertext as a medium for teaching, and to explore the positive rôle that it could play in teaching materials.

Hypertext is conventionally described as non-linear, and this aspect of non-linearity is taken to endow it with many attractive features. An alternative perception is that hypertext is a *fragmented* text form, and hence fundamentally flawed as an expository medium. The conventional rhetoric for hypertext is based on the limited concerns of information retrieval, and attempts to subordinate linearity in the text. However, an alternative rhetoric is possible, based on the aspect of hypertext which is most likely to aid learning, its *malleability*.

An attempt is made to distinguish between the parts that can be most usefully played by linear and non-linear elements in educational texts and the idea is developed of a more general *computer-based document* encompassing linear prose, non-linear hypertext and other 'multi-media' devices. A learner-centred rhetoric is possible for such documents in which the hypermedia play the rôle of *animateur* for the distant author.

TECHNOLOGY USING EDUCATION

An important starting point in any consideration of the hypermedia is the recognition that they were not purposefully designed for education. The principal foci of this technological drive have been the efficient retrieval of information and entertainment. These aspects of hypermedia are not necessarily antithetical to the goals of education, but equally they do not represent the primary aim of most educational texts. The general history of the use of new technologies in education has tended to reflect the search for panaceas rather than a serious attempt to solve problems. In a more general context, Ravetz (1971) describes how 'technical' problems can become confused with 'practical' problems. Technical problems always have a practical solution, but all practical problems do not necessarily have to have a technical solution. Because the creation of educational materials involves practical as well as conceptual issues, its problems can be mistakenly perceived as being of technological origin, and thus susceptible to a technical 'fix'.

What is it?

One of the great strengths of hypertext, but also a potential source of weakness, is that it is essentially a formless medium. It is quite possible to reinvent the scroll, book, frame-based CAL, and even the video recorder within hypertext systems. Whether this is a wise use of resources will depend on the user's goals, and to some extent on technological developments in terms of cost and the improved ergonomics of display-screen technologies. It is difficult to attempt a formal definition of such an evolving medium, but the basic features identified by Conklin (1987) of machine-supported links between blocks of text, and some measure of interaction by the reader would represent an adequate working definition of hypertext. In the context of this chapter, hypertext is best viewed as a fragmented text form whose components can be rapidly accessed.

A graphic element must also be assumed in addition to natural language. As technological developments occur, the present hypertext-hypermedia distinction is likely to blur as 'hypertext' incorporates an ever-larger graphic component of animation, simulation and video forms. A similar confusion has existed for some time in conventional printed works in that, whilst the term 'text' can formally only refer to the written word, few 'textbooks' would now be considered complete without a large graphic element. In addition, the hypertext medium itself has generally been found to require an extra, graphic 'navigational' level to help the reader move about and locate information.

LINEARITY IN TEXT

Kommers defines hypertext as "a method for browsing through extended text bases" (1990, p.1). The basic assumption underlying 'hypertext techniques' being that large texts can be parsed into "self-contained paragraphs which can be read and interpreted independently". The concerns of the developers of hypertext systems have always been primarily focused on information retrieval rather than learning, and the computer was quickly recognised to be the ideal tool for traversing such dispersed fragments of text. The question addressed in this section is whether it is a good idea to deliberately fragment educational materials in order to make them more accessible to 'browsing' in this fashion, and the following section questions the status of browsing as a form of learning.

The myth of linearity

Hypertext is often described as being 'structured' and 'non-linear', presumably in contrast to conventional 'unstructured', 'linear' text. However it is a mistake to think of conventional texts, and particularly expository teaching texts, as being purely linear. The skilful author may use the linear text form to weave an entirely non-linear pattern of associations in the reader's mind. Text linguists such as Grimes (1975) and de Beaugrande (1980) have shown how under a superficially linear form, authors may create complex relational structures. Figure 1 shows de Beaugrande's analysis of linearity in diagrammatic form, and it can be seen to be very involved.

It could even be argued that the simple pointer and hierarchical structures provided in hypertext are semantically more limiting than the complex implicit relationships created in conventional materials. Distance-teaching texts may encompass a whole academic year's worth of study, and are conceived of by their authors and readers as being 'tutorials in print' (Rowntree, 1986). These texts may properly only be described in terms of Grimes' *staging* metaphor where cycles of ideas are repeated and overlaid upon each other — for example, a central theme being repeated within progressively more complex contexts.

A line of argument will almost certainly make up more than a single paragraph. To reduce the presentation of text to the paragraph, or an arbitrary small number of paragraphs, is to make it more difficult to present a coherent view. However, the alternative of creating the 'electronic scroll', as has happened in many hypertext systems, is to completely defeat the ergonomic gains of rapid component access.

Designing prose

Nash discusses the idea of 'designing' prose, where "the paragraph functions as a viewfinder, freely used to define the groupings and transitions of a compositional design" (1980, p.8). He writes of a "free and unending play of possibilities", where "the writer may frame a dominant motif spanning a number of subordinate details, or may perhaps outline a sequence of related propositions". In direct contrast to the assumption that Kommers shows to underlie hypertext, Nash writes that paragraphs should be thought of as "units in developing discourse", and that it is "a mistake to think of them as self-contained units, the 'building blocks' of text". To dispense with paragraph structure is to lose one of the most important techniques of composition available to the writer, and means that hypertext is only likely to be suited to encyclopaedic or fragmented forms of knowledge. Equally when left without Nash's 'viewfinder' upon the author's rhetorical structure, the reader may feel lost in a maze of over-connected facts.

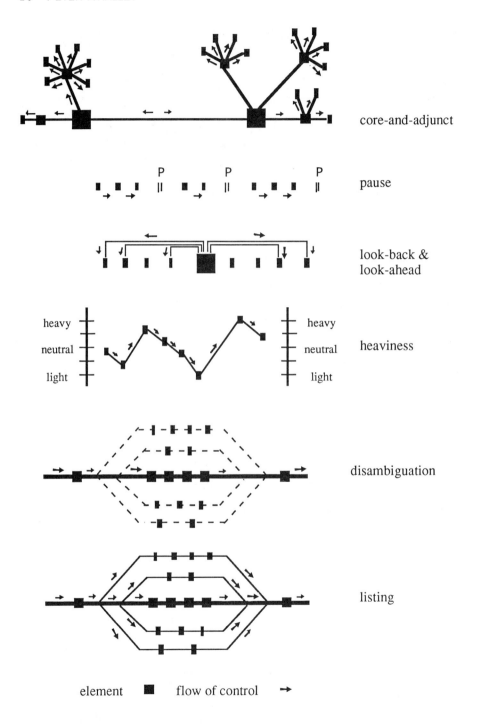

core-and-adjunct

pause

look-back &
look-ahead

heaviness

disambiguation

listing

element ■   flow of control ➜

Figure 1: de Beaugrande's seven principles of linearity (redrawn from de Beaugrande, 1980).

Van Dijk (1979) has developed an analysis of the way that linguistic and graphical cues can be used to assign the relative relevance of parts of a text. Within his framework it is possible to identify several levels where hypertext can make an original contribution, but it is important to note that such explicit cues will never be the only, or necessarily the most important, forms of non-linearity and argument structuring within a text. A direct consequence of the fragmentation effect in hypertext is that it is likely to make it more difficult for the learner to perceive the author's intended argument structure — unless certain linearity constraints are imposed on the hypertext form. For example it may be necessary to impose a certain ordering of concepts until some critical point is reached.

Text types

Where text is conceived of as a 'database of facts', then hypertext obviously provides an efficient technology for their acquisition and manipulation. However, where text is taken to express a 'configuration of ideas' and to "represent a vehicle of purposeful interaction between the writer and the reader" (de Beaugrande and Dressler, 1981), then other criteria must apply. Nash describes the organising principles underlying the creation of discursive or expository prose as the complex operation of *expounding*:

> There is a programme of assertions, examples, qualifications, but these are not presented as a series of distinctly labelled positions. Instead, they are related to each other in a progressive unfolding pattern, the turns and connections of which are demonstrated in various ways. (1980, p. 6)

It is possible to imagine a 'dimension' of text types ranging from *text as database*, where the reader has complete control, to *text as argument*, where the author guides the reader's study. This dimension is also described by the length of cohesive reference within the text, the longer the referential links the more the author's argument controls the reader.

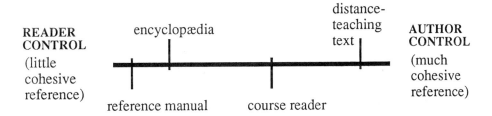

Figure 2: A dimension of text types.

The amorphous 'links' provided by hypertext do not provide any true cohesive reference. If everything is related to everything then essentially no cohesion is provided. It is only by *selective* application of the reference devices that the author turns a pile of facts into something interesting, an organised text. And to the extent that the cohesive reference is selective, the text is linear.

Malleability

The conventional rhetoric for hypertext is based on the idea of subordinating linearity, in that links and hierarchies become the main structural representation that is presented to the reader. Clearly any computer-based text form is bound to be implemented in terms of the basic computing elements of lists and pointers. The question is whether these basic structures have to be made so dominantly apparent in their raw form. The simple use of these devices stems from the limited original concerns of the designers of hypertext systems, i.e. with information retrieval rather than learning. If it was wished to devise a rhetoric for a general computer-based document intended to support learning, then the emphasis would be quite different. The most significant pedagogic feature of hypertext is its *malleability*: it may change over time and it is capable of offering multiple perspectives on a particular domain. It is possible to use hypertext to present, and then represent, ideas in ways that are difficult to achieve in print.

Examples of hypertexts based on such a learner-centred rhetoric have existed for some time, but are now beginning to be more purposefully developed. Some of the ideas that are possible can be seen in an experimental hypertext devised by the author to facilitate a 'compare and contrast' exercise (see Figure 3). The operation of the hypertext is based on the notion of *views* and *modes*, and the nature of the learning task is apparent in the structure of the hypertext. The sub-heading structure remains constant whilst the contrasted topics are aligned against it. Switching modes allows the same operation to be made, but at a higher level of abstraction. This text corpus has been widely used in experimental studies concerned with learning from prose, e.g., Schnotz (1982), Waller and Whalley (1987) and Mandl *et al.* (1991), and it is important to note that the paragraphs were written, or at least rewritten, to be able to stand alone. Whilst this makes graphic and hypertext versions of the texts possible, it is quite noticeable (cf. Nash's argument detailed earlier) that this has the effect of making them rather boring to read as prose, as there is no use of the connectives to link the ideas between paragraphs. Physical juxtaposition is one way to make conceptual relations, but it lacks the subtlety of the many linguistic devices possible.

Samarapungavan and Beishuizen (1990) describe a much larger hypertext based on similar ideas. Their system takes an introductory psychology text and allows the reader to view the content from four different *perspectives* provided by a higher-level map structure. It is in developing systems such as this that the positive future for hypertext lies.

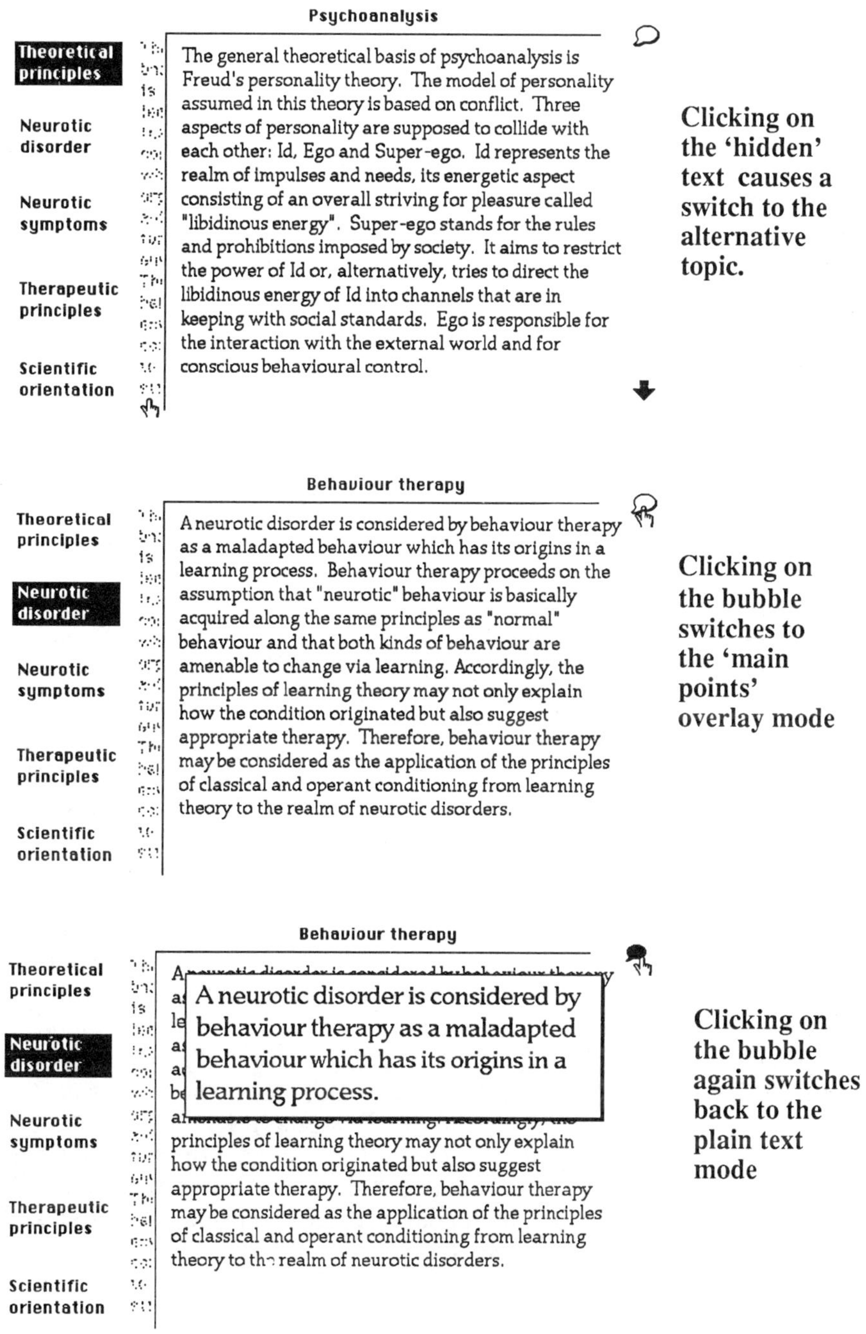

Psychoanalysis

Theoretical principles

The general theoretical basis of psychoanalysis is Freud's personality theory. The model of personality assumed in this theory is based on conflict. Three aspects of personality are supposed to collide with each other: Id, Ego and Super-ego. Id represents the realm of impulses and needs, its energetic aspect consisting of an overall striving for pleasure called "libidinous energy". Super-ego stands for the rules and prohibitions imposed by society. It aims to restrict the power of Id or, alternatively, tries to direct the libidinous energy of Id into channels that are in keeping with social standards. Ego is responsible for the interaction with the external world and for conscious behavioural control.

Neurotic disorder

Neurotic symptoms

Therapeutic principles

Scientific orientation

Clicking on the 'hidden' text causes a switch to the alternative topic.

Behaviour therapy

Theoretical principles

Neurotic disorder

A neurotic disorder is considered by behaviour therapy as a maladapted behaviour which has its origins in a learning process. Behaviour therapy proceeds on the assumption that "neurotic" behaviour is basically acquired along the same principles as "normal" behaviour and that both kinds of behaviour are amenable to change via learning. Accordingly, the principles of learning theory may not only explain how the condition originated but also suggest appropriate therapy. Therefore, behaviour therapy may be considered as the application of the principles of classical and operant conditioning from learning theory to the realm of neurotic disorders.

Neurotic symptoms

Therapeutic principles

Scientific orientation

Clicking on the bubble switches to the 'main points' overlay mode

Behaviour therapy

Theoretical principles

Neurotic disorder

A neurotic disorder is considered by behaviour therapy as a maladapted behaviour which has its origins in a learning process.

principles of learning theory may not only explain how the condition originated but also suggest appropriate therapy. Therefore, behaviour therapy may be considered as the application of the principles of classical and operant conditioning from learning theory to the realm of neurotic disorders.

Neurotic symptoms

Therapeutic principles

Scientific orientation

Clicking on the bubble again switches back to the plain text mode

Figure 3: A 'compare and contrast' hypertext.

LEARNING FROM HYPERTEXT

Research studies

It is clear that for some aspects of teaching, hypertext 'works'. Landow (1990) describes a large, long-term study where whole courses are studied in a networked hypertext system shared by both readers and writers. Used in this way as an environment to promote collaborative learning, and in particular collaborative writing, hypertext provides a powerful tool. However, as Landow points out, this is a special situation where "it is not important that readers may retain less information that they encounter whilst reading text from a screen rather than from print." Studies with other goals have had far less positive results.

Kommers describes several long-term studies made with large, very carefully constructed hypertexts. His results were uniformly bad in terms of using hypertext as a medium to improve learning, and particularly so for the less able pupils. His logged interaction data shows how browsing can easily become an activity where students can 'fail to see the wood for the trees'. Kommers writes that:

> students need extra guidance before they know how to utilise hypertext facilities. The data retrieval and data modification tools used without guidance are too open to be effective while studying in the traditional school context. (1990, p. 203)

Whilst Samarapungavan and Beishuizen (1990) using their multiple perspective hypertext found no difference in the amount of factual knowledge learnt by students using their system, they did find evidence in terms of higher-level 'reasoning' questions. Interestingly though, they note that the improved learning may not be due to linear versus non-linear aspects of their text *per se*, but might result from additional information in the graphically organised 'map' provided as an access structure in the non-linear condition. Such high-level abstractions are always going to be in danger of 'spoon-feeding' students with structures that they should be developing for themselves over the period of the course.

Mandl *et al.* (1991) report on a study using a different hypertext version of the 'compare and contrast' texts described earlier. Again their results showed that hypertext presentation favoured the most able students, which is directly contrary to the expectations and hopes of the early hypertext developers. Unless the entertainment/motivation factor for hypertext can be made sufficiently large to compensate, it would seem unwise to inflict it on less able readers.

General issues

Reflective critical reading requires the student to alternately suspend and then make judgements concerning the author's argument, and linear texts contain 'turn-taking' cues to encourage such activities. As has already been pointed out, a consequence of the fragmentation effect in hypertext is that it is likely to make it more difficult for the learner to perceive the author's intended argument structure, and consequently must make it more difficult to organise hypertext materials to support higher-level learning.

The most natural mode of study with hypertext would appear to be that of *browsing*. For information retrieval and certain aspects of learning this is an entirely appropriate study strategy. However, many educators would consider the browsing activity to be ill-suited to the courses that they wish to create, and the forms of learning that they wish to encourage. Where an author is trying to develop ideas within a particular context or framework, or where the student is being required to develop a deeper understanding, then browsing is likely to be inappropriate.

Writers of distance-teaching materials have always had to concern themselves with the problem of the 'over-organised' text. When attempting to create a complete 'tutorial-in-print', there is always the danger of pushing students into a passive rôle, and leaving them no room to think for themselves. A similar problem exists for writers of hypertexts. The author has noted elsewhere that:

> the *artefacts* introduced by the hypertext form, in order to improve *accessibility*, mitigate against its use as the principal teaching medium. The solutions to the problems of *navigation* and *orientation* within the hypertext genre will involve *providing* the very same high level structures that many educators would wish their students to be *creating* for themselves as active independent learners. (Whalley, 1990, p. 65)

It is necessary in the design of hypertext systems to devise structures that do not just hand over to the student a spurious form of 'control'. Difficulties arise in devising hypertext structures suited to browsing that will also facilitate and encourage deeper processing. The most successful uses of hypertext will involve the learner and lead them to adopt the most appropriate learning strategy for their task. They will provide guidance and encouragement to students to make more than a surface level pass through the material, and to develop higher-level learning skills.

A SYNTHESIS

Is it possible to have a synthesis between the desirable features of non-linear hypertext and linear prose? It is worth noting that one of the original hypertext systems, *Guide*, allows the author to implement a form of 'folding' and 'unfolding' of paragraphs, as well as giving direct reference structures within the text. It is perhaps only when attempting to develop a text using such systems, that the author can most clearly feel the tension between gains in accessibility and retrieval efficiency at the expense of losing continuity of exposition. A solution to this problem is to move away from the idea of 'free standing' paragraphs that appear and disappear, and to have the actual content of the text changing with the degree of folding or unfolding. This would be to have an additional intermediate level of folding where summaries stood for sections of text, rather than immediately collapsing to the heading structure. This form of hypertext could unfortunately only be achieved with greatly increased authoring effort, although the compromise of only having additional 'overview' and 'summary' levels replacing larger blocks of text might be sufficient. Where the attempt is made to directly 'port across' text written for dissemination by conventional print to a hypertext format, the appropriate use of these components is likely to be crucial to its success.

The *animateur*

In the context of the provision of distance teaching, the rôle of the course tutor has sometimes been described as that of an *animateur*: bringing the course to life for the home-based student. Some concerned with the rôle of the tutor would argue that they have a far more independent rôle than simply to act as an 'agent' for the text author. However, if one ignores the claims of AI, this title fits quite aptly the tasks most appropriate to the hypertext and multimedia aspects of course materials: presenting alternative 'views' to the student; efficient fact finding; interactive animation of diagrams and simulations; providing activities, etc. It is possible to conceive of this more prosaic, but realistic, rôle for the hypermedia within the general context of a *computer-based document*, encompassing linear prose, non-linear hypertext and the other 'multimedia' devices.

The use of the hypermedia in this supplementary rôle is likely to lead to an increase rather than a decrease in their perceived worth. The ability of such documents to reflect the author's prior expectation of the changing needs of the reader is educationally quite significant, and the equivalent devices in conventional print tend to be both rather clumsy and also expensive to produce. The importance of 'activities' in distance-teaching texts has long been recognised (Rowntree, 1986). They are seen as a vital feature to keep learners engaged, to prompt them to come up with their own ideas, and to perceive that their task is not merely to memorise facts.

Given that significant ergonomic and economic problems are overcome, it is conceivable that such a general media form might eventually supplant conventional print. However, for the present it is appears that the computer-based dynamic and interactive elements of printed course materials can best be thought of in the supplementary rôle of *animateur* for the distant author.

CONCLUSION

The adoption of such a conceptually simple technology as hypertext is unlikely to have as much pedagogic impact as was originally claimed. Non-linear hypertext is obviously a good way to package information for efficient information retrieval and is useful for some forms of interactivity. However, because of its fragmented nature, it is not a suitable medium to form the core of teaching materials. A learner-centred rhetoric is possible for hypertext based on its most important pedagogic feature, *malleability*, and its use in a supplementary rôle within the context of a more general document form offers considerable potential for education.

REFERENCES

de Beaugrande, R. A. (1980) *Text, Discourse and Process*. Norwood, NJ: Ablex.

de Beaugrande, R. A. and Dressler, W. U. (1981) *Introduction to Text Linguistics*. London: Longman.

Conklin, J. (1987) Hypertext: an introduction and survey. *IEEE Computer*, 20(9), 17–41.

van Dijk, T. A. (1979) Relevance assignment in discourse comprehension. *Discourse Processes*, 2, 113–126.

Grimes, J. E. (1975) *The Thread of Discourse*. The Hague: Mouton.

Kommers, P. A. M. (1990) Hypertext and the acquisition of knowledge. Unpublished PhD Thesis, Universiteit Twente, The Netherlands.

Landow, G. P. (1990) Popular fallacies about hypertext. In D. H. Jonassen and H. Mandl (eds.) *Designing Hypermedia for Learning*. Berlin: Springer Verlag.

Mandl, H., Picard, E., Henninger, M. and Schnotz, W. (1991) Knowledge acquisition with texts by means of flexible computer-assisted information access. Technical Report #54, Deutsches Institut für Fernstudien an der Universität Tubingen.

Nash, W. (1980) *Designs in Prose*. London: Longman.

Ravetz, J. R. (1971) *Scientific Knowledge and its Social Problems*. London: Oxford University Press.

Rowntree, D. (1986) *Teaching Through Self-Instruction*. London: Kogan Page.

Samarapungavan, A. and Beishuizen, J. J. (1990) Hypermedia and knowledge acquisition: learning from non-linear expository text. Paper presented at the EARLI 'Text Processing' Special Interest Group, University of Amsterdam, November 8–9.

Schnotz, W. (1982) How do different readers learn with different text organisations? In A. Flammer and W. Kintsch (eds.) *Discourse Processing*. Amsterdam: North Holland.

Waller, R. and Whalley, P. (1987) Graphically organised prose. In E. de Corte, H. Lodewijks, R. Parmentier and P. Span (eds.) *Learning and Instruction*. Oxford: Pergamon.

Whalley, P. (1990) Models of hypertext structure and learning. In D. H. Jonassen and H. Mandl (eds.) *Designing Hypermedia for Learning*. Berlin: Springer Verlag.

3

The Textbook of the Future

Donald J. Cunningham
University of New England, Armidale, Australia
Thomas M. Duffy
Indiana University, Bloomington, USA
Randy A. Knuth[1]
North Central Regional Educational Laboratory, USA

INTRODUCTION

Textbooks. God, how we love textbooks, books of all sorts, in fact. Whenever we visit a university or a new town, one of our first activities is to haunt the bookstores. Up and down the crowded aisles we wander, looking for that 'gem' that we have heard about, or hoping to come across one we have never heard of before that will provide new insight into a problem that is exercising us at the moment. We wince with pain as the clerk totals up our bill. Do we really need these books? Surely the library has a copy. Ah. But to own them. To put them on your shelf (already stuffed with other treasures, many unread) and browse the titles from time to time, making a mental note that you really should read them carefully. What pride we take when a colleague comments on the quality of our books, what shame we feel when the comment is made, "You mean you don't have a copy of X? Why that's the most important book to come out in years!" Off we steal again to the bookstore. Books are the academic's great addiction. We love their smell, their feel, the promise of new knowledge that they offer. To have actually produced a book is one of the academic's greatest joys, rivalling the birth of a child.

Yet we are told that in the information age, the form and character of textbooks will change dramatically. No longer will the textbook dominate the curriculum. Its static, largely unalterable format will be replaced by hypermedia and other information systems having databases that can be

---

[1] The order of authorship is alphabetical. The paper is a collaborative effort.

easily altered to fit individual needs. Shelves full of books will be replaced by banks of hard disks (or by connection to remote storage systems) filled with the 'contents' of textbooks and commentary on them. Recommendations concerning textbook design in their print form (e.g., Duffy and Waller, 1985; Hartley, 1978) will have to be revised to account for the electronic world within which future learners will find themselves embedded (see, for example, Kahn *et al.*, 1990). Emphasis will be placed on providing strategies or tools for navigating and customising these databases so that learners can explore and search out issues which are of interest, avoiding the linear mode of thinking by which traditional textbooks are bound. Individual customisation and reorganisation becomes the goal, not the communication of fixed knowledge. New tools will emerge from and be made available to students operating on these databases; we will at last be able to integrate a variety of modalities besides print and static graphics. The poor textbook sitting on our shelves looks a forlorn sort in comparison to the dazzle and wizardry of emerging hypermedia systems.

Lest we get carried away with all this techno-wizardry, we would like to propose a moment's reflection. Exactly what is it that we are trying to accomplish with all this technology? Is the printed textbook incompatible with our pedagogical aims? If the design of modern information systems makes a tool available, is the mere existence of the tool justification for its use in particular ways? We propose a short retreat into the armchair of contemplation, to consider for a moment the epistemological underpinnings of our efforts. Only with a clear sense of the theoretical foundations we hold concerning learning and cognition can we appropriately speculate about textbook of the future (Bednar *et al.*, 1991).

THE AGE OF CONSTRUCTIVISM

Until recently, theories of learning and cognition, both behavioural and cognitive information processing, were dominated by a communication metaphor. That is, some body of knowledge external to the learner, contained, say, in a textbook, teacher's lecture or computer-based lesson had to be transmitted to the student and received by him or her. If, as shown by some criterion-referenced assessment, this communication was not successful, the fault was sought in either the message (e.g., the organisation of the knowledge to be communicated), the message source (e.g., the textbook design), the transmission conduit (e.g., the student's reading ability) or the receiver (e.g., the student's level of prerequisite knowledge). Any or all of these factors could be manipulated until the efficiency and effectiveness of the communication process was optimised.

Recently, however, an alternative view of the learning process has begun to attract attention (e.g., Bednar *et al.*, 1991; Cunningham, in press). Variously labelled constructivism, experientialism and semiotics, this view holds that instruction is less a process in which knowledge is communicated to learners, and more a matter of nurturing the ongoing processes whereby learners come to understand the world in which they live. In this view, knowledge is an active process of construction, not the receipt of information from external sources. The rôle of textbooks and other instructional media shifts from one which seeks to maximise the communication of fixed content and/or skills to one in which students engage in the knowledge construction process: construct interpretations, appreciate multiple perspectives, develop and defend their own positions while recognising other views, and become aware of and able to manipulate the knowledge construction process itself. An important aspect of this approach is the insistence that learning take place embedded in the contexts to which it is most relevant in everyday life and with which the students are personally involved. Under the influence of constructivism, new words are creeping into our vocabularies: situated, constructions, reflexivity, dialogue, semiosis, anchored instruction, multiple perspectives, non-linear thinking, hypermedia, voice, ownership and so on and so forth.

This is not the place to discuss constructivist theory in detail or to debate its merits and deficits (see the discussion in the May and September 1991 issues of *Educational Technology*). But, since we consider ourselves within the constructivist 'camp', we would like to outline some of the pedagogical goals which emerge from it. Later we will consider the implications of these goals for the design of the textbook of the future.

1. Provide experience with the knowledge construction process
There is general agreement among instructional theorists that students must be actively involved in learning. Similarly, project-based learning is generally accepted. However, the nature and context of the activity is what we view as critical. Active involvement for us is not just active processing of information. Rather the student must assume responsibility for asking the questions, not just learning the answers to prespecified questions. Further, and most importantly, active construction of knowledge involves the comparison of alternative points of view or perspectives. This is critical to developing an awareness that our understanding is in fact a construction based on our experiences and point of view.

The 'constructedness' of much (perhaps all) of our knowledge of the world is invisible to us in our ordinary daily interactions. It is a pervasive and benign characteristic of human cognition that we operate with a world view that makes 'sense' to us, which seems to be 'the way things are.' It is only when we are confronted, usually in social interaction with others, with perspectives different from our own that we become aware of the extent to which our view of the world is a construction, that different people can have different views of a situation and that these views can have a sense or logic independent of our own views. Truths that we hold are shown to be only one of many possible truths.

Those who have lived in a foreign country or had extensive exposure to a culture other than their own have certainly experienced this phenomenon. An interesting way to provide such experience for students is to expose them to a variety of cultural practices, as, for example, in Jerome Bruner's controversial social studies curriculum *Man: A Course of Study* (Bruner, 1966). The differences that are observed in cultural practices can vary from the mildly odd (in most of Europe, for example, one shakes the hand of a friend upon meeting, but not a stranger, while the opposite is true in the US) to the extreme (many Africans are circumcised at puberty, while in the US this is done soon after birth). Through this exposure, students are encouraged to reconsider the inevitability of their own cultural practices.

But the constructedness of our world view is much more pervasive than this. Lakoff and Johnson (1980) have argued convincingly that much, perhaps all, of our thinking is metaphorical in nature; that is we tend to view situations as examples of something else, of some other familiar concept. For instance, many teachers and students tend to view the classroom as a workplace (Marshall, 1988), where tasks have to be completed in exchange for some sort of reward (e.g., a good grade in the course). Even the language we use to talk about classrooms is imbued with this metaphor: homework, classroom management, reading gains, teacher accountability, and so forth. In consequence, learning tends to be regarded as a phenomenon which takes place in classrooms, not elsewhere, much as work takes place in the workplace.

Experience in the constructive nature of our thinking about situations like classrooms can be provided by bringing the dominant metaphor to the students' attention and by inviting them to observe the consequences of changing the metaphor. Suppose, for example, we adopt the metaphor of the classroom as providing a consulting service. Now the agenda of tasks to be completed shifts from ones imposed by the teacher to ones generated by the students themselves. The classroom becomes one of only many places where work on this task takes place. The rôle of the teacher and other students shifts; they are now sources of insight and assistance, not authoritarian wisdom or competition. No doubt you can think of other differences which would emerge from such a shift in metaphor.[2]

2. Provide experience in and appreciation for multiple perspectives
Few issues in the world have a single 'correct' resolution. But young children (and many adults as well) tend to think that knowledge is either right or wrong, that all valid questions have answers, that authority figures (e.g., teachers, textbooks, etc.) have the answers to these questions and that experts know the truth or have ways to figure it out (Perry, 1970). Instruction designed under constructivist influences should again reveal the constructedness of knowledge, that any 'truth' begins with a set of untested assumptions which can be examined to evaluate the adequacy of the position taken. What we take as 'true' in a situation is very much a product of a

---

[2] Our purpose here is not to argue for one metaphor or the other, although we certainly favour the second over the first. Our point simply is that, under constructivism, a primary aim is to provide the students with the opportunity to experience the constructedness of their world view.

process of negotiation, often taking the form of some sort of dialogue. Positions are something we commit ourselves to, not something we adopt because (or certainly not only because) an authority figure decrees that we must.

Multiple perspectives are most commonly encountered in dialogue with other individuals. Certainly not all forms of dialogue will accomplish this goal. If one member of the group is 'certain' about her position (i.e. is an expert, or simply dogmatic) and the others not, that member will usually dominate. If the group contains more than one 'certain' individual, none of whom are willing to compromise their beliefs, then once again the dialogue will be unproductive in terms of this goal (although others in the group who are less certain may benefit). What we are interested in here is the situation where a group member is willing to reconsider his beliefs in terms of another's position and try to find a new view which accommodates them both. Surely not all views can be equally accommodated (we cannot imagine finding common ground between our views and those of the Ku Klux Klan, for example). But the development of the realisation that our view is only one of many and that an attitude of acceptance toward other views allows for the growth of our views, is fundamental under constructivism.

We have written extensively elsewhere (e.g., Knuth and Cunningham, in press; Duffy and Knuth, 1990) about the importance of providing students with the opportunity to explore multiple perspectives on an issue and about computer-based systems which support such experience. We will not repeat that discussion here since the description of Intermedia to follow will explore this issue in some detail.

3. *Embed learning in realistic and relevant contexts*
So much of what passes for education these days is relevant only to a single context — the school. Study after study shows a lack of transfer of knowledge acquired in the classroom to the real world (e.g., Bereiter, 1984; Resnick, 1987; Sherwood *et al.*, 1987). Thus, while students are able to complete the word problems at the end of the chapter in their science textbook, they are unable to use that knowledge to calculate the time it will take them to travel to Grandmother's house at a certain speed and distance.

Cognition is situated in experience. The context in which learning occurs is a significant determinant of what is learned and how it is organised in memory. While context is often thought of in terms of the physical context, it is the cognitive context that we see as being critically important. When we are in any learning situation, we are faced with a massive array of stimuli. It is our job as learner is to impose order on that stimulus environment, to make sense of it. How we do that is in large part determined by our purpose and goals — the cognitive context which is imposed or in which we place ourselves.

More specifically, the relevance of information, the interrelationships in that information environment, and the potential applications of that information that we see are all determined in large measure by the goals or purpose we bring to the learning environment. Hence, if the goal is to pass a test, relevance is determined by the school context of what might be tested. If, however, the goal is to use that information in some real world application then relevance and interrelationships will be determined in large measure by that real world task. "People make sense of concepts through engaging in the activity that circumscribes those concepts" (Brown, Collins, and Duguid, 1989b). Hence situating learning (Brown, Collins, and Duguid, 1989a); or providing anchored instruction (Cognition and Technology Group at Vanderbilt, 1990), or providing functional context instruction (Sticht and Hickey, 1988) can be seen as embedding learning in problem-solving contexts that are relevant to the real world.

4. *Encourage ownership and voice in the learning process*

So much of what we ask students to learn is of our choosing. They experience little ownership of the ideas, little sense that they are an active participant in their own learning processes. We feel that the students must come to feel a personal sense of responsibility for the products of their thinking, where their views are heard and respected by others in the situation. In other words, students must come to see that the tasks they are performing will help them accomplish the things they want, will empower them to take more complete control over their lives. Scardamalia and Bereiter (1991) discuss this in terms of the student assuming primary responsibility for working in the zone of proximal development. That is, rather than the teacher identifying the issues and direction, the teacher serves as a consultant helping the students to generate questions and issues that are relevant to them.

Perhaps one of the clearest examples of this is Paulo Freire's work in the early 1960s to promote literacy among Brazilian peasants (described in Freire, 1970). Like Perry (1970), Freire realised the importance of ensuring commitment on the part of the learners, of ensuring that the acquisition of literacy would be seen as valuable by the peasants, as something that could help them deal with real problems that they faced every day. Prior to any specific literacy training, Freire sent teams of observers to the local community to discover the character of life: what the people talked about, what they did every day, how they felt about their lives, and so forth. From these observations, Freire prepared a series of posters, visuals that were codifications of the life of the peasants, and invited his clients to 'decodify' the situations depicted, in group discussions that took place over several evenings.

The posters were carefully designed to allow the peasants to see and talk about their lives, to discover that they did in fact have the ability to influence nature and create culture. For example, the first poster in a series designed for a rural area showed a bare-footed peasant working in the field, his wife and children walking toward their hut. Beside the hut is a well. By asking questions like "Who dug the well?", "Why?", "Who built the house?", "Who made the clothes?", "Why?", the group leader started the long and painful process of showing the peasants that they did have a culture, that they were not powerless pawns of nature. Other posters stressed the importance of dialogue, a sharing of views that entailed respect for others. Freire believes strongly that dialogue is the principal means by which we come to know. By discussing these posters, hearing and contributing to the variety of views and interpretations that emerged, the peasants were able to decodify their painful social circumstance, to raise it to consciousness and examine it. In other words, the discussion made their oppression still more oppressive by enhancing their awareness of it. Still other posters provoked discussions of actions that the peasants might take to gain further control over their culture and lives, including the acquisition of literacy.

By these means, then, Freire was able to embed his literacy project in contexts and situations wherein the peasants saw value in and need for acquiring literacy. Once the peasants achieved heightened awareness of the need to acquire tools like literacy to gain further control of their lives and develop their culture, the literacy programme proper was begun using words and phrases that conveyed important themes discussed earlier in the poster sessions. Language was seen as another tool of culture, allowing them to examine their lives and gain some control over it in a cooperative endeavour requiring dialogue.

5. *Embed learning in social experience*
Many of the examples above have focused on dialogue as an important pedagogical strategy for constructivist instructional design. This is no accident, because dialogue is a major medium for providing experience in the knowledge construction process. While the individual learner is the only one who can construct his or her unique understanding of the world, this understanding emerges in a social context. Concepts take on meaning through a process of social negotiation. The differentiations that a person makes in the world — mother versus father, democracy versus dictatorship, computer versus teacher, etc. — arise from the contrast of one thing with another in some sort of social experience. Language is the key to understanding the development of these processes in humans. While it is possible to 'have a conversation' with oneself (and even desirable in some circumstances), dialogue between individuals is the primary mechanism that allows the social construction of meaning.

Vygotsky (1978) has stressed that social interaction is crucial to the intellectual development of children. Individually, any one child can accomplish certain tasks. However, many other tasks are too hard — the child simply has not yet fully developed the skills or knowledge necessary. But with the help of others the child will often be able to successfully complete many tasks that are beyond his individual ability. Gaps in the child's abilities are compensated for by others in the group. But more importantly, the child does not remain inept at the task for long because, through working with others who make up for his inability, he sees how the task is completed in its entirety and soon, through internalising the actions of others, by making new attempts, and by reflecting on experience and planning for tomorrow, the child is be able to do the task individually. This capacity to move beyond our abilities due to social interaction is referred to as the zone of proximal development or ZPD. The importance of working in one's ZPD in order to develop points out the absurdity of thinking that collaboration is simply an instructional strategy. Indeed, every learning experience occurs either explicitly or implicitly in a social context.

Of all the opportunities and resources that school settings can provide, collaborative configurations that challenge children to work beyond themselves, that is within their ZPDs, are the most abundant. We can imagine two major types of collaborative configurations. The most obvious is the expert (that is, the teacher) working with novices (students). Cognitive apprenticeship (Collins, Brown, and Newman, 1988) represents this arrangement. In teaching a cognitive skill such as reading, the teacher models the process to a small group of students by thinking out loud. Then, each student is asked to do the same process, but when a gap is encountered, the teacher scaffolds his progress and helps him to successfully finish the task. As time goes on, students receive more and more responsibility for doing the cognitive process until finally the skill is completely internalised.

The less obvious configuration for pushing students to work within their ZPDs involves grouping peers with peers. Certainly, forming student groups and letting them go at it is nothing new, and further, if these groups are left alone, the session often degrades from discovery learning to trial and error to chaos. But this need not be the case. Every child has unique skills and capabilities; every child has something to offer the group. A key to successful peer groups involves developing a classroom culture where sharing is the norm and where the teacher actively seeks out opportunities to let peers help each other. Such a classroom might take the form of a peer-scholar network where students are always engaged in authentic tasks that have a significant purpose to the child. Inquiry, not just scientific but inquiry into domains such as music, literature, and art which affect the whole child, would characterise the culture of the class. Students would have access to each other (and the teacher) to discuss and debate ideas, to search for clues, to tutor each other, to share understandings, and to provide encouragement.

One final example illustrates the ZPD concept. This chapter, written collaboratively by the three authors, is better than any one of us individually could have produced. It reflects the perspectives and strengths of each author. If all goes well, each of our weaknesses in writing will be compensated by another. And when the project is complete, each of us will be better with some respect to the task — each of us will undoubtedly better understand some of the issues within the paper. Others will become better at writing. By collaborating, we are permanently extending the boundaries of what we can each do.

6. Encourage the use of multiple modes of representation
Education throughout the world may be characterised as logocentric, emphasising talk and written language to the near exclusion of any other mode of representation. Even this paper has used discussion and dialogue as our primary examples of constructivist principles. While language is clearly the dominant form through which we construct knowledge from our experience, other modes are available and should be exploited in terms of what they can contribute to the knowledge construction process (e.g., see Howard Gardner's (1983) discussion of multiple intelligences). Within the computer context, for example, many modes of representation can be captured (e.g., graphics, photographs, animation, video, sound, etc.) and each of these can be assessed in terms of what they can reveal and what they might obscure. In another example, Michael Roth (1990) makes sure that his science students experience multiple ways of representing their experiences while conducting laboratory experiments (e.g., verbal description, equations, pictures and diagrams, demonstrations, tables of numbers, graphs, etc.), all the while encouraging them to point out the strengths and weaknesses of each mode, what is foregrounded in one representation, obscured in another. Likewise, sixth and seventh graders learning algebra through a programme known as the Algebra Project (based in Boston, MA) move through a specific sequence of representations for every mathematical concept. They always begin by experiencing a physical event, representing it pictorially, talking about it in their everyday, informal language, discussing it in structured, or formal, language, and finally representing it symbolically. In contrast, typical maths instruction begins symbolically and asks students to apply it physically.

It is critical to keep this logocentrism in mind when considering the design of instruction from a constructivist perspective. It is all to easy to fall into the trap of endless talk about issues and little consideration of alternative representations. Even within language, varieties of symbolic codes other than exposition should be explored (e.g., narrative, poetry, drama) and examined as to what they add to understanding or what limitations are revealed. Curriculum theorists like Elliot Eisner (e.g., 1982) have long encouraged educators to look beyond verbal and mathematical cognition, but such approaches have traditionally been regarded as 'frills', something to be added onto the serious business of discursive education. But as new technologies allow students not only to receive but actively create in a variety of representational modes (e.g., video, graphics, sound, etc.), the incredible potential of representational diversity may come to the forefront.

7. Encourage self-awareness of the knowledge construction process
This is perhaps the most important goal of all and has naturally arisen in discussion of previous goals. Providing experience in the knowledge construction process is an important goal, but the outcome we hope will eventually occur is awareness of the constructedness of much of our knowledge and active control over that construction process, or, to know

how we know. In other places (e.g., Cunningham, in press) this has been referred to as the development of reflexivity. There is no higher educational goal. If reflexivity were to come to serve as a primary goal in our school curricula, the subject matter of each of our courses would be the mind itself. A course in history, for example, would emphasise not simply history, but how historians know, the sign structures or systems of belief that historians use in their discipline. What are the potential effects of those beliefs on the historical analyses that are regarded as acceptable? Or take physics. How do our assumptions about the nature of matter influence our experimental methodologies, and vice versa? How do the various forms of representing our knowledge of the universe influence our theories?

One consequence of an emphasis on reflexivity in our courses would be to coalesce the various subject matters, revealing the unity underlying them and rendering their separate treatment ill-advised. More classes would be taught by teams of teachers, say a mathematician, a geographer, and a historian. The systems of belief of each of these disciplines could be juxtaposed so that, for example, the logic used to fashion some particular analysis could be examined against the tools provided by another discipline. We could ask questions like the following: Is adding amendments to the US Constitution like adding 3 apples and 2 apples, or can we think about a mathematics in which not only the number of elements but their character is represented? In what way does the climate of a country influence its historical development? Are international boundaries influenced by the way we calculate economic development?

A good example of the development of reflexivity comes again from the work of Paulo Freire (1970). The final poster in the series that Freire constructed for rural peasants depicts a group of peasants sitting in a group discussing one of the posters occurring earlier in the series. In other words, the poster is designed to have the peasants reflect on the process in which they are engaged. This is what we mean by reflexivity. Reflexive means directed or turned back upon itself or self-referential. Umberto Eco put the matter this way:

> To speak about 'speaking', to signify signification, or to communicate about communication cannot but influence the universe of speaking, signifying and communicating. (Eco, 1976, p. 29)

This notion of reflexivity is related to, but of a different order than, reflection as described by Schön (1983). We see reflexivity more as a reflection on our reflections, thinking about our thinking process, knowing how we know. For instance, we would say that when Freire's peasants recognised that the well they dug was part of their culture, they were being reflective (seeing as). But examining the process whereby they were reflective is a different order of awareness that we have come to call reflexivity. Such awareness has an important impact on the ways in which we know, observe, think and reflect.

The seven goals listed above are not exhaustive nor would all who consider themselves constructivists necessarily agree with our version. Our purpose here was to provide a general sense of the context within which we can evaluate the textbook of the future.

DESIGNING THE TEXTBOOK OF THE FUTURE

What are the requirements for the design of textbooks and other learning materials in this constructivist learning environment? To what extent do existing textbooks meet these requirements? What does hypermedia technology afford as an alternative to textbooks? In this section we will look at the design of textbooks in relation to the seven principles just outlined.

It is important to note that in a constructivist learning environment the instruction is not contained in the textbook or in any other resource. These resources are simply tools — repositories of information — for the students and teacher to use in constructing understandings. Hence, any information resource may be used in a constructivist environment. Indeed, we would hope that students will develop into life-long learners and will continue to use textbook-like materials as information resources throughout their lives. Our goal is not to reject resources but rather to look at the strengths and weaknesses of alternative resources — the opportunities and constraints they tend to afford.

Before turning to the consideration of textbook design, let us briefly encapsulate the constructivist learning environment just presented. Perhaps the key feature of a constructivist learning environment is that the student is in charge of constructing and testing his or her own understanding. This certainly does not imply 'anything goes', i.e. the student can study anything and any understanding developed is adequate. It also does not imply that the student is simply tossed into a sink-or-swim condition. Rather, it means that the goal of constructivist instruction is to aid the student in gaining the capability to ask relevant questions, to generate authentic contexts for the use of the knowledge to guide the interpretation of the information, to test his or her views against alternative views, and to be become aware of the knowledge construction process.

If these learning skills are to be achieved, learning must begin by the students generating questions, assuming some ownership for determining relevance, for developing a point of view, and for establishing the authentic context. Part of the instructional process is to aid students in evaluating the questions they generate in terms of how those questions will aid them (and others) in developing a richer and usable understanding of the issue or topic. The student is then also responsible for seeking information to answer those questions, developing a perspective or answer to the question, and evaluating that perspective against alternative perspectives generated by other groups of students. Again, this is a social process with the teacher and other students sharing their views and strategies. How well can textbooks support this type of a learning environment?

The textbook in constructivist learning environments
Text as authority

The primary feature of traditional textbooks is that they are geared to knowledge telling rather than knowledge construction. The textbook serves as an authority on a topic. There is a benefit of this in that the information is organised into a coherent, story-like presentation. Hence, it typically provides a consistent, unified point of view. However, the shortcoming is that when the textbook is used as the primary resource, as it typically is, the book assumes responsibility for the issue generation and for the development of points of view. Even if the text presents alternative points of view on an issue, it is nonetheless presenting already-developed points of view and an analysis of the differences between them.

Clearly this 'textbook as authority' design and use of textbooks is inconsistent with the constructivist principles outlined above. If the textbook is the only resource, and if the questions arise from the text (or teacher) rather than the students, then the student is relieved of the responsibility (and hence the learning experience) of generating relevant questions and issues. Learning simply becomes a matter of receiving and accepting the specified questions or point of view. Further, with the text as the relevant source, reflecting a point of view, the learners' information gathering is reduced to determining what the textbook author has decided is relevant. The students determine relevancy by analysing the textbook structure. They learn to analyse the text — underlined words, questions at the end of text, etc. — to determine what is relevant and hence what needs to be learned. There is little if any need to think about the topic or the use of the information to determine what is relevant.

Recent research by Scardamalia and Bereiter (1991) supports the view that the textbook tends to restrict the student to thinking about lower-level, fact-oriented questions. They asked 5th and 6th graders to generate questions about a topic that reflected what they wondered about and what they felt would help them to understand the topic better. Half of the students did this after looking over the lesson materials on the topic while the other half did it before seeing any text materials. Scardamalia and Bereiter then rated each question as to how much the pursuit of the question could be expected to contribute to understanding. When the topic was a familiar one, only 4% of the questions from the text-based group were rated as knowledge building while 46% of the questions for the other group were so classified. Similar findings were obtained when the topic was reasonably unfamiliar.

Situated learning

The learner must have a purpose for learning that extents beyond the simple purpose of learning because 'it is in the textbook and the teacher said it is important.' The need for this larger perspective is clearly indicated in virtually all cognitive theories of reading which stress top-down reading strategies, perhaps most clearly specified in van Dijk and Kintsch's (1983) model of text comprehension in which the student compares the text information to the 'situation' model. In the context of text comprehension, the situation model is constructed by integrating linguistic knowledge with general background knowledge about objects and actions, and with knowledge of the reference situation (Morrow, Greenspan, and Bower, 1987; van Dijk and Kintsch, 1983). In the more general sense, the situation model is the context (real world or imaginary in the case of fiction) for the use of the information, for guiding judgements of relevance.

Current textbooks attempt to provide this larger perspective by setting the context in the opening of the chapter (e.g., an overview, list of objectives, or advanced organiser) and by providing 'application' exercises interspersed throughout or at the end of a chapter. These are indeed useful tools for building the situation model, especially in those situations where the students do not have the experience to generate their own context and other potential applications. It is critical that these applications become a cornerstone of the instruction rather than a final exercise or a general introduction. The student must have a rich understanding of the situation and use that understanding to guide the reading process and the assessment of relevancy. The situation must also be rich enough to support the integration of the information in the text rather than simply the seeking of individual bits of information.

The preference in a constructivist learning environment is for the students to generate and evaluate their own purposes or goals for learning. However, the textbook may become a resource for seeking to develop a viewpoint or understanding. If an application exercise described in the text is fully discussed and elaborated by the student then this may be used vicariously to guide information seeking and knowledge construction. However, since a textbook represents a point of view, it will generally be inadequate as the only resource. The textbook must be seen as an information resource rather than as the source of knowledge.

Constructed understanding

We see students creating rather than using textbooks. That is, they will be assembling information from a variety of sources, including their own thoughts and views, to present their understanding of an issue. The textbook, in contrast, is typically seen as a complete document with the only additional input being the students underlining or marginal notes. Clearly, the physical and conceptual features of a textbook are inconsistent with this view of knowledge construction. Conceptually, textbooks are seen as complete documents. Physically, they cannot easily be rearranged, combined, or added to by the student.

Multimedia representations of understanding

We are coming to recognise the importance of alternative media as a means of presenting as well as demonstrating understanding. Indeed, Pea (in press) suggests that "Literacy skills involved in creating and using multimedia compositions may come to be regarded by society to be essential as writing is today." The textbook permits neither the presentation nor the authoring of information in alternative media. This is clearly a physical constraint and simply making the textbook available on-line would permit the presentation and potentially the authoring of multimedia materials (see, e.g., Authorware, 1991).

Hypermedia in constructivist learning environments

In contrast to hardcopy textbooks, hypermedia technology seems ideally suited to supporting constructivist learning environments (Duffy and Knuth, 1990). Of course, hypermedia is a technology and can be used in a variety of instructional contexts. Indeed, hypermedia could be used to represent that traditional textbook and support the traditional use of the textbook by using the link structure to provide elaborations on key concepts. Thus the core information or the epitome would be represented as the primary information in the database. When a student did not understand one of the concepts or principles in the epitome she could follow a link to obtain a variety of elaborations (e.g., examples, more detail, alternative representations, etc.).

This 'elaborative' function is certainly an effective use of hypermedia technology and we would expect it to be a part of most hypermedia applications. While important, however, we do not think that this use captures the power of hypermedia technology; nor is it one of the central features in what we see as the textbook of the future. In this section we will focus on the design and use of hypermedia in a constructivist learning environments.

Following links

Hypermedia is generally defined in terms of three characteristics: nodes of information, machine-supported links between those nodes, and a common user interface. The notion of an information network means that the author of a hypermedia system is freed of the constraint of creating a cohesive expository or narrative text as is required in writing a textbook. Thus a wide range of information can be included in the hypermedia system and, as the system grows, a potentially infinite number of issues and points of view can all be interconnected providing a rich semantic network in which the learners can seek information relevant to the issue at hand. The limited experiences with hypermedia databases which have been reported in the literature demonstrate the organic nature of this potential. For instance, Landow (personal communication) discovered that a database developed independently of his own, contained information about the medical history of Ezra Pound and links to that database were established.

Of course, if an individual constructs the network of nodes of information, that network will be as much a reflection of that individual's point of view as the organisation of a book is a reflection of the author's point of view. Points of view are essential. If all perspectives and contexts were taken into account, everything would be linked to everything else and the hypermedia information environment would be unusable. The important distinction between hypermedia and a textbook is that the hypermedia environment relieves the requirements of a linear presentation. While we do not see books as necessarily being used as linear documents, the linear format certainly constrains the writer to a cohesive, integrated presentation. No such constraint is imposed by the hypermedia environment. Hence while the design of the system does reflect a point of view, there is considerably more freedom for the author and, potentially, the user, in building networks of information. Indeed, as systems grow, it is expected that there will be interlinking of networks so that multiple points of view are available and the learner can seek information from that variety of viewpoints in constructing her own views on the instructional topic or question.

Authoring
We find that two additional features are essential to the use of hypermedia in a constructivist learning environment: the ability to author nodes of information and the ability to create links. Since we see learners as constructing understanding — constructing their textbook — there should be no distinction between authoring and reading. This seamless authoring-reading environment is characteristic of several hypermedia systems, notably Intermedia (Yankelovich *et al.*, 1988) and KMS (Akscyn, McCracken, and Yoder, 1988). With an authoring capability, it is not unreasonable to presume that the students will begin with an empty system. The students would tap a variety of resources seeking information and would use the hypermedia system to construct their understanding. They would actively build and/or customise their textbook or hypermedia system rather than simply receiving someone else's. More traditionally, we would expect to start with a hypermedia database that would be one source of information. The students would add to, select from, and rearrange the information in that database to construct their understanding.

Collaborating
We can identify a sixth feature that would be useful, though not essential, to the constructivist learning environment: a multi-user or networked system. This would provide the capability for a variety of collaborative activities central to the constructivist learning environment as well as support the reflexive activity of the learner. We note that this is not essential because the collaboration can occur away from the computer: in small group activities, in journals, and through other techniques used to support reflexive activity. However, capturing the collaboration on computer would generally facilitate the examination of arguments and argument development, thus aiding both the analysis of perspectives and the analysis of the knowledge construction process. We see the value of this capability most clearly in the way gIBIS support problem solving and design construction (Conklin, 1987). Conklin likens this system to a "marriage of news and teleconferencing systems, in which many people can participate in one conversation, and hypertext,

which allows people to move easily between different issues and different threads of arguments on the same issue" (1987, p. 16).

Managing complexity

Thus far we have focused on what we see to be the considerable benefits of a hypermedia system in a constructivist learning environment. However, there is one major concern: the complexity of the demands placed on the learner. Perkins (1991) has recently raised this concern about constructivist learning environments in general. He notes that we impose three types of complexity: managing oneself in the complex learning environment, facing conflicts with one's intuitive models of the world, and adapting to the 'new' approach to learning at the same time one is working in the content domain. Hypermedia is yet another source of complexity for the learner.

Earlier we noted the benefit of the textbook being that it presents a cohesive point of view that a learner can easily follow. In contrast, hypermedia systems appear to increase the complexity imposed on the learner. The problems due to complexity include: getting lost in "hyperspace", not having a sense of the "whole" and hence the proportion or topics that have been visited, and deciding what paths to follow and what information is relevant (Jonassen, 1989; Shneiderman and Kearsley, 1989; Woodhead, 1991).

There is no question that there is unnecessary complexity in many designs and considerable improvement in the interface would facilitate the use of most hypermedia systems. Indeed, there is considerable research underway on these issues. However, we would argue that the complexity of using a hypermedia system will always be a 'problem.' A hypermedia system in a constructivist environment is inherently more complex than a textbook. It is a web of information rather than a cohesive expository or narrative presentation. Also, most hypermedia systems will be considerably larger than a normal textbook and certainly will be expected to grow larger over time, hence implicating volume as well as complexity. Hence, learning to work independently and autonomously in the information environment and developing strategies for managing the learning environment must be part of the learning process. While we can and should improve the interface for hypermedia systems, the learner is still going to need guidance from classmates and the teacher in developing effective strategies for thinking about a problem and pursuing information on that problem in a hypermedia environment. The notions of cognitive apprenticeship and zone of proximal development come to the forefront when confronting this issue. Contrary to the fears that are commonly expressed, the rôle of teacher, expert, collaborative colleague and author do not disappear with the textbook of the future. Indeed they are enhanced and highlighted!

Let us state directly that we have no doubt that the instructional advantages are well worth the complexity encountered — in terms of constructivist learning environments in general (see Perkins, 1991, as well) and in terms of hypermedia in particular. Learning to manage that complexity is an essential part of the learning and instructional process. Indeed, information management may even be identified as a skill of growing importance in our society. The information age means that more information and more diverse information is relevant to a wide range of decision making. Interdisciplinary work is becoming more common in all facets of business and international impacts almost always are a consideration. In our own work thinking about constructivism and hypermedia and the issues raised in this paper, we had to sort through numerous journals and books looking for new perspectives and related information. We had to judge relevancy and rethink our position. These are the skills we hope to develop in students as they work in hypermedia-supported constructivist learning environments.

INTERMEDIA: A TEXTBOOK OF THE FUTURE

In the preceding sections we discussed our conception of the 'textbook of the future,' emphasising that it will no doubt embody hypertext functionality. We are now just completing a study of what is arguably the most fundamental example of the new textbook, a hypertext system called Intermedia at Brown University. Intermedia is used primarily by two professors at Brown, George Landow in English Literature and Peter Heywood in Biology. Each of these professors uses a different pedagogical approach in the classroom which has resulted in different structures within and uses of Intermedia. Landow's use of Intermedia was the subject of our study and will be discussed here. But it should be remembered that the following discussion highlights but one of many possible uses of a hypertext system.

Before we discuss what we have learned, we briefly describe Intermedia and Landow's use of it. Intermedia, at its most basic level, is a database manager that allows one to store and manipulate three kinds of information: word processing, graphic, and timeline documents. What makes Intermedia a hypertext system is that it embodies the three defining characteristics suggested by Conklin (1987). First, information is chunked into nodes. In this case a node is a whole document that appears in a scrollable window that is usually, but not limited to, one or two screens in length. Intermedia contains a large corpus of documents, at last count more than 5,000. These documents are most often not primary source materials (e.g., books, and whole articles) because of copyright and hard disk storage restrictions, although many poems and short stories can be found. Most of the nodes contain essays and critiques of the authors and works studied in Landow's course, written both by Landow and his students.

The second hypertext characteristic of Intermedia is the ability to create links between any chunks of information. Intermedia supports linking any portion of any document (e.g., the entire document, a paragraph, a sentence, a word, a graphic object, a timeline event, etc.) to any portion of any other document including itself. What makes hypertext particularly powerful is that a user can simply click on a link marker to retrieve (i.e. display) the 'linked-to' document or, if it is linked to more than one document, choose a destination link from a menu of choices. When a link is selected, the retrieved document appears in the foreground, often partially obscuring those in the background.

The third hypertext characteristic is Intermedia's consistent user interface for creating and retrieving documents. IRIS (Institute for Research on Instruction and Scholarship, the authors of Intermedia) chose Apple's desktop metaphor for opening, displaying and moving file and file folder icons as well as document windows. Intermedia extends the desktop metaphor by including links and a unique document type known as the 'web.' A web is a file that contains all of the links that have been established within any set of documents. More than one web can exist within a given corpus. For example, using the same set of documents, a user can create separate webs for different purposes. Landow has chosen to create one overall web document called Context32. This web is used by all of the students in his class giving them access to the same documents and links (although certainly no two students are going to read the same ones — there are simply too many).

What makes the web unique is that when opened it displays the user's recent past history of documents retrieved. The history of documents is listed in a vertical, chronological order (oldest at the top) containing both the document name and an icon to indicate its type (word processing, graphic, timeline, or web). Clicking on any document name within the web history retrieves the document. Because every student logs into a personal account, the web reveals only the history of that particular user. Further, the web history indicates how each document was accessed, for example, whether it was retrieved by following a link to it, by opening it from a file icon, or by simply reactivating it.

The web document also lists at its bottom all of the destination documents that are linked to the currently active window. For example, a document in the active window may contain many links, each to a different document. Each of these destination documents are listed in a 'tree' fashion in what we call the 'web local' view of the web document. Clicking on any document name within this list will retrieve the document.

Depending on what 'rights' have been assigned, an Intermedia user may engage in two fundamental activities: (1) retrieve documents by opening file icons, following links, or using either the web history or web local links, and (2) create new and modify existing documents and links. Landow's students spend most of their time using the capabilities of Intermedia to retrieve documents in order to write essays that reflect their understandings of authors and works. A large portion of Landow's English Literature corpus available on Intermedia consists of these student contributions. Students are not entirely free to contribute to the database nor are they permitted to make links at any time they desire. Rather, Landow solicits document contributions from his students (to ensure quality) and students may bring their link suggestions to class where they are debated and, if deemed appropriate, inserted into the corpus.

Intermedia is not the sole information source used in the course, but rather is one of many that the students access. Students read numerous novels, short stories, and poems in addition to the documents found on Intermedia. Students also rely heavily on books such as the Norton Anthologies. Intermedia's main purpose is to provide different perspectives and rich contextual information to help each student develop rich, personal understandings of authors, works, and important issues of humanity.

The assignments that Landow gives his students require effort and thought. Unlike many maths or science problems, there is not one, but many correct paths to a multitude of 'correct' solutions. The first Intermedia assignment was to create a concept map that related nine unidentified passages to Shelley's *Mont Blanc*. The students were to write clear, well-written brief mini-essays for each passage in which the relation (i.e. theme, technique, or religious, philosophical, historical, or scientific context) was explained. Landow hinted that "not all the relations you discover or create will turn out to be obvious ones." Students could use any information source available but were encouraged to use Intermedia to discover contextual relationships. The essays from this assignment may potentially end up in the Intermedia corpus linked to other works. The final assignment was to use any information source, especially Intermedia, to write a research paper essay about comparing and contrasting any authors.

In our study, we worked with eight students twice during the semester, during the weeks that the first assignment and final assignments were due, respectively. Our intent was to design and give our students tasks which were as isomorphic to their real class assignments as possible in order to capture authentic behaviours and thought processes.

During our first visit we asked the students to use Intermedia to find information within the "Context32" web that they felt would help us understand *Gulliver's Travels* by Swift. The information was to relate to the novel's theme, context, and technique. Then we asked them to construct a concept map which represented their understanding of this information and its relationships. The task for Landow's students during our final visit was to write a paper that compared and contrasted any two authors along any dimensions that they wished. The goal of the final task was to use Intermedia as the primary information source and to present a point of view in their papers that was both interesting and unique. Each student had one hour to complete both of these tasks and were asked to think aloud as they worked. The think-aloud protocols from these 16 sessions were intended to reveal patterns of Intermedia use and cognitive processes. While the students worked their computer screens were videotaped to capture the physical operations employed while working with Intermedia.

Protocols were segmented by following guidelines suggested by Ericsson and Simon (1984) which resulted in an inter-rater reliability of 0.87. Once the protocols had been segmented a categorisation scheme was derived out of the data. To determine inter-rater reliability, two encoders categorised the segments of a randomly selected protocol. Using Cohen's (1960) method the percentage agreement, adjusted for matches that occurred by chance, was calculated to be at an acceptable level (0.708).

Lakoff and Johnson (1980) make a strong argument for the rôle of metaphors in both language and cognition. Thus, the protocols were also analysed to identify the dominant metaphors used by subjects as they worked. Segments were classified into metaphor categories according to the presence of particular words and phrases (and their derivatives). For example, common words that identified particular metaphors include let's go, in, into, find, they have, under, on, and follow.

Physical operations were identified by watching the videotapes of the Intermedia computer monitor. Criteria for identifying operations were:

- Use of the mouse to point to and select (single click on) or open (double click on) an object; also included dragging windows.
- Use of the keyboard to type.
- Performance of a physical movement such as taking notes or moving the computer.

What we have learned

The primary goal of our investigation was to develop an understanding of how students approached learning tasks with Intermedia. It was not the goal to see if Intermedia 'works' or 'is better' — media comparison studies are fraught with problems and typically rather uninteresting when all the 'proper' controls are included. Clark and Salomon (1984) maintain that the introduction of new technologies changes the classroom because it allows the production of high-quality materials, novel experiences, and organisational and practice changes not available without it. Heinich (1984) calls this effect "negative entropy" to suggest that the injection of technology (i.e. energy) into an environment cannot help but result in fundamental reorganisation. Thus, it is nearly impossible to compare a course with a technology to the same course without it.

In the last few years the number of documents written about hypermedia has skyrocketed. Yet, only a handful have seriously looked at the cognitive and physical processes involved. Most of the papers are conceptual or theoretical in nature but seldom provide an in-depth look at how systems are used. One of the most prevalent beliefs about hypertext environments is that users will browse the hyperspace, serendipitously acquiring knowledge and the structure of the database as represented in the links. In other words, by traversing the links within the hypertext a user will acquire the content and form of the database. Our study reveals that when involved in ill-structured, constructive tasks, browsing and acquiring knowledge in this fashion is not a major strategy. Instead, a student's engagement with Intermedia is a complex interaction of the user's motives and goals, the user's prior knowledge, the user's understanding of the task, the affordances and constraints of the Intermedia system, the available documents, prior work with Intermedia, self-knowledge, and a number of other factors.

In order to make sense of the think-aloud data, we used a framework proposed by Leont'ev (1981). In his Theory of Activity, Leont'ev suggests that there are three distinct, yet related, levels of human engagement. The most global description is at the activity level. An activity is always associated with a motive. Example activities include "play, instruction or formal education, and work" (Wersch, Minick and Arns, 1984, p.154). It is important, therefore, to understand what activity subjects felt they were engaged in. For example, a subject whose motive is only to receive payment for participation has a different motive than one who believes the activity will help with class assignments and will therefore employ a different set of actions and operations. Therefore, we designed the tasks in this study to be as isomorphic to the ones Landow uses in class to increase the likelihood that subjects would be engaged in a 'learning' activity.

An intermediate level of analysis described by Leont'ev focuses on goal-directed actions. Whereas activities are associated with the 'why,' actions deal with setting and achieving goals, or in other words, decision making. While working with Intermedia, each student establishes goals and specifies actions to achieve them, but not the particular physical means required. For example, in deciding to go to Indianapolis for a business meeting, the activity is work, the action is getting to Indy, but the means of getting there (driving, flying, the train) is not specified. In the think aloud protocols actions take the form of decision statements as well as interpretative statements and represent an iterative interaction of cognitive processes involved in an 'inner dialogue.'

Four types of decisions categories emerged from the protocols:

(1) decisions about the overall plan ("Let's compare Soyenka and Tennyson..."),
(2) decisions about choosing a document from the database ("Let's open the Swift Overview..."),
(3) decisions about Intermedia operations ("Let's move the web over here...") and
(4) decisions about cognitive strategies ("I need to re-read this...").

The first three decision types influenced the overall document retrieval form of the session interaction. That is, these decisions were responsible for both which documents were retrieved (i.e. the content) as well as when they were retrieved (and how long they were viewed). The final decision type guided the overall interpretation and sense-making processes of the subjects.

The interpretative segments in the protocols related to the sense-making attempts of the subjects. They occurred after a decision had been made and when the subject was interacting with the content of a document, the database, Intermedia, or their own thoughts, knowledge, and understanding. These segment categories fell into six groups:

(1) Comments,
(2) Questions,
(3) Prior Knowledge and Evaluations,
(4) Read,
(5) Discussion, and
(6) Cite Reason.

One of the most interesting insights that this study has reinforced is that knowledge construction via Intermedia is a complex phenomenon, where attention is continually shifting according to the immediate demands of the task, and an inner dialogue involving decisions, debate, and reflection progresses through time.

While activities and actions are cognitive phenomena, the basic level of description, operations, is concerned with the physical conditions under which goal-directed actions are achieved. Operations are the means by which actions are carried out and are due directly from the constraints and opportunities that the Intermedia interface affords. For example, to achieve the goal-directed action, "Let's go to Swift," a user could employ one of many possible operations on Intermedia. One could search through the folders, reactivate the Swift Overview, or search the web history for Swift documents. Operations occur at the level in which students 'operate' the mouse and keyboard to click, drag, point, and manipulate windows. Videotapes of the computer screen enabled us to identify and catalogue the operations used. Unfortunately space does not permit a discussion of the operations level.

A critical component of our model of Intermedia interaction is attention. Two major views regarding attention exist in the cognitive science literature (Glass and Holyoak, 1986). One suggests that people have a certain 'amount' of attention to pay which can be divided up among many task components simultaneously. The other view suggests that attention can only be paid to one task component at a time, but that a person can switch from task component to task component while putting the others on hold. Although we believe that both views have merit, the latter model seems more compatible with our observations. While engaged in an Intermedia task a user's attention shifts among the various levels of the task depending on the immediate circumstances and they tend to objectify the various aspects that they are paying attention to. For example, subjects refer to Intermedia itself, their knowledge, their feelings, their progress, and their obstacles as if all of these were actual objects. The following excerpt from a protocol illustrates how attention is shifted between various aspects:

(Reads text) Oh, wow! (Reads text) So Soyenka was a revolutionary fighter. (Reads text) That could be sort of like, um, Tennyson. Tennyson was a dwarf, wasn't he? One of those writers was. I could compare him to Tennyson, with like, the physical situations that isolate them from society... Oops. OK, I won't do that. I don't understand what's going on... Back this way. (Reads text)

Notice that the subject, after first reading the text, focuses on an emotional reaction to the text by exclaiming "Oh, wow." Then she draws an inference. Attention has shifted from the text (or the reading of the text) to the subject's constructed understanding of what she has read, and then back to the text. Then attention is aimed at the subject's prior knowledge about another author, Tennyson. This leads to a shift of attention to the overall plan for achieving the task, that is, a suggestion to compare Soyenka and Tennyson in terms of "the physical situations that isolate them from society." And then a breakdown occurs. As this happens, the subject's attention is shifted to Intermedia itself, as a mis-click accidentally scrolled the text out of the document window. Attention then shifts to a 'fix-up' strategy (scrolling to get "back this way") to alleviate the breakdown. And then attention is focused once more on reading the text.

In just over a minute and a half the subject shifted attention ten times, yet only one small section of a single document was dealt with. Throughout the duration of the session, subjects shifted attention to an even wider array of 'objects.' In addition to the above, subjects focused on 'objects' including decisions ("Let's go to Introductory Comments"), worth of the document ("This has nothing to do with Soyenka"), self-knowledge ("I usually have no particular strategy when I do this"), task progress ("So, I have one of my contacts"), questions about the content ("There's more than one supreme Uba?"), and emotional state ("I get so sick of looking at the screen").

This shifting of attention supports a notion suggested by Heidegger (cited in Winograd and Flores, 1986) about the use of tools. When a person first begins to use a tool, attention must be paid to how to use it. In Heidegger's words the tool at this stage of skill is "present-at-hand." The user must be conscious of it (i.e. pay attention to it) in order to use it properly. With continued practice, however, less and less attention is required by the tool and it becomes a transparent extension (Winograd and Flores, 1986) of the user or "ready-at-hand." In a short time, Intermedia becomes ready-at-hand, freeing the student's attention to higher-level aspects of task completion. However, there are times when Intermedia acts in an unexpected fashion, or takes a long time, or the user simply forgets how to do something. Then, the user's attention shifts from the task to the tool as a breakdown occurs. Breakdowns occur in cognitive actions as well as at the operation level, for example in forgetting an author's name or when a cognitive strategy does not work.

The primary model of hypertext use that we propose is one where the student is engaged in a dialectical conversation with herself to achieve goal-directed actions. Hypotheses are continuously formed and tested, progress is monitored and evaluated, and decisions about what to do next, although influenced by an overall plan, are made according to the immediate situation (Suchman, 1987). This process is remarkably similar to the way that knowledge is socially constructed in the real world. Vygotsky (1978) believed that everything that a person does individually is first learned socially. The same kind of critical thinking, analysis, and synthesis of ideas that Landow models and then requires of his students in the classroom manifests itself in the inner speech of his students as they use Intermedia. This suggests to us that tools such as Intermedia are but one part (albeit an important one) of a larger educational environment that must be embedded in a social context.

The 'objects' that students focused their attention on are revealed in their inner speech. That is, the object of attention is specifically referenced to in the metaphors that subjects used while thinking aloud. The metaphor that appears in just about all of the protocols is one we call the 'Intermedia-as-vehicle' metaphor. In this metaphor users refer to documents as if they are 'out there' on some virtual landscape. Subjects refer to the functions of Intermedia as the means, or vehicle, for getting to them, and links between documents as 'roads.' Some of the most typical decision statements that illustrate this way of understanding Intermedia include: "Let's go to...", "Let's go back to...", and "Back this way..."; Questions about the landscape are also present: "Where's the English thing?", "Does this go anywhere?", and "Where does this arrow lead me?" Finally, subjects commented about the progress of their journey: "Did I already go to...?", "I already looked at this...", "What did I go to?", "I was just here...", "Great, I'm just heading myself in circles" and "It's not going to let me go there."

Although the 'Intermedia-as-vehicle' metaphor is predominant, the protocol data do not strongly support the related metaphor used by designers to characterise hypertext systems: navigation. While it is true that subjects spoke of 'going to' documents, no mention is made of critical navigation concepts: distance between documents, direction (e.g., north) to documents, or landmarks to recognise position. Further, very few comments suggested that the user got lost (e.g., "Where am I?"); rather, it was the document that became lost ("Where was it?"). In other words, attempts were seldom made to answer two of the five questions that Barbara Allen (cited in Fischer and Mandl, 1991) suggests they should always be able to answer: Where am I? and How did I get here? Instead, the users ask, "What have I found on my journey?" and "Have I seen this before?"

This was somewhat puzzling. How could Intermedia be thought of as a vehicle but not in a navigational sense? One possible answer is that complex phenomena are understood in terms of mixed metaphors (Lakoff and Johnson, 1980). In addition to the 'Intermedia-as-vehicle' metaphor, most users also conceptualised Intermedia as a container in which documents are looked for and retrieved. Typical 'container' statements include: "Let's get another one", "Let's look for...", "There's not much in here", "Why is this in here?" and "There's too much stuff [in here]."

The importance of the metaphors used by subjects is that they largely determine how students approached the task. If Intermedia was thought of as the Yellow Pages, for example, we would find users looking up functional topic headings, then searching alphabetically and reviewing the titles and descriptions. However, Intermedia was thought of as a tool set (vehicle and container) by the subjects and hence each user was subject to the constraints and affordances of this tool metaphor.

According to Vygotsky (1978), tools mediate human effort to affect the physical world. That is, tools are used to increase our mechanical, chemical, electrical, and other types of advantage in such a way that we can accomplish tasks not otherwise possible. For example, the ox and plough allowed farmers to cultivate a plot of ground in a short amount of time not possible by hand. While the objective is to affect the physical world with a tool, an inevitable consequence is that the psychological world of the tool user is also affected. The ox and plough enabled the farmer to think reflexively about his life and his relationship to the rest of the world; now he could think about raising different kinds of crops and do other kinds of farming in his newly found time. In short, with each new tool that we use, our view of ourselves and our world is forever changed.

In the case of Intermedia as a tool, the physical world affected is quite different than that of most traditional tools. Intermedia allows users to rapidly access and construct visual sign systems. Signs, according to Vygotsky are like tools in that they are mediating devices. Instead of having an external orientation, however, signs are aimed internally, that is, at "mastering oneself" (Vygotsky, 1978, p. 55). For example, we read newspapers, articles, and books (all visual sign systems) to develop an understanding of our existence and to shape the way we think and behave. Sign systems are simply those man-made systems of symbols and rules for combining symbols that are used both explicitly and implicitly by humans to represent something other than itself (Eco, 1976).

The documents within Intermedia employ the two main types of sign systems that humans have used extensively throughout history: written language and pictures. Each document in Intermedia was meant by the author to represent his or her particular perspective on the topic at hand. A document is an argument — a persuasion — to influence another's understanding of an issue. Except for the portraits, the graphical pictures found within Intermedia represent a person's beliefs (or group consensus) about the relationships between documents and authors. Furthermore, the links found between documents represent the link creator's perspective on document relationship.

Intermedia, like all computer systems, represents a high-tech marriage between tools and sign systems. Intermedia, as a tool, mediates the quick and easy retrieval to and construction of written language and pictorial sign systems. It is unique in that it introduces two new kinds of sign systems: links between documents and the web. We are beginning to understand how the particular way that tool and sign are married in Intermedia might allow it to mediate cognitive processes, especially the practice, development, and application of critical thinking in a social context.

In addition to examining the metaphors that subjects used to conceptualise Intermedia and the task, we were also interested in the references made to self and to others. We found that almost every subject had inner speech that was oriented both socially and individually. Subjects referred to themselves singularly as in "I'll go to this now" as well as socially as in "Let's go to this now." We think that this is significant because this reference system mirrors that used by people when working in a group to achieve a task. In other words, the subject's attention focuses inward on self as well as outward toward the whole group to monitor performance and set goals. Some of the protocols were almost exclusively "I" oriented, some mostly "we", while others were about even. While this phenomenon might be attributable to habits of speech it is nonetheless interesting to note that these habits reflect a social orientation.

The individual orientation shows up pretty much as one would expect: "I'll do…", "I'm gonna do…", or "I need to…". In addition to goal setting, subjects used self-references when making judgements about their abilities, knowledge, memory, likes and dislikes. Again, these kinds of comments are the same ones found in social speech. We might hear someone say to a group, "I don't remember the main idea," referencing himself. Often an individual reference was found next to a social reference. For example, one student referred to herself by saying "I hate it when I do all this stupid stuff," and then addressed the virtual group: "Let's go to Works."

As in a social setting, an idea is 'discussed and debated' and then a decision is made whether to follow the suggestion. This was the first indication to us that what was going on when subjects used Intermedia was very much commensurate with Vygotsky's view of internalised behaviour. In other words, social speech used in the classroom and elsewhere becomes transformed into inner speech which each subject uses to guide themselves through the task. This social speech becomes mixed with an internal orientation. It is interesting to note that the essays found on Intermedia are also written in a "we" orientation, suggesting that this convention becomes internalised by the users.

CONCLUSION

The results of our study support our belief that learning is a constructive process that occurs personally but within a social domain. Measuring 'how much' each subject learned during the sessions was not attempted. Perhaps it is the wrong question. Scrutinising the think-aloud protocols shows that insights — indicators of new understandings — occur as the subject actively enters into a mediated dialogue with oneself. The subject shapes her own knowledge by solving the ill-structured problem and by taking advantages of the affordances and working around the constraints that this textbook of the future provides. As one part of the learning environment, we are convinced that Intermedia can be a powerful mediator to fostering learning and critical thinking.

How does Intermedia support the principles discussed earlier in the chapter? A point that needs reiteration is that Intermedia is a part of the larger learning environment that is commensurate with this philosophy of education. In Landow's class, Intermedia plays a major rôle in allowing students to experience knowledge construction. Indeed, each assignment requires students to blend various perspectives into logical wholes, hopefully resulting in new and wider understandings. The context for learning is now no longer contrived because students are actively preparing themselves for authentic discourse with their peers. Thus students are given a large measure of freedom — and responsibility — for what perspectives they visit and how they go about constructing knowledge.

Intermedia's weakest contribution to constructivist principles is its narrow range of representation. The version of Intermedia used in our study affords only the traditional sign systems: text and graphics. However, we have seen experimental versions that include animation and motion video, as well as collaborative writing spaces, that are very exciting. One can easily imagine extending the Intermedia concept to include voice, music, three-dimensional representations, mathematical nodes (e.g., spreadsheets) and so on.

It has become apparent to us that the reason for Intermedia's success as well as the point of its utility is its embeddedness in a social context as arranged by Landow. The think-aloud data make clear that constructing meaning mirrors social interaction. Thus, we emphasise our commitment to developing 'textbooks' which support and help develop the kind of dialectical thinking we have seen Intermedia support.

A FINAL WORD

In this chapter, we have tried to project the type of learning environment which is possible given recent advances in technology and a constructivist view of learning and learners. We want to stress once again that technology, in and of itself, will not bring about the sort of educational revolution we are seeking. Many of the constructivist principles outlined above can be followed without any of the tools we have described here and elsewhere (Knuth and Cunningham, in press; Fishman et al., 1991; Jones, Knuth, and Duffy, in press). Likewise, these tools which seem so well-suited to serving constructivist principles are easily adaptable and quite useful in the service of traditional instructional goals.

The combination of technology and constructivism, however, offers possibilities undreamed of until recently. We believe that the most important idea presented here is the notion that the textbook of the future will be a construction of the learner, drawing upon the database and authoring, linking and customising tools provided. Instructional software will be of a different type: instead of selecting, organising and presenting content, software will provide tools that enable students to select, construct, organise and customise information from a variety of sources and representational modes.

We are unsure of the impact of these ideas upon the future of education in general and instructional design and development in particular, but we are sure that the times ahead will be exciting and challenging.

ACKNOWLEDGEMENTS

The research reported in this chapter was supported by a grant from the Proffitt Endowment to the School of Education, Indiana University. We would like to thank the Institute for Research on Information and Scholarship, Professor George Landow, and his students at Brown University for their enthusiastic cooperation and participation.

REFERENCES

Akscyn, R., McCracken, D. and Yoder, E. (1988) KMS: A distributed hypermedia system for managing knowledge in organizations. *Communications of the ACM*, 31, 820–835.

Authorware, Inc. (1991) *MacWorld Interactive*. Minneapolis, MN: Authorware, Inc.

Bednar, A. E., Cunningham, D., Duffy, T. M. and Perry, D. (1991) Theory into practice: How do we link? In G. Anglin (ed.) *Instructional Technology: Past, Present, and Future*. Denver, CO: Libraries Unlimited.

Bereiter, C. (1984) How to keep thinking skills from going the way of all frills. *Educational Leadership*, 42, 75–77.

Brown, J. S., Collins, A. and Duguid, P. (1989a) Situated cognition and the culture of learning. *Educational Researcher*, 18, 32–42.

Brown, J. S., Collins, A. and Duguid, P. (1989b) Debating the situation: A rejoinder to Palinscar and Wineburg. *Educational Researcher*, 18, 10–12.

Bruner, J. (1966) *Toward a Theory of Instruction*. Cambridge, MA: Harvard University Press.

Clark, R. E. and Salomon, G. (1984) Media in teaching. In M. C. Wittrock (ed.) *Handbook of Research on Teaching* (3rd edition). New York: Macmillan. 464–478.

Cognition and Technology Group at Vanderbilt (1990) Anchored instruction and its relationship to situated cognition. *Educational Researcher*, 19, 2–10.

Cohen, J. (1960) A coefficient of agreement for nominal scales. *Educational and Psychological Measurement*, 20(1), 37–47.

Collins, A., Brown, J. S. and Newman, S. E. (1988) Cognitive apprenticeship: Teaching the craft of reading, writing, and mathematics. In L. B. Resnick (ed.) *Cognition and Instruction: Issues and Agendas*. Hillsdale, NJ: Lawrence Erlbaum Associates.

Conklin, J. (1987) Hypertext: A survey and introduction. *IEEE Computer*, 20(9), 17–41.

Cunningham, D. J. (in press) Beyond educational psychology: Steps toward an educational semiotic. *Educational Psychology Review*.

van Dijk, T. A. and Kintsch, W. (1983) *Strategies of Discourse Comprehension*. New York: Academic Press.

Duffy, T. M. and Knuth, R. (1990) Hypermedia and instruction: Where is the match? In D. Jonassen and H. Mandl (eds.) *Designing Hypermedia for Learning*. Berlin: Springer-Verlag.

Duffy, T. M. and Waller, R. (1985) *Designing Usable Texts*. New York: Academic Press.

Eco, U. (1976) *Theory of Semiotics*. Bloomington, IN: Indiana University Press.

Eisner, E. W. (1982) *Cognition And Curriculum: A Basis for Deciding What to Teach*. New York: Longman.

Ericsson, K. A. and Simon, H. A. (1984) *Protocol Analysis: Verbal Reports as Data*. Cambridge, MA: MIT Press.

Fischer, P. M. and Mandl, H. (1991) Introduction: Toward a psychophysics of hypermedia. In D. H. Jonassen and H. Mandl (eds.) *Designing Hypermedia for Learning*. Berlin: Springer-Verlag.

Fishman, B., Duffy, T. M., Brown, B., Chaney, T., Prigge, W. and Welsh, T. (1991) Tools for Classroom Restructuring: What Do Teachers Really Need? Instructional Systems Technology Occasional Paper. Bloomington, IN: Indiana University.

Freire, P. (1970) *Pedagogy of the Oppressed*. New York: Herder and Herder.

Gardner, H. (1983) *Frames of Mind: The Theory of Multiple Intelligences*. New York: Basic Books.

Glass, A. L. and Holyoak, K. J. (1986) *Cognition*. New York: Random House.

Hartley, J. (1978) *Designing Instructional Texts*. London: Kogan Page.

Heinich, R. (1984) The proper study of instructional technology. *Educational Communication and Technology: A Journal of Theory, Research and Development*, 32(2), 67–87.

Jonassen, D. (1989) *Hypertext/Hypermedia*. Englewood Cliffs, NJ: Educational Technology Publications.

Jones, B. F., Knuth, R. and Duffy, T. M. (in press) Constructing rich learning environments for professional development. In T. M. Duffy, J. Lowyck and D. Jonassen (eds.) *The Design of Constructivist Learning Environments*. Heidelberg: Springer-Verlag.

Kahn, P., Launhardt, J., Lenk, K. and Peters, R. (1990) Design of hypermedia publications: Issues and solutions. In R. Furuta (ed.) *Proceedings of the International Conference on Electronic Publishing, Document Manipulation and Typography*. Cambridge: Cambridge University Press. 107–124.

Knuth, R. and Cunningham, D. J. (in press) Tools for constructivism. In T. M. Duffy, J. Lowyck and D. Jonassen (eds.) *The Design of Constructivist Learning Environments*. Heidelberg: Springer-Verlag.

Lakoff, G. and Johnson, M. (1980) *Metaphors We Live By*. Chicago: University of Chicago Press.

Leont'ev, A. N. (1981) The problem with activity in psychology. In J. V. Wertsch (ed.) *The Concept of Activity In Soviet Psychology*. Armonk, NY: Sharpe.

Marshall, H. (1988) Work or learning: Implications of classroom metaphors. *Educational Researcher*, 17, 9–16.

Morrow, D. G., Greenspan, S. L. and Bower, G. H. (1987) Accessibility and situation models in narrative comprehension. *Journal of Memory and Language*, 26, 165–187.

Pea, R. (in press) Multimedia works: Student learning through multimedia tools. *IEEE Computer Graphics and Applications*.

Perkins, D. N. (1991) Technology meets constructivism: do they make a marriage? *Educational Technology*, 31(5), 18–23.

Perry, W. (1970) *Forms of Intellectual and Ethical Development in the College Years: A Scheme*. New York: Holt, Rinehart and Winston.

Resnick, L. (1987) Learning in school and out. *Educational Researcher*, 16, 13–20.

Roth, W. M. (1990) Collaboration and constructivism in the science classroom. Paper presented at the American Educational Research Association, Boston, April, 1990.

Scardamalia, M. and Bereiter, C. (1991) Higher levels of agency for children in knowledge building: A challenge for the design of new knowledge media. *The Journal of the Learning Sciences*, 1, 37–68.

Schön, D. (1983) *The Reflective Practitioner: How Professionals Think in Action*. New York: Basic Books.

Sherwood, R., Kinzer, C., Hasselbring, T. and Bransford, J. (1987) Macro-contexts for learning: Initial findings and issues. *Journal of Applied Cognition*, 1, 93–108.

Shneiderman, B. and Kearsley, G. (1989) *Hypertext Hands-On! An Introduction to a New Way of Organizing and Accessing Information*. Reading, MA: Addison-Wesley.

Sticht, T. G. and Hickey, D. T. (1988) Functional context theory, literacy, and electronics training. In R. Dillon and J. Pellegrino (eds.) *Instruction: Theoretical and Applied Perspectives*. New York: Praeger.

Suchman, L. A. (1987) *Plans and Situated Actions: The Problem of Human–Machine Communication*. Cambridge: Cambridge University Press.

Vygotsky, L. S. (1978) *Mind And Society: The Development of Higher Psychological Processes*. Cambridge, MA: Harvard University Press.

Wersch, J. V., Minick, N. and Arns, F. (1984) The creation of context in joint problem-solving. In B. Rogoff and J. Lave (eds.) *Everyday Cognition*. Cambridge, MA: Harvard University Press.

Winograd, T. and Flores, F. (1986) *Understanding Computers and Cognition*. Norwood, NJ: Ablex Publishing Corporation.

Woodhead, N. (1991) *Hypertext and Hypermedia: Theory and Applications*. Wokingham: Addison-Wesley.

Yankelovich, N. Haan, B., Meyrowitz, N. K. and Drucker, S. M. (1988) Intermedia: The concept and construction of a seamless information environment. *Computer*, January, 81–96.

4

Learning with Hypertext: Problems, Principles and Prospects

Nick Hammond
Department of Psychology, University of York, UK

OVERVIEW

Hypertext presentation systems, on their own, are a poor vehicle for many learning situations; they fail to support some of the key principles for effective understanding and memorisation. However, they do provide the basis for a new generation of exploratory learning systems. In this chapter we review cognitive principles underlying learning from hypertext-based systems, and consider the implications for design. Basic hypertext needs to be supplemented by more directed mechanisms for information access, for learner guidance and for a variety of simulation and creation tasks. Different learning situations may require quite different tutorial approaches and facilities, and we argue that hypertext systems potentially provide an organising structure for supporting a broad range of learning activities.

INTRODUCTION

Computer-based learning (CBL) has not been immune from the missionary zeal so characteristic of applications of hypertext and hypermedia. Claims and counterclaims of the supposed effectiveness of hypertext and multimedia for learning abound, usually pregnant with unstated assumptions about the nature of learning. Ted Nelson, whose vision has done so much to fire the field, sums up the philosophy:

> Anyone can choose the pathway or approach that suits him; with ideas accessible and interesting to everyone, so that a new richness and freedom can come to the human experience. (Nelson, 1981)

This can be realised within the new wave of multimedia technology:

Computer-supported multimedia is a new technology-based medium for thinking, learning and communication. Users can browse, annotate, link, and elaborate on information in a rich, non-linear, multimedia database [which] will allow students to explore and integrate vast libraries of text, audio and video information. (Ambron, 1988)

But do learners, or indeed teachers, really want to do this? How many learning situations actually require integration over a vast panorama of knowledge? Certainly, as argued by Alty (1991), there is an important rôle for browsing and exploration within the learning process, but is free-range browsing always preferable to battery feeding? Is there a happy medium? It may be fun, and perhaps instructive, to open every door and peer inside, but there are many situations where learning is most effective when the freedom of the learner is restricted to a relevant and helpful subset of activities: think only of arm bands for the young swimmer or stabiliser wheels for the budding cyclist. This contrasting 'training wheels' philosophy of restricting the initial freedom of the early learner has been successfully applied by Carroll and his associates (Carroll and Carrithers, 1984; Catrambone and Carroll, 1987) who demonstrated that learning with an initially simplified system can lead to sounder understanding and problem-solving even after transfer to the full system. An extension, termed the spiral curriculum approach, has been developed by Rosson, Carroll and Bellamy (1990) in which each learning block builds on previous learning experiences. These examples are restricted to the learning of a variety of computing skills; however, more general application of the 'minimalist' approach to instruction, of which constrained exploration is one avenue, is reviewed in Carroll (1990).

There are other assumptions in the use of hypertext for learning. For instance, while proponents of the intelligent tutoring systems may claim that the course of learning must be driven by explicit models of learners' and experts' states of knowledge, the hypertext philosophy assumes that there is no need to model the student, and that effective learning is achieved by allowing learners maximum freedom to explore information bases, to discover relationships for themselves and to form integrated structures as their learning goals demand. Thus strict intelligent tutoring has been criticised on the grounds that:

to treat the learner as a dumb patient and the computer system as an omniscient doctor is both perverse and arrogant. (Megarry, 1988)

On the other hand, strict hypertext-based learning can hardly be effective if learners merely ramble through the knowledge base in an unmotivated and haphazard fashion.

The point is that these and other assumptions need to be considered in terms of what we know about the determinants of effective learning in different situations. For the author of educational artefacts, it is a fact of life that human learning is extraordinarily varied. An exploratory approach might be optimal in one situation but counterproductive in another; in a third it might be appropriate to give the learner the choice of whichever approach suits best. Learning is not unitary; there is room for a spectrum of approaches to CBL in general and to learning from hypertext in particular. Generic prescriptive guidelines for educational design have only limited utility, and the author must take account of many of the characteristics of the learning situation and how people are likely to learn from the artefact in question.

One might hope that research on the fundamentals of learning would provide guidance for the instructional designer. However, it is also a fact of life that we know very little about the detailed mechanisms of learning; specifying a precise model of the cognitive changes which occur during a close encounter with an artefact as mundane as a textbook is not as yet a feasible exercise. But all is not lost: the more we are concerned with the practical aspects of instructional design, the less important this ignorance becomes. What matters is that we have some understanding of the situations and conditions that promote effective learning, even if we don't really understand what is going on in the learner's head. It is the engineering rather than the science of learning that is important. From this perspective, current psychological and educational theory can provide some helpful pointers for designers of educational materials. It is certainly the case that a solution to an instructional design problem driven entirely by the fads of current technology is unlikely to be the best way forward.

This chapter starts by identifying some of the major issues in the use of hypertext for learning. I then review a number of principles derived from psychological and educational theory which are important in determining effective learning, and finally discuss the implications of these principles for the design and use of hypertext for learning.

HYPERTEXT AND LEARNING

The use of hypertext tools in education and training is growing. In some cases, hypertext serves as the sole mechanism for delivering information to the student: I shall term this basic hypertext. Basic hypertext systems present information to the learner in the form of a linked network of displays (whether frame-based or window-based), allowing exploration through browsing. Learners are guided in part by their goals and in part by the imposed structure of the information network. More sophisticated presentation systems include additional facilities, for example for search or overview, to guide the learner through the material, to provide tutoring information, or to support other types of learning activity such as question answering, assessment or problem solving. Finally, some systems allow learners to generate or interlink materials for themselves, either by allowing access to the full authoring capabilities of the system or some structured subset of these facilities.

Experience with using hypertext systems for learning has revealed a number of problems and critical issues (for example, Hammond and Allinson, 1989; Jones, 1987). These are discussed in the following sections; they are not of course apparent in all cases, but they do give some insight into issues of general importance.

Navigation and search

One set of factors concerns how learners navigate around the information. (A general review of hypertext navigation can be seen in Oborne, 1990.) It is certainly the case that learners can get lost or disoriented in large hypertext structures. The information base may be large and its structure unfamiliar, and the links provided will not be suitable for all individuals and for all tasks. Once in an unknown or unexpected part of the knowledge base, the user may have difficulty in reaching familiar territory, although the provision of backtrack facilities may alleviate this. More critical, perhaps, is that learners may also have problems finding specific information they know to be present. The hypertext may not be structured in the way that they expect, or their lack of knowledge might mislead them. Jones (1987) has pointed out that the sheer number of alternative choices often makes appropriate selection difficult. A related problem is that of uncertain commitment, where the user is unsure where a link will lead or what type or amount of information will be shown: the impression for the user may be of an adventure game, where he or she is uncertain what can be selected and what will happen, but at least it could be something interesting and unexpected.

These navigational difficulties tend to arise when learners are unable to match their task goals to the structure of information and activities offered by the system; for instance the user of a tutorial on the anatomy of the brain may want to prepare notes on the plasticity of the nervous system, but have little clue as to where relevant information can be found or how the information sought relates to the overall structure. Problems may be compounded if the system fails to include facilities for gaining an overview of the information available and its organisation. Learners may fail to see how parts are inter-related and even miss large relevant sections entirely. In one experiment, we asked individuals to explore a small knowledge base for a fixed time using a variety of hypertext tools (Hammond and Allinson, 1989). After twenty minutes' use, we asked them how much of the material they thought they had covered. All users had available the basic hypertext mechanism for traversing links from one frame of information to another, but some users also had access to additional facilities such as *maps* (providing an overview), an *index* of keywords or a number of *guided tours* through the material. Compared with users of systems with these additional facilities, users of the basic hypertext version thought they had seen the *most* material when in fact they had seen the *least*. It was evidently hard for these users to get an overview of the available materials or a view of where they had been.

Guidance and control

Another important issue concerns the guidance the system provides for the learner. When learners are left to their own devices, there is the danger that they will ramble at random through the hypertext, with choices motivated by moment-to-moment aspects of the display which happen to attract attention. While serendipity may be a by-product, a system which gives a multiplicity of choice but the minimum of guidance may not be ideal for helping learners ask themselves the right questions (for instance, see Gay, 1986). Haphazard meanderings may be avoided when the learner has clear and explicit goals, and these can be realised with the tools available; but a more likely state of affairs is that the learner, uncertain of his or her goals and of how to attain them, will indeed search the environment for clues on what to do next. This may be both more fun and require less effort, but not necessarily conducive to structured learning.

Engaging the learners and their needs

A feature of basic hypertext presentation is that it is by nature passive: the learner may fail to engage with the materials in ways which result in effective learning. It is a truism that conceptual learning is much more effective if learners understand and think actively about the materials, their structure and relationships, and basic hypertext does not promote such processing by default. Material is there to be viewed, sure enough; but there is nothing to guarantee that the learner adopts a productive strategy for understanding and remembering. For instance Meyrowitz (1986) notes that some users of the Intermedia system showed no learning benefits and suggests that this may have been because they used the system passively rather than actively. Multimedia presentation, though often vivid and persuasive, is rarely 'interactive' in the sense that learners are required to engage actively with the content in relation to their learning goals. Plowman (1988) questions the claims made for so-called interactive video and suggests that the passive learning strategies it induces need to be bolstered by "cognitive enhancers". Multimedia environments in which the student is given tools to 'repurpose' existing materials (assemble snippets into a kind of multimedia essay) obviously allow more opportunity for engagement.

A related problem common to many CBL systems is that a given approach typically only supports a small range of the activities that could be usefully brought to bear on the learning situation. Learners may wish not only to browse material, but also to interact with demonstrations, solve problems, assess their knowledge, and generate or assemble materials for themselves. In some respects the open philosophy of hypertext systems may make it better suited than other approaches to support a range of learning activities, but there is still a danger of labelling an approach as 'hypertext only' and thereby artificially restricting its capabilities. It may be more helpful to take the view that hypertext provides one set of tools from the educational technologist's toolbox, to be used judiciously alongside others. Supporting a range of learning activities may go some way to resolving the problems of engagement: if learners can choose (or be directed to) an activity appropriate for their task and for their level of expertise, they are much more likely to think carefully about what they are doing.

Optimising the interface

Hypertext authoring systems are general-purpose tools with necessarily complex interfaces. All too often, the interfaces of hypertext systems for learning share this abstract quality and are not well adapted to the specific task in hand. Getting the interface right is crucial in learning situations so as to prevent needless squandering of the student's resources on coming to grips with the system. It can sometimes be helpful to encapsulate the interface facilities within a familiar metaphor as a way of minimising the learning required and maximising the transparency of the interface and use of the facilities (Hammond and Allinson, 1987).

Matching instructional approach with the learning need

A final point, already mentioned in the introduction, is that situations differ and not all will be suited to a particular CBL approach. Some, where the domain can be formalised and a 'best path' exists, may be best served by intelligent tutoring in which the system guides the course of the session on the basis of inferences about the learner's state of knowledge in relation to an 'expert' model of the knowledge to be learned. Other situations, where the optimal route through the domain is linear, may be suitable for programmed learning. Here the system presents information to the learner in a fixed sequence interspersed with tests, with branching back to earlier, or remedial, information if the tests indicate inadequate learning. An exploratory microworld approach, or even drill and practice, may be the best bet in yet other situations. Hypertext seems particularly suited to learning situations where flexibility in sequencing of exposure to materials and in the choice of learning activity is required. It may well be possible to incorporate a variety of instructional approaches within a hypertext framework, but this certainly does not absolve the instructional designer of the responsibility for matching learning need to educational provision.

We have identified a number of key points in the use of hypertext for learning: issues of navigation and search, and their relations to the learners' tasks; issues of guidance and control; issues of engagement and of learning activity; issues concerning the interface; and finally issues concerning the learning need. In the next section we step back to take a broader view of the underlying factors which may determine the effectiveness of learning before considering how some of these factors might inform the design of educational hypertexts.

PRINCIPLES FOR EFFECTIVE LEARNING

Understanding, learning and remembering

On the whole, learning of conceptual material occurs as a by-product of understanding it. This accords both with everyday views of learning and with psychological theory. Learning is not an optional activity that can be switched on or off independently of comprehension; the task implied by asking students to learn about, say, the greenhouse effect is that they should explore and understand the key issues, not that they should rote learn a specific text. The learning occurs without an explicit effort of memorisation, and by processes that are largely opaque to introspection.

Learning of procedural knowledge — of actions and how to do things — shares some of these properties. Again, learning may occur without a specific intention to learn and without insight into the acquisition process. However, since learning occurs as a by-product of performing the actions, rote practice (perhaps appropriately varied and contextualised) is often effective.

These impressions are backed up by a large body of psychological research that demonstrates that attempts to learn meaningful material by rote memorisation are rarely helpful (for example Craik and Watkins, 1973); that requesting people to learn rarely results in superior performance to study with no explicit instruction to learn (Nelson, 1976; Postman, 1964); and mnemonic strategies which add meaning to otherwise impoverished materials vastly improves learning (for example Sweeney and Bellezza, 1982). The implication for CBL is that conceptual materials should be presented to be as meaningful as possible for the learner. This in itself is rather a vacuous statement; its utility comes from considering just how material can be made meaningful. The following sections consider the factors which influence meaningfulness together with other influences on learning.

Effects of prior knowledge

An expert seems to be able to pick up new knowledge quite effortlessly. Mayes (1992) cites the example of the football devotee, reeling out the results of last Saturday's matches, who would be astonished to be regarded as having had to make any kind of effort to learn the information. Superior remembering by experts is attributed to the fact that they develop highly sophisticated frameworks or *schemas* which enable new facts to be slotted into the existing structure and immediately elaborated and enriched; the framework and the elaborations of the newly acquired knowledge together constitute a highly effective means for retrieving the information at a later date. Thus a particular football result is likely to have all sorts of interesting ramifications for the devotee which are quite lost on the tyro.

The power of schemas and elaboration in aiding memorisation cannot be over-emphasised. Chess masters are able to reconstruct a board position of more than 20 pieces after only five seconds' study, but only if the position is legal; for randomly positioned pieces the masters perform no better than novices (de Groot, 1965). It has been estimated that chess masters have acquired about 50,000 different (legal) chess patterns that they can quickly recognise (Simon and Gilmartin, 1973), and it is this schematic knowledge that supports their skill. Other examples include the heroic subject who increased his digit span (the number of digits one can correctly repeat back after a single presentation) to over 80 items after many hours of training by developing a structure based on times for athletic events (Chase and Ericsson, 1982), and a waiter able to memorise complete dinner orders from tables of up to eight guests (Ericsson and Polson, 1988). An interesting feature of both these last two experts is that, following a session (an hour's testing for the former, an evening shift for the latter), they were able to recall nearly all of the material from the entire session.

The factors that make such feats possible are obviously not characteristic of most learning situations; learners just do not have the background expertise to call upon. Nevertheless, there remain considerable advantages in harnessing their prior knowledge in more modest ways, for instance through the use of familiar examples or of analogies based on familiar situations.

Task specificity, situated action and affordance

There is a particular sort of knowledge learners will bring to the situation; their learning objectives and their view of the tasks to be performed in order to achieve these objectives. A CBL system which fails to meet the general objectives of the learner is hardly likely to be effective, but does this mean that the system should attempt to match every goal and task step of the learner? Is this in any case feasible? Recent years have seen something of a change of emphasis in the modelling of plans and their execution: there has been a swing from the somewhat formal view that people largely plan their goals and actions in advance (and that these can in principle be modelled) to the view that much action is 'situated', that is determined by a mix of high-level goals and of the specifics of the immediate situation. Thus one might have a general plan for crossing a busy road, but one's actions and short-term goals when half-way across are determined by the dynamics of the situation which may include quite unforeseen contingencies.

In the context of CBL, learning is situated in the sense that the way someone learns, and the cognitive resources they call upon, depend on the nature of the learning situation, possibly changing from moment to moment. Part of this situation is internal to the learner: their objectives and prior knowledge; part is determined by the system itself: the display of information and the alternatives offered to the learner. The learner's view of his or her objectives and task strongly colour the way the external information is interpreted; every teacher is familiar with the student who is unable to grasp some seemingly simple concept because of their particular perspective. The message for CBL is that as far as possible learning materials should be structured in a task-based fashion. Mere availability of information is likely to be insufficient. Given that planning is effortful except in highly familiar domains, people are inclined to determine their actions on the basis of external cues where possible. This accounts for the tendency of hypertext users, mentioned above, to follow the whim of the moment in selecting routes rather than following a more motivated path.

The notion of situated action is tied in with a related concept, that of *affordance*. This term refers to the fact that the artefacts we deal with in the world themselves embody information about how they are to be understood and used, and thus our actions are a product of both our internal knowledge and this external information. To take a simple example, a door handle is shaped and positioned such that is has an affordance for grasping, and our actions on approaching a closed door is determined by the coupling between our internal knowledge of doors in general and the specifics of the handle in front of us. The use of affordance in interface design is discussed by Gaver (1991). The notion is that the design of artefacts should naturally invite task-appropriate usage. In the case of a system for learning, the design of materials, activities and their presentation should lead the learner into the most effective strategies for learning. Hypertext systems often offer mis-affordances: features that invite actions which turn out to be suboptimal for the task in hand. Attractive-looking buttons to press will be pressed, regardless of the good intentions of the learner's plans.

Depth of processing

The sections above discuss the importance of the learner's existing knowledge and goals. Of equal importance is how learners should be encouraged to deal with novel information. The idea that the main determinant of memorability is the extraction of meaning is a central tenet of the principle of *depth of processing*. This term was coined by Craik and Lockhart (1972) to reflect the extent, or depth, to which a person processes the meaning of the material to be learned. Later work has demonstrated that depth is better conceived of as the number and nature of the elaborations the learner generates, and how these elaborations relate to the situations under which the material is to be remembered (Anderson, 1990; Eysenck and Keane, 1990). Nevertheless, depth of processing remains a useful heuristic concept. Whatever the details of the underlying mechanisms, the important point for CBL is that the more the learner thinks about the material, the better they will remember it — where 'more' does not mean simply for longer but in greater depth and variety.

This is why both active engagement in materials and task relevance are so important. A cursory browsing of materials will result in shallow processing, few elaborations and poor retention. Materials which are perceived as distant from the learner's task perspective may well not stimulate engagement, but even if they do they will not be elaborated in a way which 'binds' the material to wider aspects of the task. This issue of relevance is discussed further in the section on encoding specificity and encoding variability below.

Learning-by-doing: enactment and generation effects

Two further effects, both probably related to the underlying concept of elaboration, are particularly relevant to CBL. Both illustrate that learning is enhanced by doing rather than just by reading or observing. If one group of subjects is asked to remember the descriptions of simple actions (such as breaking a match) and another group actually performs the actions, subsequent recall is higher for those that performed the actions (Cohen, 1984). This is known as the *enactment effect*.[1] The cause of the effect is currently a subject of debate, and some of the laboratory findings are rather unexpected. For instance, although memory for enacted events is superior, the forgetting rates for enacted and non-enacted material is similar (Nilsson, Cohen and Nyberg, 1989); and while recognition and cued recall of non-enacted events are normally highly dependent, these two process are largely independent for enacted events (Svensson and Nilsson, 1989).

The *generation effect* also concerns superior learning for material which has been acted upon, and refers to the finding that people tend to be better at remembering material that they have generated for themselves than equivalent material provided by someone else (for example, Gardiner, 1989; Greene, 1988). Again, there are arcane theoretical disputes on the underlying mechanisms (probably the critical factor is the nature of the resulting elaborations), but the point is that in general better learning results.

The implications for CBL are clear enough. Learning-by-doing, whether through performance of task-relevant actions or through the generation of materials, tends to lead to good retention of information. Learning-by-doing, together with minimising the baggage of verbal instructions and descriptions, has been a central theme of the highly effective minimalist approach to the training of computing skills pioneered by Carroll and his associates (Black, Carroll and McGuigan, 1987; Carroll, 1989; Carroll *et al.*, 1988). Obviously learning through the performance of task-relevant actions is likely to be particularly helpful when the knowledge to be acquired includes the very same skills, but even with the learning of abstract conceptual information it is often possible to include activity-based learning activities: interactive demonstrations or simulations, the generation or manipulation of materials, or even a requirement to generate teaching materials for someone else.

Encoding specificity and encoding variability

Information is learned for a number of purposes. The learner might have a specific examination or assessment in mind, requiring recollection and perhaps a reworking of the material; the learning may be directed towards some specific task or procedures; or the learner may view the material as a component within some broader perspective of education. The situation in which the information will be used is an important determinant of how it

---

[1] Terry Mayes was the first to point out the relevance of this effect to computer-based learning in 1991.

should best be learned: other things being equal, the greater the similarity between the conditions of learning and the conditions of use, the better the demonstrable learning. This is an informal version of a far-reaching principle of memory performance, the principle of encoding specificity (Tulving, 1983). The principle is grounded within a theory of memory which assumes that retrieval of information depends on the learner generating (or having available) memory cues — fragments of the original information — which enable more of the learned information to be recovered. The more potential cues available, and the more specifically they refer to the required learning experience rather than to other experiences, the greater the chance of successful recall of the information.

This principle has two general implications for learning. The first is that the learning situation should contain cues that will be helpful during use of the information. The second is that such cues should help the learner pinpoint the particular information required. Thus material using distinctive concrete examples which the learner can easily bring to mind is likely to be a good bet. Material which is homogeneous in form and content will be less so. If the CBL material is to support some specific task, then as far as feasible the materials should reflect the intended tasks and its situation. It may be important for the situation of learning to be made as realistic as possible; for instance learners might find information embodied within a game context hard to generalise from since the context of learning is rather different from the context of information use.

Interestingly, the theory predicts that the general context will influence learning as well as the specifics of the material. The general context covers aspects not related to the particular material, such as the room in which learning occurs, the time of day or the mood of the learner; similar contexts for learning and for recall are generally found to result in better performance, though at times the difference is quite small. While the laboratory experiments demonstrating these effects tend to use very simple materials, such as lists of words, there are some studies using more realistic situations which replicate the findings (eyewitness memory of a staged crime is one such example: see Davies and Milne, 1985). In CBL, unless the student is learning a computer-based task, many aspects of the context of learning are bound to differ from the context of use; however, this may not be any more than for material studied in a library or delivered in a lecture. If CBL is the exception rather than the rule, then this difference itself can be capitalised upon as a distinctive cue.

In education, particular facts or concepts are often studied on multiple occasions, perhaps from different perspectives or by different methods. From the arguments above, one might suppose that studying material in a number of different contexts or from a variety of perspectives would be advantageous, since at least one of the study contexts would be likely to match with the context of use, and multiple perspectives might result in key points standing out against the shifting background. This effect has been demonstrated to be robust, and the underlying principle is termed encoding variability. Indeed, merely spacing out practice in time, and thereby increasing the differences in context between one learning trial and the next, tends to improve memorisation (Madigan, 1969).

It is hard to better Anderson's conclusions about encoding variability:

> The implications of these results for study habits are almost too obvious to require comment: we should space our study of particular material over time; and when such spacing is impossible, we should change the context of repetitive study. At a physical level, we can change the location in which we study. At a more abstract level, we can try to change the perspective we take on the to-be-learned material. (Anderson, 1990)

CBL may well be able provide that variety of perspective, particularly if material is studied from different viewpoints by conventional and by computer-based means.

Explicit versus implicit learning

The distinction between explicit and implicit forms of learning is particularly relevant to hypertext-based learning, since hypertext and multimedia provide a potentially rich environment for implicit learning during exploratory tasks. When knowledge is explicit, it can be expressed directly by the individual — in words or using some other form of expression; an example is knowing who the President of the USA is. Implicit knowledge cannot be described directly, but its presence can be inferred from the person's actions; knowing how to ride a bicycle is an example. A similar distinction can be made between explicit learning, where the learner is aware of the facts, rules or other information which they are learning, and implicit learning, where the learner is not aware of some of this material. It is claimed that much childhood learning and adult learning occurs implicitly, and particularly the learning of skills. Some have argued for a clear distinction between explicit and implicit modes of learning (Hayes and Broadbent, 1988); certainly there can be a dissociation between the two types of knowledge in memory performance (Graf and Schachter, 1985). Models of learning based upon connectionist principles (Pike, 1984) or on multiple-trace memories (such as Hintzman, 1986) give a spur to the idea that rules and structures can be abstracted from experiences without the need for them to be represented or taught explicitly.

This distinction between two ways of expressing knowledge, explicitly or implicitly, is closely related to a common distinction between two forms of knowledge representation, declarative and procedural representations. Declarative knowledge (essentially knowledge of facts) is usually expressed explicitly; procedural knowledge (knowledge of how to do things) is generally expressed implicitly, through performance. The correlation is not perfect however: experts may acquire or express what would normally be classed as declarative knowledge with little explicit awareness. For instance, Chase and Ericsson's subject (1982), who extended his digit span to 80 or more items, was initially well aware of how he encoded the digits (using an elaborate system based on times for athletic events). However after about 100 hours' practice, when he had a span of about 40 digits, he was unable to report details of how the digits were held.

The idea of implicit learning is an appealing one for the proponents of hypertext-based learning; if just by browsing through the information network the learner can soak in information like a sponge, and without the mental effort characteristic of explicit learning, then a truly revolutionary learning medium has been found. However, it is necessary to identify just when implicit rather than explicit learning is appropriate and possible, and what the optimal instructional approach for each type of learning might be. Implicit learning seems to be characteristic of skill-based tasks, where actions are learned through repeated performance, and also of other tasks where rules of structures can be abstracted from repeated instances. Thus aspects of language learning, like the implicit use of grammatical rules, can be implicit. Implicit learning is no substitute for the hard thinking required for much conceptual learning.

Individual differences

Different individuals will adopt different learning styles for the same materials, and a single individual may change learning styles from one occasion to another. Such differences are highly informative of the underlying processes of learning and their variability, and have some practical consequences for the provision of optimal learning for a range of individual styles. However, all too often the design aspects of CBL systems to be resolved are of such a basic nature that consideration of individual differences is something of a luxury. The issues will not be discussed here; we have raised some of the issues in Allinson and Hammond (1990).

Metacognition

A final issue of particular relevance to hypertext-based learning is the extent to which learners can choose their own strategies and learning activities. Metacognition refers to people's ability to self-regulate their cognitive processes, and in many respects metacognitive skills can be considered much like other skills in that they can be learned and refined with experience. For instance, even young children possess quite sophisticated metacognitive skills for remembering to perform future actions. Kreutzer, Leonard and Flavell (1975) found that five-year-olds demonstrated at least some techniques for reminding themselves to do things, whilst older children have a wide range of mnemonic strategies at their disposal.

Hypertext-based learning makes a number of assumptions about metacognitive skills. In particular, it supposes that learners can make well-motivated choices over the sequencing of exposure to materials and the best strategy for organising learning activities. As we have seen above, these assumptions may at times be over-optimistic. However, within appropriate constraints, learning can often be effectively self-directed, with exploratory behaviour resulting in a kind of cognitive experimentation. Mayes (1992) argues that learners are intrinsically motivated to seek and explore explanations, and that this should be capitalised upon by engaging the learner in challenging tasks.

EXTENDING HYPERTEXT-BASED LEARNING

The message from the section on hypertext and learning above is that basic hypertext systems may fail to provide learners with the support, direction and engagement that learning requires; the section concerning effective learning outlined some of the principles which reflect on these partial failures and suggested some implications for the design of hypertext-based learning. In this section we suggest a framework for thinking through how some of these principles can be applied to the kinds of tools typically provided by hypertext systems and the kinds of learning tasks they support. This framework is shown in Figure 1.

The figure summarises three relevant dimensions along which hypertext-based learning systems, and computer-based learning in general, vary: control, engagement and synthesis. Control refers to the degree to which the learner rather than the system controls exposure to learning materials, the particular learning activity or strategy. Engagement refers to the extent that learner is required to process the materials actively rather than passively. Synthesis refers to the nature of the learning activity: does it require the learner to create materials or relationships rather than merely observe them? These last two dimensions are not independent since creative tasks generally require active engagement, although the converse is not true.

In the figure, these dimensions define a cube, crudely divided into eight regions by dichotomising each dimension. Basic hypertext systems can be located in the lower back left region since these typically allow learner control, provide only passive engagement and merely present materials to the learner. However, more advanced hypermedia facilities and variations in learner tasks allow 'movement' along the dimensions.

As we have seen, the level of learner control available within hypertext systems is a two-edged sword for the learner; self-regulation may be possible, but at the risk of haphazard browsing. The problem is too often an implicit assumption that the learner's goal of understanding can be equated with the designer's goal of information provision. If learning also needs thought, then it is often the case that more explicit direction and control, to restrict the learner to realistic goals and to a sensible part of the domain knowledge, needs to be judiciously mixed with freedom of action. System guidance may vary from the explicit step-by-step constraints of programmed learning, through optional fixed sequences, such as guided tours (Hammond and Allinson, 1989) or other path structures (Zellweger, 1989), to provision of advice over learning activities or sequencing of materials. The provision of navigation tools (maps, indexes, overviews and so on) can also help learners define their goals and actions.

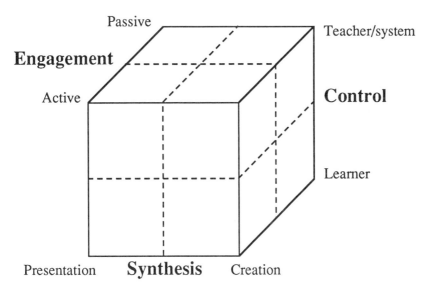

Passive

Engagement

Teacher/system

Active

Control

Learner

Presentation   **Synthesis**   Creation

Figure 1. A cube representing relevant dimensions of computer-based
learning. The three dimensions of the cube, height, width and
depth, represent the degree of learner control, synthesis and
engagement respectively.

The second dimension, engagement, identifies the potential problem
that presentation can result in merely passive browsing. One strategy is to
provide learners with external motivation for making the best of the
information available, perhaps through imaginative learning assignments.
Another strategy is for the system itself to provide the learning challenge and
engage learners more actively as they move around the hypertext structure.
This is the philosophy behind the StrathTutor system (Mayes, Kibby and
Anderson, 1990). Alternatively, the system can provide a range of learning
activities which move outside strict hypertext: problems to solve, interactive
demonstrations, simulations, self-assessment and so on.

In terms of the synthesis dimension, allowing the learner access to
authoring facilities provides a creative capability, although letting the novice
learner loose with the full complexity of an authoring system is not likely to
be a productive enterprise. More limited and directed facilities for creativity
may be more educationally effective. These could focus on re-working the
materials themselves, such as creating multimedia essays, the specification
of learning sequences such as self-generated tours, the use of annotation
facilities, or the creation or manipulation of structural overviews. This last
possibility is supported by a variety of concept mapping tools, such as
Learning Tool (Kozma, 1992), and their use is discussed in Trapp and
Hammond (1991) and Trapp, Reader and Hammond (1992). A more
constrained synthesis task, termed knowledge jigsaws, is described by

Hammond (1992). Different learning requirements will benefit from each of these tools.

The message is that the hypermedia designer needs to think carefully about how learners will use his or her system. Learning is not the same as retrieving information, and depends on subtle interactions of the learning context, the materials, the tools provided and the learner. The hypertext approach is one of many in the armoury of the educational technologist — we describe a heuristic method for assessing the pros and cons of different approaches in Hammond and Trapp (1992). However, as well as supporting an educational approach based on learner exploration and choice, hypertext provides a framework within which a range of tools and techniques can be coordinated and deployed, posing both unique challenges to the educational designer and unique potential to the learner.

REFERENCES

Allinson, L. J. and Hammond, N. V. (1990) Learning support environments: rationale and evaluation. *Computers and Education*, 15, 137–143.

Alty, J. L. (1991) Multimedia — what is it and how do we exploit it? In D. Diaper and N. V. Hammond (eds.) *People and Computers VI*. Cambridge: Cambridge University Press. 31–44.

Ambron, S. (1988) What is multimedia? In S. Ambron and K. Hooper (eds.) *Interactive Multimedia*. Redmond, WA: Microsoft Press.

Anderson, J. R. (1990) *Cognitive Psychology and Its Implications* (3rd edition). New York: Freeman.

Black, J. B., Carroll, J. M. and McGuigan, S. M. (1987) What kind of minimal instruction manual is the most effective? In J. M. Carroll and P. P. Tanner (eds.) *CHI+GI '87 Proceedings*. New York: ACM. 159–162.

Carroll, J. M. (1989) An overview of minimalist instruction. Technical Report RC 15109 (#67329). IBM Watson Research Center, New York.

Carroll, J. M. (1990) *The Nurnburg Funnel: Designing Minimalist Instruction for Practical Computer Skills*. Cambridge, MA: MIT Press.

Carroll, J. M. and Carrithers, C. (1984) Blocking learner error states in a training-wheels system. *Human Factors*, 26, 377–389.

Carroll, J. M., Smith-Kerker, P. L., Ford, J. R. and Mazur-Rimitz, S. A. (1988) The minimal manual. *Human-Computer Interaction*, 3, 123–153.

Catrambone, R. and Carroll, J. M. (1987) Learning a word processing system with training wheels and guided exploration. In J. M. Carroll and P. P. Tanner (eds.) *CHI+GI '87 Proceedings*. New York: ACM. 169–173.

Chase, W. and Ericsson, K. A. (1982) Skill and working memory. In
    G. H. Bower (ed.) *The Psychology of Learning and Motivation,
    Volume 16*. New York: Academic Press.
Cohen, R. L. (1984) Individual differences in event memory: A case for
    nonstrategic factors. *Memory and Cognition*, 12, 633–641.
Craik, F. I. M. and Lockhart, R. S. (1972) Levels of processing: a framework
    for memory research. *Journal of Verbal Learning and Verbal
    Behavior*, 11, 671–684.
Craik, F. I. M. and Watkins, M. J. (1973) The role of rehearsal in short-term
    memory. *Journal of Verbal Learning and Verbal Behavior*, 12, 599–
    607.
Davies, G. and Milne, A. (1985) Eyewitness composite production: A
    function of mental or physical reinstatement of context. *Criminal
    Justice and Behavior*, 12, 209–220.
Ericsson, K. A. and Polson, P. G. (1988) An experimental analysis of the
    mechanisms of a memory skill. *Journal of Experimental Psychology:
    Learning, Memory and Cognition*, 14, 305–316.
Eysenck, M. W. and Keane, M. T. (1990) *Cognitive Psychology: A Student's
    Handbook*. Hillsdale, NJ: Lawrence Erlbaum Associates.
Gardiner, J. M. (1989) A generation effect in memory without awareness.
    British Journal of Psychology, 80, 163–168.
Gaver, W. W. (1991) Technology affordances. In S. P. Robertson,
    G. M. Olson and J. S. Olson (eds.) *CHI '91 Conference Proceedings*.
    New York: ACM. 79–84.
Gay, G. (1986) Interaction of learner control and prior understanding in
    computer-assisted video instruction. *Journal of Educational
    Psychology*, 78, 225–227.
Graf, P. and Schachter, D. L. (1985) Implicit and explicit memory for new
    associations in normal and amnesic patients. *Journal of Experimental
    Psychology: Learning, Memory and Cognition*, 11, 501–518.
Greene, R. L. (1988) Generation effects in frequency judgement. *Journal of
    Experimental Psychology: Learning, Memory and Cognition*, 14,
    298–304.
de Groot, A. D. (1965) *Thought and Choice in Chess*. The Hague: Mouton.
Hammond, N. V. (1992) Tailoring hypertext for the learner. In
    P. A. M. Kommers, D. H. Jonassen and J. T. Mayes (eds.) *Mindtools:
    Cognitive Technologies for Modelling Knowledge*. Berlin: Springer-
    Verlag.
Hammond, N. V. and Allinson, L. J. (1987) The travel metaphor as a design
    principle and training aid for navigating around complex systems. In
    D. Diaper and R. Winder (eds.) *People and Computers III*.
    Cambridge: Cambridge University Press. 75–90.
Hammond, N. V. and Allinson, L. J. (1989) Extending hypertext for
    learning: an investigation of access and guidance tools. In A. Sutcliffe
    and L. Macaulay (eds.) *People and Computers V*. Cambridge:
    Cambridge University Press.

Hammond, N. V. and Trapp, A. L. (1992) Matching CBL approach to learning need: A heuristic methodology for instructional design. In P. Brusilovsky and V. Stefanuk (eds.) *East-West Conference on Emerging Technologies in Education*. Moscow, April, 142–146.

Hayes, N. A. and Broadbent, D. E. (1988) Two modes of learning for interactive tasks. *Cognition*, 28, 249–276.

Hintzman, D. L. (1986) "Schema abstraction" in a multiple-trace memory model. *Psychological Review*, 93, 411–428.

Jones, W. P. (1987) How do we distinguish the hyper from the hype in non-linear text? In H.-J. Bullinger and B. Shackel (eds.) *Human-Computer Interaction — Interact '87*. Amsterdam: North-Holland. 1107–1113.

Kozma, R. B. (1992) Constructing knowledge with Learning Tool. In P. A. M. Kommers, D. H. Jonassen and J. T. Mayes (eds.) *Mindtools: Cognitive Technologies for Modelling Knowledge*. Berlin: Springer-Verlag.

Kreutzer, M. A., Leonard, C. and Flavell, J. H. (1975) An interview study of children's knowledge about memory. *Monographs of the Society of Research in Child Development*, 40(1).

Madigan, S. A. (1969) Intraserial repetition and coding processes in free recall. *Journal of Verbal Learning and Verbal Behavior*, 8, 828–835.

Mayes, J. T. (1992) Mindtools: a suitable case for learning. In P. A. M. Kommers, D. H. Jonassen and J. T. Mayes (eds.) *Mindtools: Cognitive Technologies for Modelling Knowledge*. Berlin: Springer-Verlag.

Mayes, J. T., Kibby, M. R. and Anderson, T. (1990) Signposts for conceptual orientation: some requirements for learning from hypertext. In R. McAleese and C. Green (eds.) *Hypertext: State of the Art*. Oxford: Intellect. 121–129.

Megarry, J. (1988) Hypertext and compact discs — the challenge of multimedia learning. *British Journal of Educational Technology*, 19, 172–183.

Meyrowitz, N. (1986) Intermedia: The architecture and construction of an object-oriented hypertext/hypermedia system and applications framework. In *OOPSLA '86 Proceedings*. Portland, Oregon.

Nelson, T. H. (1981) *Literary Machines*. Available from the author, 8480 Fredericksburg #138, San Antonio, TX 78229, USA.

Nelson, T. O. (1976) Reinforcement and human memory. In W. K. Estes (ed.) *Handbook of Learning and Cognitive Processes, Volume 3*. Hillsdale, NJ: Lawrence Erlbaum Associates.

Nilsson, L.-G., Cohen, R. L. and Nyberg, L. (1989) Recall of enacted and non-enacted instructions compared: forgetting functions. *Psychological Research*, 51, 188–193.

Oborne, D. J. (1990) Browsing and navigation through hypertext documents: a review of the human-computer interface issues. *Interactive Multimedia*, 1, 23–32.

Pike, R. (1984) Comparison of convolution and matrix distributed memory systems for associative recall and recognition. *Psychological Review*, 91, 281–294.

Plowman, L. (1988) Active learning and interactive video: A contradiction in terms? *Programmed Learning and Educational Technology*, 25, 289–293.

Postman, L. (1964) Short-term memory and incidental learning. In A. W. Melton (ed.) *Categories of Human Learning*. New York: Academic Press.

Rosson, M. B., Carroll, J. M. and Bellamy, R. K. E. (1990) Smalltalk scaffolding: A case study of minimalist instruction. In J. C. Chew and J. Whiteside (eds.) *CHI '91: Human Factors in Computing Systems*. New York: ACM.

Simon, H. A. and Gilmartin, K. (1973) A simulation of memory for chess positions. *Cognitive Psychology*, 5, 29–46.

Svensson, T. and Nilsson, L.-G. (1989) The relationship between recognition and cued recall in memory of enacted and nonenacted information. *Psychological Research*, 51, 194–200.

Sweeney, C. A. and Bellezza, F. S. (1982) Use of keyword mnemonics in learning English vocabulary. *Human Learning*, 1, 155–163.

Trapp, A. L. and Hammond, N. V. (1991) Concept mapping tools: a different approach. *Psychology Software News*, 2, 10–11.

Trapp, A. L., Reader, W. and Hammond, N. V. (1992) Tools for knowledge mapping: a framework for understanding. In P. Brusilovsky and V. Stefanuk (eds.) *East-West Conference on Emerging Technologies in Education*. Moscow, April, 306–312.

Tulving, E. (1983) *Elements of Episodic Memory*. London: Oxford University Press.

Zellweger, P. T. (1989) Scripted documents: a hypermedia path mechanism. In *Hypertext '89 Proceedings*. New York: ACM.

5

Enhancing the Usability of Text Through Computer Delivery and Formative Evaluation: the SuperBook Project

Thomas Landauer, Dennis Egan, Joel Remde, Michael Lesk, Carol Lochbaum and Daniel Ketchum
Bell Communications Research, Morristown, USA

OVERVIEW

The SuperBook project grew out of the convergence of two sources of interest in the use of computers for the delivery of text. The first was a set of research studies concerned with the psychology of information access by humans, studies initially done in the context of document retrieval and interfaces to databases. These studies attempted to analyse the factors involved when people look for and assimilate information, and in particular to identify important reasons for failures. Out of these studies, in turn, grew a number of schemes for improving human performance in search tasks. These schemes used computers to support indexing, querying, navigation and display in new ways that are difficult, if not impossible, to accomplish with paper and ink technology. The other source of the SuperBook concept was the ongoing evolution of computer-based methods for composing and publishing textual materials. Word processing and automated printing technology now make the vast majority of newly produced textual materials potentially available in machine readable form. Moreover, the option of storing and distributing large volumes of text electronically has become not only feasible but economically attractive.

The SuperBook project, as such, began around 1985. By that time, various subgroups of the cognitive science research group at Bellcore had progressed from psychological studies of information access to the development of research prototypes of new search and navigation tools. Some of these had been separately evaluated in controlled laboratory experiments and shown to be effective. Trying them out as components in an integrated text enhancement system was appealing. At the same time, text and reference books produced by Bellcore for telephone company use had become available in machine readable form. Moreover, there were distinct murmurs of interest in completely electronic delivery of these documents to business computer terminals for use. But there were also reports that previous attempts to deliver text electronically had foundered on usability defects. Not only was text on screens hard to read, but it also appeared to produce severe problems of disorientation.

Thus there was both an enticing applied research opportunity and a challenging practical problem to be attacked in trying to find a way to make computer-delivered text as usable as the paper versions it would replace. This modest but important goal has shaped the SuperBook project throughout. We have adopted a strongly empirical approach, in which the actual usability of prototype versions and of their component functions and features have been evaluated in detailed behavioural studies and compared repeatedly with the use of the competing paper and ink technology. The lynchpin of the work has been user-centred behavioural research aimed at discovering what kinds of computer aids will actually help people to use text more effectively.

It is perhaps useful to contrast this approach with other efforts in hypertext (see Nielsen, 1990). The SuperBook project differs from most hypertext research efforts in that its intent has been to study the use of computers for improved delivery of ordinary textual materials, rather than to create tools for new ways of authoring and organising information resources. Most hypertext research efforts have adopted as self-evident the assumption, often attributed to Vannevar Bush (1945), that authoring and structuring information in modules connected by a network of easily traversed links would greatly improve its value. The research task has been taken largely to be the implementation of this idea: the design of tools for creating and delivering text structured in novel ways. In contrast, while the SuperBook system has always included the support of certain kinds of hypertext links, they have never been its *raison d'être*. Indeed, we have retained a rather conservative attitude towards the concept of intertext links in general, a matter to which we will return later.

In this chapter, we will review some of the background research in the psychology of information access, along with the experimental work on prototype information search tools that preceded and contributed to the initial design of SuperBook. Then we will describe a series of versions of the SuperBook system along with the usability studies that compared its use to that of paper and print and whose detailed analyses drove the iterative development. We will also describe several other accessory studies done along the way that helped to guide design choices. In addition, we will report tests of the system with several different kinds of users using different kinds of materials in different sorts of tasks, ranging from the use of textbooks for open book exams in chemistry and statistics to reference materials as job aids in telephone business applications. We have found that the design of text-delivery tools can depend heavily on the kind of text and what the user wants to do with it — no surprise — and we illustrate some of the design issues that result. We will also briefly describe ports of the SuperBook system to a number of different platforms, and some of the usability design problems that have been raised, although not necessarily solved as yet, by dealing with hardware, software and standards constraints.

Finally we will describe a new set of experiments, including new prototype delivery interfaces that incorporate some rather different techniques from those expressed in SuperBook. This last study is part of a cooperative research project in which substantial quantities of text in the field of chemistry will be delivered to faculty and students at Cornell University in electronic form.

RESEARCH ON FINDING AND ABSORBING INFORMATION IN TEXT

In this section we describe what may seem to be a grab-bag of miscellaneous studies on information searching, not a clearly articulated program of research directed at issues in hypertext or at the creation of a system. Indeed, the studies were not conducted with any such goal, or any single goal, in mind. However, they all did in the end contribute ideas and constraints to the design and development of the SuperBook browser. What unites them conceptually is that they all dealt with aspects of the problems people have in finding information or with the evaluation of proposed computer-based solutions to such problems. We begin this account by setting the stage, first with a brief general discussion of the use of printed text as an information medium, then of the state of the art in computer-based information retrieval.

Textual information presentation before computers

Before discussing research relevant to electronic text delivery, let us start by reminding ourselves of some of the goals, issues, problems, solution techniques, functions and features represented in the use of traditional text. It is important to do this because in designing new ways of delivering textual information we will run the risk of changing well-evolved traditional techniques in deleterious ways.

Of course, all text is intended to convey information of some sort to the reader. Authors, by which we mean here the entire authoring profession of writers, editors, indexers, compositors, printers and librarians, are engaged in an attempt to communicate. The goal of their craft is to move information that is scattered, unavailable or obscure into a location and form in which it can be more easily grasped by the minds of others. Authors try to use language that is at once sufficiently precise to express ideas unambiguously (or in some cases with just the ambiguity intended), while at the same time being as comprehensible as possible to an intended group of readers. People read only a little bit at a time — probably only one word at a time (see McConkie and Raynor, 1975) — forget rather rapidly as they go, and accommodate new information very strongly to what they knew or believed before they started, so good authors need to frequently repeat and rephrase information in just the right times and places. Authors try to organise and arrange information so that certain kinds of logical or expositional contingencies are maintained, for instance that the facts, concepts or vocabulary whose comprehension depends on other facts, concepts or vocabulary are introduced in the appropriate order. Within and between sentences and paragraphs the 'grammar' of discourse matters. Knowledge in the reader's mind does not grow simply as a heap, but often is more like a growing crystal; there are only some propositions that can be attached to the existing structure at each point (Kintsch and van Dijk, 1978). There are a host of more or less well codified discourse order conventions that help authors deal with these cognitive constraints in conveying meaning to readers. For example, narrative accounts tend to mirror the temporal order of events they describe in the order of presentation in text, argumentative discourse proceeds from premises to conclusions, scientific reports go from problem to observation to inference, and so forth.

When the body of text and ideas grows beyond rather small limits, the likelihood that any given reader will read the whole thing end to end, in one sitting, and with overall comprehension diminishes rapidly. Some readers will already know enough about some parts and want to skip them, others will have limited time, others limited ability to comprehend. Such readers will need guidance as to where in the text what information is to be found. Even skimming, an important activity in the face of overabundant text, can only succeed if the sampled input guides the reader to regions of concentrated interest. Structural guidance can also be very helpful for those who actually read the text word for word and beginning to end. It is well established that "advanced organizers" (Ausubel, Novak and Hanesian, 1978), summaries and review questions (Rothkopf, 1972; Frase and Kreitzberg, 1975) improve the comprehensibility and memorability of text.

Authors and readers may have additional problems in reconciling needs for greater quantity and detail of information with smoothness and clarity of exposition. Excursions into related or explanatory topics, scholarly citations, examples and illustrations can be both helpful and disruptive, and the degree to which they are can depend on the reader and the current reason for reading. Devices such as footnotes and parenthetical references have long been used, but little systematic knowledge exists about their relative merits and optimal use. Even the use of figures and graphs can have either beneficial or adverse effects that are not understood much beyond the level of art and craft (Dwyer, 1972; Schallert, 1980).

To make it easier to comprehend long texts, or to find component information, authors often provide headings, subheadings, tables of contents, typographical and layout cues to the relative importance, subordination, or relation between parts. Beyond a certain length of document, they are likely also to provide indices. Collections of books or articles may be further categorised and catalogued. For collections of short documents like journal articles, abstracts and keywords may be added as both identifiers for search and advanced organisers for reading, and a variety of categorisation and search tools may be provided for finding sets of articles relevant to a particular purpose.

How well does all of this work? How well text communicates depends, of course, on the intent of the particular text. The intent, in turn, is much more easily defined and measured for factual expository text than it is for text whose goal is to motivate, persuade or entertain. In most of the work to be reported here, we have concentrated on text uses whose success is relatively easy to assess. Our assumption has been that the arts and crafts of written communication are hard to better but easy to spoil. Thus assessment is crucial.

Information retrieval

Much of our basic work has been done in the framework of information retrieval, that is, the use of user queries to match documents of presumed relevance. There is a closer relation between this traditional field of research and the problems underlying issues of hypertext design than has often been credited, and much useful knowledge and methodology exists. After all, the first step in getting information is always to find documents (read modules or nodes if you wish) with wanted information in them.

Extensive empirical data on the success of searchers finding relevant documents (actually, usually abstracts of longer documents) in small to very large collections is both consistent and depressing. There is always a direct relation between finding lots of things that are wanted and getting lots of things that are not. Finding half of the documents in a collection that are really relevant while collecting only half 'junk' is about the best that can be expected from state-of-the-art methods. More typically, searchers find 10–40% of the relevant materials while getting back 30–60% unwanted things. These search difficulties have been remarkably resistant to technological improvement; the numbers seem to be about the same for the most advanced computer retrieval techniques as they are in paper access in libraries (Salton, 1971; Salton and McGill, 1983; van Rijsbergen, 1981; Cleverdon, 1984; Spärck Jones, 1971).

Now, suppose a reader has found a book sized document on a topic of interest, and within it wants to find the answer to particular questions. As research that we will report below shows, even when there is a text segment present that will answer the person's question, the chance of finding it within a reasonable amount of time is hardly better than 50–50. Moreover, having found a page, or even a paragraph, containing desired information, readers still miss the information with considerable frequency. This is also illustrated in data reported below, but is probably familiar to anyone who has taken a reading comprehension test.

This cursory discussion only scratches the surface of a deep topic: how traditional text communication functions to convey information and wherein it succeeds and fails. But it should be enough to indicate that attempts to improve the process, and its technology — which has had a 500-year evolutionary history — may require more than armchair speculation or just throwing a computer at it.

Why do people have so much trouble finding information in text, and what can be done about it? Let us begin by describing research that exposed a fundamental factor in the difficulty of search, the noncorrespondence of the language used by authors and readers.

The vocabulary mismatch problem

We were first made aware of the depth and extent of this problem when trying to devise new command names that would be more easily learned by novices. 'Natural' names were solicited from a number of typists for the actions needed in a word processor. But renaming commands with the most popular terms did not materially help new learners. A big part of the reason was that no one term was especially popular for any action. Indeed, the chances that any two people would choose the same name for a command were less than 20%, and the most popular term was chosen by only 30% of potential users. This observation was extended to the use of terms for queries in databases of several kinds, from classified ad listings to recipe files and program names. Now, almost all retrieval systems, be they library subject catalogues, dial-up query systems, relational databases, or computer file systems, require the user to enter some words which must match words used as identifiers by authors or indexers. The data from our various studies (Furnas et al., 1983) showed that any two people were unlikely to agree on a 'best' term, so the common expedient of a one word command, file name or table label will usually fail to put a user in touch with data stored by someone else. Moreover, while, on average, each person can think of four or five different terms that might suit an 'information object', the total number of terms so offered by, say, 100 people is in the order of 30. The chance that any of the four or five terms offered by one person will match any one of the four or five offered by another is no greater than 50%. Thus, even when authors provide multiple index terms, categories or keywords, retrieval accuracy based on word matching will (and does) fail more often than it succeeds.

The data from these studies (Furnas et al., 1983) also made it possible to simulate various solutions to the problem. The one that appeared best was to try to collect as many as possible of the terms people would actually apply to a piece of text and index by all of them. This technique was called "unlimited aliasing" or simply "rich indexing". Simulations showed that it would improve interactive search success (recall) by a factor of four, from about 20% to about 80% on average without much adverse effect on precision.

Probably no one would dream of such an approach in the paper and ink world, because the prospect of 30 catalogue cards for every book or 30 index entries for every paragraph in text would seem excessive. But the storage and access problems for such a solution would be quite manageable using a computer, so we tried it. And it worked. For example, in a collection of 188 recipes searched by homemakers, the starting success rate, using more or less standard indexing and retrieval methods, was the usual 20%. When we added all the terms offered as good titles for each recipe by a set of eight representative cooks, the success rate rose to over 70% with targets being found at least as quickly with the richer vocabularies[1] (see Gomez, Lochbaum and Landauer, 1990).

Moreover, we found that we could achieve at least the same level of success by using every word contained in each recipe as an index to it, i.e. using a form of full text indexing. Full text indexing, in general, however, is only a partial solution to the problem; it has two deficiencies. First, in many instances searchers will use a different vocabulary from that of the author, so that even all of the author's words will not serve to connect the two. Second, in large databases, full text indexing can lead to a severe precision problem; too many items, too many of which are irrelevant, are returned. Some way to reduce and improve the hit rate in the set of items returned is needed. One way of conceiving of the underlying problem here is that all the words that match between a user query and those simply used in a document are not necessarily good for discriminating it from other documents. When users, as in some of our studies, actually nominate words as good names for a piece of text, the terms are much more likely to be characteristic and discriminating. That is, given that someone has used the word "information" to find an item about information retrieval or information theory, other people who use "information" in a query will be more likely to be satisfied by the same item than by some other item that merely contains the word "information" (e.g., one that begins, "This brochure presents information about driver's license exams.")

One solution that has often been attempted for the low precision of full text indexing has been to allow users to specify combinations of words rather than single words, that is, Boolean expressions on terms. There are two critical problems in this approach. The first is that most people find it extremely difficult to construct logically correct expressions or sentences. For example, Greene, Gomez and Devlin (1986) found that even when people could easily recognise a target datum that met certain simple logical conditions, they were rarely able to generate a correct query to specify it. The second, and perhaps even worse problem, is that given the low agreement between the words used by different people, the probability of the user offering two words that match exactly two words in a wanted item is very small indeed. Simulation studies with the data from our recipe

---

[1] We believe the proper measure of success in interactive retrieval systems is time efficiency such as the median time needed to find a target.

experiments showed that Boolean ANDs of two of the words used by actual searchers reduced recall levels drastically. All of this meshes well with the common experience of users of Boolean query languages who often note that while a single term returns too much that is uninteresting, a Boolean AND returns almost nothing. The right compromise between too much chaff and not enough wheat, i.e. the really desired functionality, is simply not attained by the Boolean approach. Designers of information retrieval systems have apparently been misled by observing that it is easy to differentiate relevant from irrelevant documents by Boolean combinations if the right words are used in the right expression. But for this to work, the user must know what the right words and combinations will be in the unknown text. The problem is not finding an algorithm that can be applied successfully to the text, but a method that will connect what the user thinks and can express with what is in the text. It is, thus, fundamentally a matter of the psychology and statistics of word use. Boolean techniques have also appealed because of computational efficiency, of course. This probably accounts for the continued reliance on these query methods in commercial systems despite widespread dissatisfaction on the part of information searchers and researchers alike. But, if we are to improve on the utility of traditional methods, there is little point in computational efficiency if it does not yield a desired result.

We have evaluated three approaches to enhancing full text indexing. The first is a scheme called "adaptive indexing" (Furnas, 1985). An interactive retrieval system begins with an access scheme of some traditional kind, author-supplied keywords or full text indexing on abstracts, for example. However, whenever a user tries one or more query terms that do not find a match, but then eventually succeeds, the system asks whether the failed query terms should be added as index pointers to the found item. In this way the system adds more and more terms by which an item is known, not simply because the terms are contained in it, but because users actually use them in trying to find it. This may be the optimal way of assigning search terms to documents. Trials with the use of such a system have found it remarkably effective; after only a few hundred uses, the retrieval effectiveness of one online directory using this scheme was improved by 50%. Part of the dramatic success was due to the fact that the objects for which new terms are added first are just those that are most often searched for and most often searched for with just the words most in need of being added. This scheme is most suitable for relatively stable information collections, and ones of relatively small size and many frequent users.

Another approach is statistical analysis of the use of words in text to improve the selection or weighting of the terms by which it is indexed. A now classical, demonstrably very effective instance of this is the term weighting used by Salton and colleagues (see Salton and McGill, 1983; Salton, 1989) in ranked retrieval systems. In these schemes the matching of one word and another is improved by counting matches more strongly if they involve words that are more discriminating, i.e. appear often in some documents but are not widely spread across the collection. Recently we have gone a step beyond these weighting schemes in a method called Latent Semantic Indexing (LSI). LSI uses a powerful statistical technique to establish the degree to which each word is similar to each other word in its use to communicate on similar topics (for example, because they appear in paragraphs containing many of the same words). This allows documents to be found that do not share any particular words with the query, but that do use words that are often used in the same contexts as those found in the query. In tests with standard document collections for which exhaustive relevance judgements are available, LSI improves retrieval effectiveness by about 25% as compared with the best previous methods. (For more detail, the interested reader is referred to Deerwester *et al.*, 1990.)

Still another approach is currently used in the SuperBook browser to be described below. Here the straight word matching technique is used for full text indexing, but the user is provided with a new method for narrowing the set of returned items. This is accomplished by combining the information returned by a full text query with the information provided by an expandable, hierarchical Table of Contents. The Table of Contents view of a document is often insufficient by itself to form the basis of effective search for particular facts or text segments of interest, and people often ignore or make little use of it (see observations from the open book essay task in the evaluation of SuperBook Version 1 below). However, tables of contents do offer valuable semantic guidance in choosing which of a number of full text query hits are of actual interest. For example, if you enter a common ambiguous word such as "lead" as a query against a nine-volume telephone switching manual produced by Bellcore, you get 96 hits. However, "lead" the metal, as in lead batteries, is found very quickly (4 mouse clicks) in section 13.1 DC Power Systems and is the only paragraph in all nine volumes where the metal is intended. The other 95 paragraphs containing "lead" are about wire connections or conditions that "lead" to problems. These include some 19 paragraphs including both "battery" and "lead" where "lead" is used in the sense of a wire connection.

In a manner of speaking, this is a kind of Boolean combination, an AND of (text word with search word matches) AND (topical matches in the Table of Contents). However, the AND is done in a much more tractable way for users because they do not have to generate words to define both terms of the intersection. Instead they can select one of the 'terms' by recognition from the semantic structure and labelling of topic headings. While this technique is primarily a precision enhancing method — a way to cut down on the number of false leads (sic) — it actually can improve recall — finding more of the relevant material — because it lets the user start with broader search terms than would otherwise be feasible. Moreover, the topic headings may suggest additional search terms.

Navigation and menus

This illustration of the use of a Table of Contents as a search aid leads into a closely related set of topics, the use of menus and graph structures for retrieval and navigation. As an alternative to word-based queries, it is often proposed to give users some kind of verbal or visual map of the available information space and a method for traversing it. Such maps are often employed or proposed for hypertext systems. Commercial advertisements for systems often equate hierarchical menu access with 'user friendliness'. The proffered rationale for this approach is that users will not need to know the specialised vocabulary, or to type in words, but will merely have to recognise which option to choose. In hypertext theorising, it is often assumed that node and link graphs will reflect users' conceptions of knowledge structure and thus facilitate traversal. There is not a great deal of direct empirical evidence on the value of such guides in hypertext. But there is some relevant research on menu-based search techniques in their more familiar information retrieval applications.

Where the searched-for target is well known and well defined, as for example a known name in a telephone directory, and there is a commonly understood and highly regular organisation, such as alphabetic or numeric order, people can use hierarchical menus quite effectively (Landauer and Nachbar, 1985). Unfortunately, well-defined domains with well-defined targets and organisation are rare. Menu-based search only works if the user is able to recognise the correct answer when it is found and can pick the right alternatives on the path to it. Finding names in an alphabetic list succeeds fairly well, finding spellings in a dictionary less so, and finding suppliers of goods or services in a large heterogeneous collection very poorly indeed (see Dumais and Landauer, 1984). In this last case, success rates are usually as dismal as they are in keyword search methods (Tullis, 1988; Dumais, 1988; Paap and Roske-Hofstrand, 1988). Even the best case, finding names on a list, is probably not superior to schemes in which the user attempts to type in the correct alternative and is provided with some kind of completion or near-neighbour search aid, as is done in the systems actually used to help directory assistance operators find telephone numbers.

Where a menu is used as access to a poorly conventionalised organisation of objects, as for example in videotex information systems, experience has shown very poor results. Dumais (1988) reviews the reported literature. Typically, menu selection schemes have a branching factor of four to ten options; more often than not, users stray from the path to their target by the third hierarchical level. Put differently, if there are more than about thirty items in the database, the chances of finding the right one in a single error-free traversal drop below half. There are some known methods for improving success slightly (Tullis, 1988), but performance with large databases is never very good. Moreover, in large databases, error rates and frustration are increased by the fact that once off the correct path the recovery route can involve extremely long, confusing, and repetitious cycles back to previous nodes.

Dumais and Landauer (1984) explored some of the underlying problems in menus for *ad hoc* collections of items. In a series of experiments, they tried various ways to organise and label information objects, for example the headings found in a typical 'yellow pages' directory. They had people, ranging from college students to professional indexers and psycholinguists, divide sets of items into categories of the kind that would be needed for a hierarchical menu system. They found several different problems. First, there was very poor agreement among different judges as to how to divide up the items. Second, given any classification of the items, the ability of other people to properly place a new example in the right category was not good. Third, people did not agree on what labels to assign to the categories, another instance of the verbal disagreement problem described above. And fourth, other people did not succeed well in assigning new items to categories identified either by label or by well-chosen examples. The high rate of categorisation errors observed in these controlled studies agrees quite well with observations from use of actual videotex hierarchies.

In discussions of the rationale for hierarchical search techniques, the classification tree of the animal kingdom is often used as an example. Unfortunately, this tree is a rare species. There are probably few, if any, others that will support accurate classifications by the general public. Even the animal kingdom tree is probably quite limited in this regard, once the set of animals goes beyond a moderate number of familiar species and families. Support for this assertion comes from the extensive literature in similarity scaling in which only some, usually small and carefully selected domains yield good hierarchical clustering fits to human ratings (see Pruzansky, Tversky and Carroll, 1982). Menus are frequently offered as a way to traverse *ad hoc* collections of items without any well-formed conventional structure. In these cases the ability of users to choose the right alternative at each step is almost certainly too low to support desirable levels of performance.

Note that all of these problems apply in some degree to the construction and use of node-link structures in hypertext. In following links, users must be able to determine from some provided description or link typing whether a node selected by following a link is on the path to some other node of interest. This is a much more problematical cognitive requirement than is usually imagined. In using overall maps of a large hypertext collection, the user must be able to infer correctly the content of nodes from the structure and labelling of the graphical presentation, which is also likely to be difficult and error prone for anything but very well-known, well-structured (i.e. not fuzzy) and relatively complete (so that elements are not expected that are missing) sets of information. The provision of preview and backtrack facilities can probably alleviate this problem to some extent, but not remove it entirely.

Dumais and Landauer had hoped to find ways to improve menu search techniques by applying statistical methods to the categorisation and labelling problems. They eventually abandoned this pursuit, concluding, at least provisionally, that menu traversal methods are fundamentally, and probably irremediably, flawed as a primary method for information retrieval. As conceived by humans, almost all categories are essentially fuzzy; most items belong only partially or with only moderate probability to any one category, and can often fit reasonably well into several. Moreover the hierarchical structure of categorisation is by no means universal; many concepts and categories are related only by partial orderings or graph structures with less useful constraints. The relations between humanly conceived categories in a (fuzzy) domain may require labelled edges for proper representation, and as we have said, actual verbal realisations of such labels are frequently misinterpreted. Human categorical conceptions may contain cycles, that is circular definitions, or may not be well captured at all by graphical representation. People seem to have imagined that the tidy categorisation into which (many) animals can be put would hold elsewhere, and it just ain't so. We should note here that the matter of human category cognition has a deep and active — and controversy laden — literature. Smith and Medin (1981) give a good review.

On the other hand, the situation is not entirely bleak. Experts and authors are frequently able to impose structure on a domain of knowledge by judicious selection, arrangement and exposition. As a result, well authored and organised text may offer an exception in being amenable to at least useful, if not sufficient, hierarchical, menu-like guidance in the form of headings and tables of contents. Moreover, as described next, there are ways to enhance the utility of such organisation by the use of computers.

Fisheye views

Closely related to the menu or graph guidance approach, is a model and method devised by George Furnas (1982, 1986) for improving navigation in structured domains. The model describes how a person's awareness or need for information is distributed over a domain. Some facts or concepts are more important or fundamental than others and some sets of facts are more closely interrelated than others. The model proposes that the degree to which an object is likely to be available to or needed for thought processes depends on both its 'distance' from the current focus of attention and on its *a priori* importance. This relation is called a 'degree of interest function'.

In many cases the degree of interest function that describes the relevance of information has the characteristics of a 'fisheye' lens, that is objects at the point of focus are seen with great detail, those farther away with successively less. Furnas often shows a famous cartoon of the New Yorker's view of the world as an example. The map shows the streets and buildings of Manhattan in detail, the neighbouring state of New Jersey as a whole, but only the relative positions of Chicago, Los Angeles and China.

In reading a document, one's attention is necessarily focused on the sentence currently being read. But comprehension of and thinking about its meaning may depend on knowing the content of surrounding lines, the topic of the section in which they occur and the general subject of the chapter. Thus the hierarchical structure typical of many well organised textbooks provides the underpinnings of a fisheye view. Higher level headings like chapters and sections have more *a priori* prominence than do lower-order headings and paragraphs and sentences, yet locality is also important; generally the farther away one paragraph is from another the less relevance the two have to each other.

This analysis leads to an important insight with regard to using an outline as a guide to a text. The value of different parts of an outline or Table of Contents varies in a systematic way as the user reads the text. In a paper and ink book the Table of Contents is a static map where all the information at all levels of detail are always available. Furnas proposed that with a computer display the information could be changed from moment to moment. At a given time, the system can present only the most useful parts, those above a threshold in the 'degree of interest' function, defined as a combination of linear distance in the text and level in the heading structure. Momentarily irrelevant detail can be hidden. Such a fisheye view, it was hypothesised, should both improve comprehension and reduce the reader's difficulties in search and selection when moving from one part of the text to another.

Furnas went on to carry out a series of empirical studies. First, he verified the model as a description of people's relative awareness of different information. Then, of more direct interest here, he implemented and tested computer-based 'fisheye views' as navigation guides for several kinds of information, including text. In one study, some students tried to move from topic to topic in a text with a dynamic fisheye heading structure; only the current section heading, its siblings, the immediate superordinate heading and its siblings, etc. were shown. Other students navigated in the same text with a traditional static Table of Contents in which all levels of all parts were always shown. Performance with the dynamic fisheye viewer was significantly better.

Spatial location of information

A frequently proposed accessory to the graph structure organisation of categories as an access method is the provision of a visual, spatial analogue map as a guide. Perhaps the most ambitious attempt to use this approach was that of the SemNet interface used in the CYC knowledge base project described in Lenat and Guha (1990). Kim Fairchild (Fairchild, Poltrock and Furnas, 1988) provided a very sophisticated graphical interface to help expert knowledge engineers in understanding old and adding new concepts to the knowledge base. The three-dimensional colour space supported 'fly around' traversal; users could zoom in and out and around views of labelled nodes and arcs representing concepts. However, as Lenat and Guha rather sadly report, when the number of objects in the space became large, the tangle and confusion of the visual guide became hopeless and was abandoned.

Dumais (Dumais and Wright, 1986; Jones and Dumais, 1986) explored another use of spatial cues as an aid to finding information that has a certain currency in the folk beliefs of the human interface community. The belief is that it is very useful to distribute information access points, such as file folders and command icons, across the surface of the screen, in analogy to the spatial locations they might occupy on a desk or in an office or suite of rooms. Because people do put things in physical places when not using a computer, and do (at least sometimes) find them, it is hypothesised that spatial location is an important storage and search device. Dumais set out to investigate factors that might influence how well this approach works. In several experiments she asked users to store items of information in spatial filing schemes ranging from arrangements of 'folders' on a screen to actual location of real folders in real offices. What she found was that the value of arranging folders spatially, in addition to having a minimal (two or three letter) verbal label on each folder, vanished with more than a handful of items. In the absence of a verbal label, the utility of spatial cues was extremely low. Only a small number of items could be retrieved reliably on the basis of their spatial location alone. She speculates that the apparent common reliance on spatial location is not a reflection of effectiveness, but of some combination of necessity and sloth. At any rate, this method also failed to provide an attractive route to the large-scale improvements in information finding we wanted. Rich indexing remained the one really promising technique by which computer power could offer leverage, with fisheye views as an attractive accessory.

Extracting information from text

Suppose the user has actually found a document or text segment that in some sense does truly contain information of value. How likely is it that the information will get from text to users' minds, and what factors are influential? On this issue we lack strong conclusions from the research literature. At a very detailed level, it has been shown that the order of presentation in a syllogism (e.g., Tom is shorter than George, George is shorter than Dennis, Sue is shorter than Tom) can have a dramatic effect on people's ability to draw correct inferences from the printed statement (e.g., Is Tom shorter than Dennis? Is Sue shorter than George?) (see Clark, 1969; Sternberg, 1980). At a slightly higher level of complexity, Kintsch (Kintsch and van Dijk, 1978) and colleagues have shown that similar logical entailments among the elements of propositions inherent in natural sentences have substantial effects on comprehension and recollection of factual information in passages of text. Work relating such analyses to construction and comprehension of hypertext might be quite useful.

One could also hope to get guidance in the construction of electronic text from knowledge of the effects of typography and layout, text organisation and heading structure, and so forth, and from the effectiveness of various techniques provided as guidance for professional and technical writers. Unfortunately, although there is a literature on such topics, there appear to be few if any consistently strong effects. Generally when different organisational and typographical structures are studied, their single effects on the reader are marginal and their combined effects are unknown (see summaries by Hartley, 1981, 1985; Todres and Wilson, 1989; Wright, 1978, 1985). When the effectiveness of prose produced by technical writers is studied, it is often found sufficiently wanting that the guidelines and computer-based writing aids used to produce it are rather suspect (Todres and Teibel, 1990; Klare, 1977; Coke, 1982).

A more useful source for guiding electronic text design might be the disciplined methodology known as 'instructional systems development'. This is a system of steps and procedures (e.g., Gagné and Briggs, 1981) followed in trying to take a domain of knowledge and convert it into a set of instructional materials. There is evidence that the method can be very effective in producing technical courses that convey needed information efficiently. The central effective techniques in this methodology involve careful analysis of what the student needs to know and does not, construction of the logical sequence in which the sub-parts of the knowledge need to be addressed, presentation of these in an orderly fashion, starting with advance organisers to tell the student what is coming, the use of reasonably tight structure to maintain orientation, and the use of frequent review and repetition before moving on to new dependent topics. Often, some use is made of branching and cycling; testing the student's knowledge and requiring repetition or remedial activities before progressing. The principles used in designing such branching might offer useful heuristics for hypertext link construction. On the other hand, the prescription of disciplined sequencing techniques in this technology implies that *ad hoc* link construction should be approached with caution.

Illustrations

Even the matter of the use of illustrations is not simple. The empirical literature on effectiveness of illustrations in conveying knowledge to readers is a mixed bag (Dwyer, 1972; Schallert, 1980). Sometimes adding illustrations, diagrams and other figures markedly improves comprehension, sometimes it diminishes it. Results surely must depend in part on what is being illustrated, the quality of the illustration, and the information intended to be conveyed to the reader. It also appears likely that certain kinds of illustrations may have different effects on readers of different ability. Low-ability readers can be tempted to pay too much attention to illustrations, that they fail to understand, because they have not comprehended the text that accompanies them. Even the question of whether to have pictures embedded in the text or separated is empirically an unsettled matter. We report a small study of the issue later, as well as some observations from SuperBook usability studies that raise interesting issues about whether and when following graphics links should be compulsory.

Paper versus electronic text

The design of electronically delivered text offers opportunities for finding ways to improve human performance through the use of computer technology. The available, previously 'perfected' print techniques leave room for improvement. Especially attractive is the opportunity to improve the users' ability to find text segments containing particularly interesting information. While there is probably as much room for improving users' comprehension and memory for the material once located, ways to do so with computers have yet to be developed.

On the other hand, electronic delivery brings with it some substantial handicaps. In the first place, there is the matter of space, resolution, and screen speed. The available space on today's most sophisticated terminals is considerably less than that available on a printed page. The resolution, and thus clarity and definition with which characters and illustrations can be displayed is much less. As a known result, the speed and comfort with which people can read from all but the best terminal screens (which are not yet in commercial use) is significantly lower than for print (see Gould *et al.*, 1987). Additionally, it is possible to turn pages in a print book more rapidly than they can be replaced on most systems, and rapid 'page' flipping is not available at all electronically. Display changing is especially slow if graphics are involved. Moreover screen presentation requires the reader to sit still and watch a box in one position. For some people whose main work is on a computer screen, adding textual information sources in the same medium may be a genuine benefit as compared to separate presentation in a paper book, but for others it may be a serious interference.

Given all these problems and issues what is the 'box score' for previous attempts to present text electronically? How well have actual systems for electronic delivery fared when compared with paper and ink versions of the same information? Other chapters in this volume contain more detailed reviews of the relevant literature, but comparison of online and print text formed the baseline for the SuperBook effort in a very real sense, so we will summarise the pre-SuperBook state of affairs. The earliest work that we know of comparing online and paper delivery of textual materials was a study by Rouse and Rouse (1980) of a simulation of a section of a manual for aeroplane emergency procedures. Subjects attempted to carry out sequences of procedures as instructed by the text. Those using the online version were about 20% faster but made 33% more errors. A version of the online instructions that simulated integration with the actual controls so as to provide feedback on user actions dramatically reduced errors. This last is a very interesting observation, but unfortunately hard to extend to most text usage situations.

The first comparison involving a full-sized book of ordinary text is contained in the thesis by Steven Weyer on his "Dynabook" experiment. Dynabook put a history textbook into electronic form with a windowed display that gave both keyboard and mouse-selection access to the author's index, and from there to the referenced text section, posted nested hierarchical headings, and highlighted selected subject terms in the text. Weyer (1982a, 1982b) reported that students looking up answers to preset questions were equally as accurate with Dynabook as with the original paper version of the text, but were "significantly" faster. Unfortunately the data on which the later conclusion was based have never been published in a refereed source, and the results given in the thesis itself seem questionable. The average advantage of Dynabook over paper was less than one second out of over five minutes per question. It would seem wise to count this experiment as a tie on both accuracy and speed.

Most other comparisons have been considerably less encouraging. Perhaps most dramatic was the study by McKnight, Dillon and Richardson (1990), in which they compared a hypertext version of a document specifically constructed as hypertext with a paper document generated by printing the text files in a somewhat arbitrarily chosen order. Information retrieval from the electronic text was significantly inferior to the paper version, and the users preferred the paper strongly. Marchionini and Shneiderman (1988) and Gordon et al., (1988) have also reported studies comparing hypertext presentation with paper versions. In both cases the nod goes to paper in terms of efficiency of information search, and hypertext was preferred by users only in the Marchionini and Shneiderman study. Since participants in studies of new technologies tend to be generally favourable to novel or higher 'tech' methods, and to respond favourably to the 'demand characteristics' of the evaluation context, preference data require cautious interpretation. The one study of hypertext (other than those on SuperBook to be reported below) in which the electronic medium triumphed, was one by Watt (1988) which involved a single carefully reconstructed and rather small technical instruction manual.

Although many of these studies actually appeared well after the beginning of the SuperBook browser project, they do confirm our original view that the development of an electronic delivery tool that improves on paper is a difficult challenge. Those doubts were bolstered by informal knowledge that some attempts to deliver documents electronically had been unpopular with users. Sales of electronic full text sources to date would seem to confirm these rumours. Nonetheless, we believed that better understanding of the underlying problems and of what was and was not likely to help, would justify another try. But it was equally clear that any attempts would have to be carefully evaluated against the pre-existing standard of print technology.

SUPERBOOK AND THE FORMATIVE DESIGN EVALUATION PROCESS

We believe that the design of good computer-based tools to aid people in intellectual tasks is an extremely difficult and complicated matter. The information processing capabilities of human minds are very complex and very little understood. Few generalities or laws are available to provide significant help in the design of cognitive tools. Moreover, the computer systems on which such tools are based are themselves extremely complex. The design space for possible cognitive tools is so huge and so full of pitfalls that getting one right the first time is virtually impossible. The situation is at least as daunting for first principle design as is the construction of aeroplane wings or ship body shapes. There is no alternative in such circumstances to guided trial and error. The use of evaluation experiments to produce useful design guidance, however, is still more art than engineering (Nielsen, 1992). What is required from such experiments is much more than evidence on how well the system worked overall, whether it is good enough to market, or better than some alternative. The data must reveal what parts of the process were easy and difficult for the user, where users went wrong and why, where and why they were able to do things more efficiently than previously.

A particularly important part of usability design, we believe, involves simplification of functionality, feature space and operation. It is easy to think of techniques, approaches, gadgets and features that users *might* find effective for dealing with online text. But even if every one of say, 50 different features was actually effective by itself, offering them all might make the aggregate system very hard to use. The user's every decision as to what feature to use will be made slower and more difficult the more options there are. In general, the more options the more cluttered the display will be, the smaller must be the location in which the controls are located and thus the harder and slower to operate, or the deeper the menu that will be needed to reach an option, and thus the less likely the user to find it. At a minimum, more options usually mean more key strokes or mouse clicks. One important goal of iterative design, then, is to identify the most effective subset of possible functions and operations.

We will try to illustrate the uses of formative design evaluation more concretely as we proceed. However, to begin with we present the overall usability results from the main series of three full-scale evaluations conducted during the development of SuperBook. Figure 1 shows time and accuracy for finding information using Versions 0, 1 and 2 of the SuperBook text browser. These data are from evaluation studies in which college students used a printed textbook or its SuperBook form to answer questions about an online statistics and graphics system. We will present the details of these experiments shortly. For now we call attention merely to the fact that while the first attempt was not better than the printed book standard, by the third iteration there was a 25% advantage in both speed and accuracy, and corresponding differences in subjective ratings of usability. Thus, at the end of the day, we accomplished what we had set out to, the production of an electronic delivery system that improved significantly on the previous paper technology. Let us now review how we got there.

The SuperBook browser: Version 0
The first experimental prototype of the SuperBook browser was programmed in Franz Lisp in 1985 by Joel Remde (see Remde, Gomez and

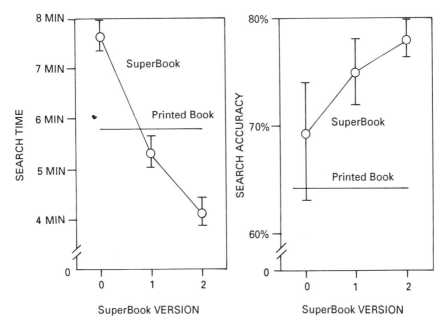

Figure 1: Results of evaluating successive versions of SuperBook. Left panel compares time taken to complete search tasks using the same 500-page textbook in SuperBook and in printed form. Right panel shows the accuracy of finding information.

Landauer, 1987). It ran on an early model Sun workstation using the experimental prototype window manager mgr[2] written by Steve Uhler at Bellcore. The SuperBook program has two parts, a text preprocessor and a display manager. The goal of the preprocessor is to take machine-readable text in the form that it comes from a word processing file and convert it automatically into the formats and data structures needed to support rapid search and flexible display and interaction. The display module includes the search engine, on-the-fly text formatting for variable window configurations, and interface management. The program accepted text in UNIX[3] *troff* mark-up, as used extensively in Bellcore documentation. The *troff* formatting tags were converted to a much simplified SuperBook tag set, and the text was indexed in a compressed Btree. The text was displayed, by default, in a set of four windows as shown in Figure 2. Across the top was a title window that included 'buttons' for help and other commands. A second window contained a 'dynamic Table of Contents'. A third window contained text formatted and sized by SuperBook from the ASCII files. The fourth window contained a history of interactive search.

---

[2] © Copyright 1987 Bellcore. All rights reserved.
[3] UNIX is a registered trademark of AT&T Bell Laboratories.

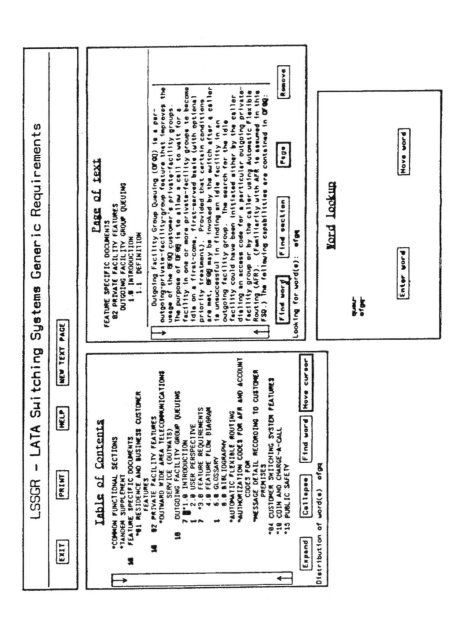

Figure 2: SuperBook Version 0 displaying results of looking up a term, posting the frequency of term occurrences against topics in the expanded Table of Contents, and opening the text page to show the term (emphasised by boldface font) in the text.

SuperBook Version 0 design features
By design, the important aspects of functionality provided were the
following:

Good search tools
An attempt was made to approximate the principle of unlimited aliasing
described above. First, full text indexing was provided. By default, every
occurrence of every word in the text is indexed. (There is an optional stop
list, but the utility of stop lists for users is questionable, and we have
generally employed them only when space was at a premium. We prefer to
let users have the choice. Quite a popular query for our online Shakespeare
texts is "to be or not to be", of which no word would be found if standard
stop lists were in force.) Words to be looked up can be typed in either full or
truncated form, or they can be selected from the displayed text with a mouse
click, or from a history of previously looked up words, also by a mouse
click. As an additional aliasing mechanism, words can be declared
synonymous by doing successive searches, then using mouse clicks to
equivalence search terms.

   Note that this set of search facilities does not fully capture the
unlimited aliasing principle. Many search terms that users will try will not be
found in relevant text portions because authors use different vocabulary. We
had not, and have not as of this writing, found a smooth way to integrate
either true adaptive indexing or Latent Semantic Indexing, as described
above, into the browser. The synonym creation facility (improperly labelled
'aliasing' in the interface) declares two words to be equivalent everywhere
in the text. In adaptive indexing, 'aliasing' declares a term to be a pointer to
an information object; in a browser, that would be a segment of text. Using
synonyms instead of aliasing is probably a significant flaw in the design.
Synonyms can reduce precision through the multiple meanings of the added
words; whereas aliasing, adding new index terms only to segments to which
they have been applied by at least one user, greatly improves recall while not
much affecting precision (see Furnas *et al.*, 1987).

   In most of our SuperBook evaluation studies, the synonym creation
feature was turned off. We pursued this strategy because we believed that
training people to use the feature appropriately would be difficult, and
because we did not believe strongly in its utility. We did include the
synonym creation feature in our first study of the Chemistry Online
Retrieval Experiment (the CORE project, see below). We felt that chemists
might productively associate chemical compound names with their
abbreviations (e.g., "trimethylenemethane" and "TMM"). The study showed
that synonym creation was used mostly inappropriately, and by the third
session of the study, only two of the 12 chemists in the study used it at all.

   The interface also allows users to type in multiple word queries. These
are treated in the following way. Every paragraph containing at least one
occurrence of each of the words in the query, no matter in what order or in
what place, is marked for return. SuperBook deliberately chooses not to

provide the ability to specify the order of the words, or that they occur adjacently or within some 'scope' of characters, words, etc. The single, cruder, default is offered as an optimising compromise for both performance and usability reasons.

As mentioned above, there is considerable evidence that ordinary users find complex query constructions, like those involved in Booleans or scope operators extremely difficult to use (Greene, Gomez and Devlin, 1986; Egan and Gomez, 1985). In our experience, users' attempts to specify exact strings of words are often misplaced in that actual text that is relevant to the query may contain the same words in different orders or with many others interposed. Although the user can think of one or a few precise strings that would satisfy, thinking of all satisfactory strings is very difficult. Moreover, the number of irrelevant paragraphs returned, e.g., paragraphs not relevant to "information retrieval" but nevertheless containing both "retrieval" and "information", in practice appears to be small. Thus, offering a somewhat looser match than some users might sometimes want to specify appears to be helpful more often than it is harmful. Note that this approach implicitly defines a kind of AND operator, but does so in a way that relieves the user of having to construct a Boolean logical expression. Similarly, the mechanism for defining synonyms creates an implicit OR at the paragraph level, also without requiring logical expression from the user.

Following a search, (a) the total number of paragraphs meeting the search criterion is posted, (b) the number of paragraphs containing hits is posted next to each section in the Table of Contents, and (c) each occurrence of any of the words in the query is highlighted in paragraphs where the whole query matches and in succeeding paragraphs of the same section.

While word truncation is supplied, more 'sophisticated' stemming or morphological analysis is not attempted. Again this is for both performance and usability reasons. Empirical evaluations of stemming algorithms for information retrieval have had conflicting results; sometimes they help a little, and sometimes they hurt (see Harman, 1991). The popularity of stemmers among designers of information retrieval systems seems to be due to a trick of human memory related to the 'fisheye view' nature of thought. Because of strong contextual association effects, it is easy to think of positive cases, but hard to think of negative ones. For example, suppose you want to look up "spelling", as in "spelling correctors" in a text-editing environment. It easily springs to mind that you will also want "spell" as in "spell checkers". It is much harder to realise that the same base, "spell", will bring back articles on magical spells and spells of bad weather or insanity. We originally set the default in SuperBook to stem users' search words, but our evaluation studies (see Egan, Remde, Gomez et al., 1989) revealed that some users consistently tried to override the default, leading to extra confusion and keystrokes. We have since changed the default to be literal search with stemming taking an additional step to activate. (We have not yet attempted to help our users with spelling or typing errors.)

Structured search feedback
We admitted above that full text indexing in very large databases may bring too many hits, of which too many will be uninteresting. And we claimed that the traditional precision tools of Boolean query construction were both unusable and ineffective, and therefore we have only provided rudimentary and simplified forms of them. So what about the precision problem? Suppose a hypothetical user is looking for information on what it will cost to connect two local area networks with phone lines. If the user enters "network" as a query against one of our large telecommunication documents, there are 729 hits. The SuperBook browser highlights each of these hits in the text, but the user will probably not want to march through them one at a time! And even supposing that it might work or that a real user could do it, we have not allowed a query of the form "network AND (cost OR price OR tariff OR charge) AND (local OR metropolitan OR interconnect)". Instead there is a novel precision tool, which we have named "structured search feedback". As shown in Figure 2, the number of paragraphs in which the search term (or set of search terms) occurs in each section or subsection of the document is posted against the displayed dynamic Table of Contents. (How the dynamic Table of Contents works will be described shortly.) This allows the user to subselect by recognition those paragraphs that not only contain the search term but also occur in appropriately labelled parts of the overall structure of the text. The user does not have to prespecify the intersecting qualifiers that will reduce an excessively large return set. Instead, the search can be narrowed as needed, using much richer semantic information provided by the system.

Dynamic Table of Contents
The SuperBook preprocessor extracts a 'Table of Contents' from the heading structure in the document provided by the author. That is, it does not use a separate Table of Contents as is commonly constructed for a paper book. Rather, the program parses the tags, e.g., ".H1, .H2", and so forth by which the troff text formatter is instructed to render typographic and layout conventions for various levels of heading. (In succeeding developments of the browser, filters for converting a variety of other tag sets to a very simple set of SuperBook tags have been programmed. At present writing, source text has been converted automatically from several UNIX formatting languages, Microsoft Word, LaTex, Interleaf, several versions of printer tape formats, and several different stylistic expressions of heading structure in flat ASCII. Most recently filters have been written to convert versions of SGML mark-up into SuperBook mark-up.)

As shown in Figure 2, the Table of Contents is not presented as a linear structure, but rather as an approximation to a fisheye display. When a document first comes up, only the highest hierarchical level of headings is displayed. Next to each heading under which there are subheadings is an asterisk, indicating that the user can expand that section to its next lowest level by a mouse click. (Only the middle button of the three button Sun mouse was used in the original SuperBook design, the other buttons being reserved for operations on windows not associated with the browser.) The user can open up as many different parts of the Table of Contents at the same time as desired. In Version 0, to collapse the Table of Contents the user clicked on a superordinate heading, then clicked on a "collapse" button to cause all headings under the superordinate to be collapsed. Scrolling through the Table of Contents was also provided (as was scrolling through the opened window of text). In Version 0, once the user had identified a section or subsection in the Table of Contents that was of interest, it was necessary to actively select that section to have its first text segment displayed.

Getting to a page of text
To navigate with the Table of Contents in the early version of SuperBook, users clicked on its sections as described above until one of interest was found, then clicked on a "Find Section" button to bring up the beginning of the indicated section in the "page of text" window. To go to a new section they went back to the Table of Contents and repeated these operations, sometimes also closing up sections, opening others, scrolling and so forth. For a query-based search, the users clicked the search button which activated a fill-in slot in the search window; they then typed a word or words. They could also enter a one-word query by clicking on a word in the text. Thus, each word constitutes a kind of anchor for links to every other paragraph containing the same word, with posting against the Table of Contents acting as a semantic guide to the nature of the destination nodes. If the search found one or more paragraphs in which the query word or words occurred, the number of hits was reported. To see them posted against the Table of Contents the users clicked another button. Then if this display provided sought guidance, they clicked on the appropriate part of the Table of Contents and then on the "Find Section button" on the text page window. If a query failed to return any hits, the procedure could be repeated; click on the search button, enter terms, etc.

When a section or subsection was selected from the Table of Contents, it was displayed, with the beginning of the section at the top of an opened window of text. Above the text were displayed the three directly ancestral headings superordinate to the displayed text. This provided additional orientation. Any number of new text windows could be opened by first clicking on a soft key in the top window and then sweeping out a new window. The last window opened or clicked was active, and would display newly selected text. In this manner a user could keep open many different windows. If desired, each could be from a different part of the text (in later versions, even from different documents).

The combination of the Table of Contents, in which a cursor follows along as the user navigates through the text (either by clicking in the Table of Contents or by scrolling[4]), and the heading information provided in the page of text, which also changes appropriately, is designed to prevent disorientation. Informal reports of users of previous online systems, as well as some empirical data from experiments with early hypertext systems (Mantei, 1982) indicate that "getting lost" — not knowing where in the overall information structure of a document the current window of text is located — is a severe problem. As long as the author of the original text has structured the document reasonably well and provided well-labelled headings, the SuperBook browser provides a great deal of orientation and context information. In fact, we have observed few usage difficulties traceable to disorientation (but see the 'wandering' problem in the CORE study below).

Command buttons
All four windows, or more, were configurable under user control at startup time, with the default configuration shown in Figure 2 which shows the browser opened up to full screen size. In later versions, it was sized to whatever initial window it was invoked from, providing that the window exceeded certain minimum dimensions, and new windows could be added at any time. Buttons in the command window were labelled as shown.

The "Help" button brought up descriptions of the functions of whatever window was clicked just after clicking on help. The "New Text Page" button allowed users to create additional text pages of any size by using the mouse to sweep out small rectangles anywhere on the screen. Each text page came with its own set of buttons at the bottom. These allowed users to jump to occurrences of highlighted search words, open to the section indicated in the Table of Contents, change the text page being displayed, and remove the text page entirely. Three of these buttons popped up a menu of alternatives from which the user could select an option by sliding the mouse pointer. For example, the "Page" button popped up a five-alternative menu from which the user could go forward one page, back one page, move forward or backward through a personal 'history' of pages already seen, or clear the page. The word lookup window included a button that popped up a dialogue box into which one or more search words could be typed. The Table of Contents window included buttons for expanding and collapsing hierarchical section headings, posting the frequency of occurrence of the current search words against the section headings, and changing the focus of the Table of Contents in three different ways.

---

[4] The reader may notice that somewhat unusual scroll controls were provided both in the page-of-text windows and in the Table of Contents window. The basis of this first design was an intuition that the arrows should correspond to the direction that the text moved when you clicked that part of the scrollbar. Suffice it to say that many users complained about this, the design has been changed several times since, and that at the time it was first implemented no widespread conventions for scroll bars existed.

User–system interaction protocol
A critical, although not always explicitly designed, characteristic of user interfaces is the necessary and typical order of operations performed by the user and system. With a window-menu-icon-mouse-keyboard-graphics interface there is so much flexibility in user–system interaction trajectories that it may seem impossible or unnecessary to describe them. But we believe that these matters can have substantial effects. Good, explicit design of interaction sequences can reduce wasted time, confusion, errors and poor user strategies. The philosophy is sometimes followed that users should just be given plenty of options, and allowed to find the best methods for themselves. We think this approach is unwise. Rather, we believe, there are better and worse strategies, ones that are in general better or worse for all users, and that only some users will discover or habitually use good strategies in the absence of 'designed in' guidance. We will discuss this point further below.

This belief in the different effectiveness of different strategies and the difficulty people have in finding optimal strategies is not just an opinion. In a study by Lee *et al.* (1986), 94% of users preferred to have a choice between keyword and menu access at all points (even though they probably didn't choose the most effective method on many occasions). Note that SuperBook, as described below uses a combination of full text (an enhancement to keywords we will argue) with a dynamic Table of Contents (likewise considered an enhancement of menu access). Moreover, SuperBook integrates the two uses in a novel way, by posting keyword hits against the Table of Contents. Later versions incorporated dialogue and instructional features designed (successfully, tests show) to encourage optimal strategies that used this "structured feedback" method. Barnard (1987) and others (MacLean, Barnard and Wilson, 1985; Hauptmann and Green, 1983) have shown that users do not always select optimum methods, and our own data have demonstrated large differences in user-effectiveness that have been modified by design changes. Indeed, we believe that we got many aspects of this part of the design wrong in Version 0.

In designing the browser we imagined three typical scenarios for its use. In one, the user brings up a book and reads it through by scrolling in the text window. In a second, the user explores the Table of Contents by opening successive headings and subheadings until one of interest is found, then clicks to bring up its first page. In the third, the user does query-based search. We have outlined how each of these three strategies was carried out by a user. We did not know, before testing, the relative utility of the three methods, how often they would be chosen or how they would be intertwined by users, with what effects. In addition, simple examination and our own use did not reveal what later turned out to be improvable characteristics of the three methods.

Summary of design motivation

To achieve the practical goals of easy production of online documentation, the preprocessors and text mark-up filters for SuperBook were built to allow authors or organisations to continue to produce text in exactly the way they presently do, using the word processing and text formatting systems currently in use for producing print. The SuperBook preprocessor automatically produces its own version for computer delivery, usually with little or no added manual effort. Thus users and organisations are not required to learn new philosophies, styles, or mechanisms for producing text. Insofar as they want to use the search and display facilities of the browser to support new authoring devices, such as diversions and 'links' that can be followed by mouse clicks, they can do so by altering the content of the text appropriately. For example, to provide an explicit link between two text segments, they could include a unique anchor identifier of some sort, e.g., "A.12", or a unique parenthetic remark, e.g., (DEF., LINK-A), in both the origin and termination sections of the text. Users would follow these with the same mechanisms as usual for navigation, that is, they would click on one such string, see in the Table of Contents where its other occurrence was, decide from the structure and heading information if they really wanted to pursue the link, and if so continue the search as usual. Authors might also use footnote and other diversion conventions differently given the much more powerful search facilities of the browser as compared to print.

Enhanced usability goals were pursued in several different ways. First and foremost, we tried to provide the best available information retrieval style search tools for finding relevant sections of text. Some guess-work was required, as little research has been done on information retrieval in continuous text as opposed to discrete document identification. There were two primary recall tools. The first was full text indexing of the entire text accessible either through typed or mouse-selected words, supplemented by a synonym-defining facility. The second was a dynamic Table of Contents, an approximation to a fisheye viewer, for top-down navigation. This set of features was designed to approximate the 'unlimited aliasing' principle previously demonstrated to be extremely useful in interactive document retrieval. However, we judged, and still judge, the achieved approximation to be too crude; without adaptive indexing or some other means to enrich the mapping of words to text objects beyond the original author's usage, recall will not be optimised. For precision enhancing tools, we offered disguised forms of simple ANDs as multiple word entries, and simple ORs as explicitly declared synonyms, with a common implicit 'best bet' scope of a single paragraph, while avoiding the requirement of any explicit construction of logical expressions by the user. We also provided a novel precision tool in the posting of term hits against the expandable Table of Contents. While all of these precision tools were motivated by known user problems with previous methods and had a certain amount of intuitive theoretical justification, their actual utility had not been proven.

Enhanced orientation was provided by the expandable dynamic Table of Contents, which was always on display, with the current text point indicated by a cursor, and dynamically updated headings in the text window. The dynamic Table of Contents was intended to approximate the proven navigation facility of a fisheye view, but again falls short of the tool that had actually been shown effective. In particular, the browser's display structure was manually determined by the user, rather than automatically opening to a fisheye view of the text being displayed. This was done because the Table of Contents was intended to be used as a search device prior to actual reading of text, as well as an orienting and navigating tool.

We also provided a variety of miscellaneous features and facilities, primarily on the grounds that the printed text that we wanted to replace contained them, that they were 'wanted' by us or other potential users, and that there seemed attractive ways of providing them by computer. These included history mechanisms for prior searches and the trail of previous pages of text seen, multiple screens of text, icon-marked and clickable links to diversions such as footnotes, tables and figures that appeared in pop-up windows, graphically context-sensitive help facilities, and a user annotation facility. (A click in the margin brings up a window with a default text editor, which leaves behind a file containing the annotation reached by an icon link in the margin. The text of the annotation was not searchable in Version 0, but was dynamically added to the full text indexing in later editions.) There were also means for changing various command and display options at start-up, for sending displayed text to files and output devices, etc. It is important to emphasise that the actual utility for users of these features, bells, and whistles had never been empirically demonstrated, that they merely appeared desirable, and that the effect on user performance of the way they were presented and controlled, either singly, or, perhaps more critically, in combination was unpredictable. Moreover, the overall combination of all these functions and features in terms of display and control layout on the screen, and required sequences of user and system actions in interaction, and underlying system processes in support of all this, added up to a whole of considerable complexity. Thus, while many of the components were known to be effective cognitive tools when used in isolation, and we had high hopes for several more, the full combination, as usual, offered extensive opportunities to confuse, frustrate and thwart users.

We were, of course, perfectly delighted with our design. When shy, mild-mannered Joel Remde first emerged from his office with a demonstration of the text browser for us to try, we were so overwhelmed with its obvious superiority to anything we had previously seen, and so pleased with our early in-house use that we dubbed it "SuperBook". Moreover, as customary in such circumstances, we immediately began technology transfer efforts, efforts to make this marvellous new tool available to other organisations at Bellcore who were heavy text producers and users, so that they could profit from its use while demonstrating its value to the world, and perhaps even help by giving us feedback to iron out some small flaws. In fact two members of the design group transferred temporarily to a documentation-producing organisation for just this purpose. Fortunately, showing the system to newly arrived Dennis Egan, with whom other group members had previously collaborated in empirical analyses of usability issues (see e.g., Gomez, Egan and Bowers, 1985) reminded us of some our public pronouncements about (and past experiences with) the necessity of evaluation studies.

Evaluation of Version 0
The goal of the first and succeeding evaluation studies was to discover how to refine and improve the text browser, and in particular to understand in what ways it did and did not improve on print presentation of the same content. Ideal characteristics of a research study for this purpose would include (1) textual material to be delivered that was representative of its intended use, (2) real users in so far as possible, and (3) a setting that was at once as 'natural' as feasible and that permitted the collection of detailed data and observations. Obviously, not all of these desiderata can be perfectly achieved at once. Some have even argued that sufficient naturalness of setting, task and participants cannot be achieved in conjunction with the collection of objective, controlled, aggregate data. We do not believe that the situation is nearly so hopeless. However, as the reader will see, we do believe that in the long run a variety of different tasks and settings need to be studied in order to confirm the robustness of conclusions. The study design attempted to provide a reasonable approximation to each of these goals.

For content material we chose a book describing the online statistics and graphics system, S, developed at Bell Laboratories. This book combines elements of a textbook on the statistical methods and procedures it describes, a user's instruction manual, and a reference source for the online system. In print form the book, *An Interactive Environment for Data Analysis and Graphics*, by Richard Becker and John Chambers (1984) is generally well-written, has a hierarchically organised structure, a good Table of Contents and index, etc. It was available to us electronically in a standard UNIX format. The experimental users of the system were students from nearby colleges. They had had at least one course in statistics, but had not previously used the S package.
A set of representative and analytically interesting search tasks was developed which required users to find information in various sections of the book (see examples in Table 1). The search tasks were constructed by crossing two factors presumed to make information harder or easier to find in print and SuperBook. One factor was whether or not the question shared words with the heading of the section containing the target information. We hypothesised that performance using the printed book might be very sensitive to this factor. In printed books, heading words have a special status: they are much more likely to be indexed; they are displayed in the Table of Contents; and they are emphasised (typically by use of white space and different type font) in the text itself. The other factor was whether or not the

Table 1: Types of Search Questions

Words in Question Taken from:	Example Search Question
Text + Heading	"Find the section discussing the *basic concept* that the **value** of any *expression* however **complicated**, is a **data structure**."
Text	"**The dataset 'murder'** contains **murder rates** per 100,000 **population**. Find the section that says which **states** are included in this **dataset**."
Heading	"Find the section that describes *pie charts* and states whether or not they are a good means for analysing data."
Neither	"Find the section that describes the first thing you have to do to get S to print pictorial output."

Note: Words in boldface are taken from the text, while those in italics are taken from the headings. No highlighting was used in the presentation of questions to the users.

question contained words in common with the text of the target section. We hypothesised that SuperBook users would take better advantage of any words in the question that occurred in the vicinity of the target information, whether or not they were heading words. Thus, we expected an interaction between the question factors and form of documentation (the printed book or SuperBook).

Results (see Tables 2 and 3) of the evaluation generally showed the predicted interaction: performance with SuperBook was quite good when questions included words taken either from the text or the relevant heading, whereas the printed book worked well, and in some respects better than SuperBook, when problems were stated using words chosen to overlap the heading of the section containing the target information. Users of the printed book also tended to perform better than SuperBook users on questions that shared no content words with either the text or the heading of the target information. When the data were pooled across all types of problems, SuperBook had a small, statistically nonsignificant advantage in search accuracy, whereas the printed book had a significant 23% advantage in search speed.

Version 1

Analysis of the time-stamped key stroke data, which was collected in such a way that user sessions could be subjected to statistical classification and summarisation, were very useful in diagnosing inefficiencies in the use of SuperBook and in suggesting improvements. For example, about two-thirds of the average time difference for searching in SuperBook and print could be

Table 2: Proportion of Correct Responses —
Version 0: Before Improvements

Form of Documentation	Words in Question Taken from:				Mean for All Types
	Text + Heading	Text	Heading	Neither	
SuperBook	.90	**.70**	.86	**.31**	.69
Print	.84	**.43**	.80	**.55**	.66

Note: Adjacent boldface pairs in the same column differ reliably across forms of documentation

Table 3: Mean Search Completion Times in Minutes —
Version 0: Before Improvements

Form of Documentation	Words in Question Taken from:				Mean for All Types
	Text + Heading	Text	Heading	Neither	
SuperBook	5.1	**6.6**	7.2	11.6	7.6
Print	3.9	**8.6**	4.3	7.8	6.2

Note: Adjacent boldface pairs in the same column differ reliably across forms of documentation

traced directly to slow system response time. That is, there were many occasions on which users entered search terms and waited for a return set, or tried to expand the Table of Contents or open new pages of text, and then waited for a response by the system. The dead time occasioned by these occurrences was 15 to 20 seconds for each search or text page update. Now, of course, we were aware that the initial system, programmed as it was in Lisp, would be slower than strictly necessary. But we had not anticipated the degree to which users would be actually waiting for the system, and especially the extent to which this would lower the efficiency of finding information. Indeed, commercial information retrieval, text browsing and hypertext systems often have search response times considerably longer than Version 0 SuperBook did, so the large impact of this factor on utility relative to print appears to be easy to underestimate.

By reprogramming in C for Version 1, we were able to reduce all of these waiting times to less than two seconds, thus reducing their contribution to user time substantially. But the log data also suggested other ways to reduce time. Over the four sessions of the experiment, users got much faster at finding answers with SuperBook. How so? The log data revealed that most users, and those who were most effective, came to use a strategy in which they first looked up a search word, then posted it against the Table of Contents, then selected a page of text to view. Since this strategy appeared to be particularly effective, its use was streamlined and made more attractive by modified interface features and by instructions for subsequent versions of SuperBook.

The new tutorial for Version 1 emphasised searching by word as the primary search procedure rather than searching by expanding topics in the Table of Contents. The new interface emphasised the results of word search by employing inverse video instead of the less salient boldface font to highlight hits. The new interface also highlighted hits on heading words in the Table of Contents whereas Version 0 did not. This design change was implemented in response to the search time data (Table 3) showing that the printed book was faster than SuperBook when words in the question to be answered overlapped words in the topic heading of the section containing the answer.

The second point[5] in Figure 1 shows the overall improvement in search time for Version 1. When results were pooled across all types of problems, SuperBook had a significant advantage in search accuracy, and a small, nonsignificant advantage in search speed compared to the printed text baseline. As mentioned above, we estimate that about two-thirds of the improvement between Version 0 and Version 1 was due to system response time improvements, but note that these were made in those places where we knew that users were waiting. The rest of the improvement came from improving the highlighting and encouraging the use of the empirically best search techniques. The frequency of using optimal search strategies from the opening experimental session increased reliably with Version 1 compared to Version 0. The more frequent use of optimal search strategies apparently accounts for the increase in search accuracy between Version 0 and Version 1.

In the evaluation of Version 1 additional tasks were added. We had subjects write open book essays in order to obtain data from a task which required something more complicated than finding a single definite target piece of text. We assessed incidental learning, because many people had suggested that the electronic medium might limit the acquisition of important information that was learned 'for free' without explicit attention when using printed materials. Finally, we included some assessment of users' affect for the documentation, the statistics system being documented, and the general study of statistics.

---

[5] The usability evaluation for Version 0 was done as a within-subject design; that is the same users used both the paper and the SuperBook version for different questions, half in one order and half in the other. In succeeding evaluations we have always used between-subject designs, in order to be sure that users are as familiar as possible with one system, and are more representative of real users who rarely learn two different versions of the same system. The baseline, or bench mark performance data for the print version was based equally on data collected during the evaluation of Version 0 and Version 1. The print baseline performance for those two studies was very similar, so the average of the two studies is used.

Results of these tasks favoured SuperBook over the printed book in interesting ways. Results of blind scoring of the essays by a statistics subject matter expert showed that the SuperBook essays averaged much higher scores than those written by the students using the printed book (5.8 vs. 3.6 out of 7 points maximum, p < .01). We did not know immediately what was responsible for this difference. Certain explanations could be ruled out: the essays written by the two groups were approximately the same length, and the two groups of students spent about the same amount of time writing. We conducted another experiment (see Egan, Remde, Landauer *et al.*, 1989) to try to pin down the difference. In brief, we recruited new subjects and videotaped them as they used the printed statistics textbook and then compared very detailed records of the activity of these new subjects with the SuperBook subjects. The textbook was anchored on a camera stand outfitted with a video system that taped and time stamped all interactions. Thus, we had a detailed record of which book sections had been found, how much time was spent on each section, how much the index and Table of Contents were used, etc. These data allowed us to rule out further explanations. For example, subjects using SuperBook and the printed text read approximately the same number of sections and had approximately the same number of word lookup episodes.

Two candidates for the SuperBook essay advantage emerged from this detective work. First, the students may have made use of important contextual information contained in the SuperBook Table of Contents as they looked up information for the essays (our experiment showed that students hardly ever used the printed book's Table of Contents, but they used the SuperBook Table of Contents an average of five times in the course of writing their essays). Second, the dynamic page formatting and highlighting of search words in the text almost certainly helped attract the students' attention to important facts on a text page that they may have missed otherwise. Indeed, our experiment verified that students often got to a critical page of the printed book, and failed to include facts on that page in their essays, whereas the same information was almost always included in the SuperBook essays.

Incidental learning measures were similar for SuperBook and the printed book, except for one dramatic difference. Students using SuperBook remembered the headings of the Table of Contents much better than students using the printed book. This result makes sense given that the SuperBook Table of Contents is displayed continuously and used very often to gain entry to the text. An interesting hypothesis is suggested by this result: students may acquire important organisational information about the content of a book presented via SuperBook. If this hypothesis is true, then some of the benefits attributed to "advanced organisers" (Ausubel, Novak and Hanesian, 1978) such as improved long-term retention and better transfer may accrue to those using SuperBook documents. We have not explicitly tested this hypothesis.

Students using the SuperBook text also liked it better than did students using the printed text. Interestingly, the higher affect extended not only to the usability of the text itself (ratings of 5.8 vs. 3.1 out of 7 for SuperBook and Print respectively), but also to the usability of the statistical system described by the text (4.9 vs. 2.9) and to the general study of statistics! That is, the affect for the documentation influenced the affect for the system being described in the text and for its general subject matter. This result must be replicated over a much longer experiment to assure that it is not just a novelty or demand effect, but it is certainly a result warranting replication.

Version 2

The creation of Version 2 was motivated by a request for a practical modification. A large group of potential users wanted to present text on PC-sized terminal screens, rather than on the large, high resolution screen of the Sun workstations for which it was originally implemented. We were concerned that putting the SuperBook interface on such a platform might degrade its usability. Consequently, we devoted considerable energy to careful redesign. The SuperBook windows to this point had operated somewhat independently. Coordinating the windows (e.g., reflecting the results of a word lookup in the Table of Contents, or making the pointer in the Table of Contents consistent with the currently displayed text page) required an action by the user. Analysis of the log files and observations suggested how the SuperBook windows might be coordinated automatically — a necessity for good interaction with overlapping windows in a limited space — with resulting efficiencies for the user.[6]

From the log files of the study of Version 1, we found that subjects posted the hit frequency against the Table of Contents following 64% of all word lookups. The actions taken to complete the posting operation, i.e. to view the overall hit frequency, decide to do the posting operation, move the mouse to the Table of Contents window, click the button, get the results, took on average 10.8 seconds. This pattern suggested automating the posting operation, and arranging the windows so that the Table of Contents would be visible simultaneously with the word lookup window. Automatic posting not only reduces the needed user actions, but also attracts the user's attention to the Table of Contents, a strategy whose usefulness was evident in the log data of relatively efficient users.

Another frequently observed pattern of coordinating activity was for users to request the text page window to jump to the next occurrence of a search word immediately after looking up the word in the look-up window.

---

[6] In retrospect, one reason that we had not thought to automate procedures earlier was that the slow response time of Version 0 did not make automation attractive. That is, if automatically posting the results of word lookup or automatically opening to a text page took, say, 15 seconds, we would not necessarily improve user efficiency through automation, because the automated steps were not always necessary. When the system response time "cost" of automation became much lower in Version 1, automating several user steps became much more effective.

Users also were frequently observed opening the text page to a new location following an operation in the Table of Contents window. These activities were automated in Version 2; following every word lookup, the text page automatically opened to the next section containing a hit and highlighted the hit. The text page window also automatically tracked Table of Contents operations — pointing at a topic in the Table of Contents immediately opened the text to that location.

The default organisation of the overlapping windows is shown in Figure 3. This design not only occupies only 20% of the screen area used by the original design (hence the nickname "MiteyBook"), but it is also set up to encourage the use of the look-up, Table of Contents, then page-of-text search strategy. The number of command buttons was reduced to a minimum, hiding infrequently used functions behind a single "other" button.

As a result of these modifications, the typical interaction protocol for Version 2 compared to Version 1 had many fewer user steps between entering a search term and bringing a desired page of text up in the window.

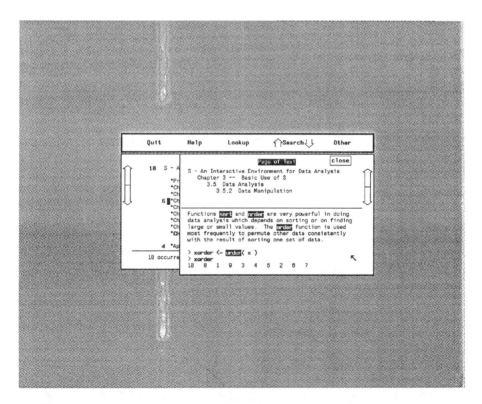

Figure 3: MiteyBook window configuration with page of text overlapping the partially visible Table of Contents. Display shows results of looking up the words "sort order", with frequency of occurrences posted and search terms highlighted.

And many interactions required fewer decisions and less time on the part of the user.

Results of the evaluation of Version 2 are presented in the third data points of the graphs in Figure 1. Performance on all types of questions taken together show that searches are 25% faster and 25% more accurate with SuperBook Version 2 compared to the printed text baseline. Searching using Version 2 was faster for every type of problem when compared to Version 1. Although Version 2 was designed in order to run SuperBook in a smaller screen space, the new design proved so efficient that we have since migrated its features to the larger, full-screen versions of SuperBook as well.

EVALUATION OF TEXT/GRAPHICS COMBINATIONS

Graphical material is an often used adjunct to many kinds of text. In the scholarly journals of disciplines such as chemistry and astronomy, graphics (figures, drawings, and reproductions of photographs) occupy perhaps a quarter of the area on a typical printed journal page. In our own internal Bellcore documents, graphics occur somewhat less prominently, averaging about 9% of the total page count in a random sample of documents (98% of the graphics in our sample of internal documents occurred on separate pages that included no regular text). Graphical material undoubtedly is much more prevalent in certain magazines and probably less so in legal documents.

Not much is known about the effectiveness of graphical adjuncts to print or electronic texts. Ultimately, it will be possible to animate electronically presented graphics, combine graphics with other media, and program graphical presentations to interact with users — features that are difficult or impossible to incorporate in printed graphics. For the present, however, the graphics generally available in computer readable form are very simple, typically bitmaps or vector representations of the corresponding printed graphics. A first step toward understanding the usability issues surrounding graphics is to compare these simple electronic graphics with their printed counterparts and learn how to use them effectively.

We carried out an experiment[7] seeking to evaluate how well users could find a variety of information in a document that contained both text and graphics. Four combinations of a 500-page Bellcore text (the content of the text concerned the technical and economic feasibility of many new network services) along with its 101 graphical items (figures, bar charts, flow charts, simple network diagrams, etc.) were prepared. The four text/graphics combinations were (a) Print/Embedded — printed text presented in a binder in which each graphic was included on the page where it was introduced in the text; (b) Print/Separated — the same printed text with the graphics collected on separate pages at the back of each section of the text; (c) SuperBook/Pop-up — text presented via SuperBook with bitmap graphics appearing in a pop-up window adjacent to the text; and

---

[7] Therese Gerhard collaborated with us on this study.

(d) SuperBook/Binder — SuperBook text with a separate paper notebook containing the printed figures. Each of these combinations is a realistic alternative. Our Bellcore document sample showed that both print-based combinations were used extensively. The SuperBook/Binder combination might reasonably simulate a 'dumb' terminal implementation of SuperBook supplemented with printed graphics, whereas the SuperBook/Pop-up combination might be used on graphics workstations, and is most similar to common designs for hypermedia documents (Nielsen, 1990).

A pilot study suggested that our original scheme for presenting SuperBook graphics (via a window that popped up automatically whenever SuperBook opened to a page containing a graphic) made user interaction difficult. The graphic window would overlay the SuperBook Table of Contents, and this contention for screen real estate led to user confusion and many extra actions to bury or get rid of the graphics when the user wished to see the Table of Contents. We devised a means of displaying graphics that led to much less user difficulty and tried to anticipate when it would be most productive to display a graphic continuously. When a graphic was accessed as a result of a user interaction on the text page, e.g., scrolling or jump searching (clicking the search forward or backward buttons to request the next or previous occurrence of the search term), the graphic popped up and remained displayed until removed by a user action (moving to a new section or closing the graphic window). When a graphic was accessed as a result of a Table of Contents action or word lookup, our presumption was that the user wished to continue viewing the Table of Contents rather than the graphic. In this situation, SuperBook briefly popped up the graphic and then automatically buried the graphic window beneath the Table of Contents. The graphic still could be accessed by a mouse click, but it did not overlay the Table of Contents window.

We designed one set of search questions to replicate the materials used in our formative design studies with the statistics book. We had users search for information that could be found in a part of the text that had no graphics. Results very closely paralleled those of the second formative design study[8] discussed previously: both versions of SuperBook led to significantly greater accuracy (SuperBook/Pop-up = 76%; SuperBook/Binder = 68%; Print/Embedded = 60%; Print/Separated = 54%). Search times averaged approximately 6.8 minutes and did not reliably differ across the four text/graphics combinations. The SuperBook and print combinations interacted with the heading and text cues almost exactly as they had in the formative evaluation studies.

A second set of questions required users to search for text-based information contained in sections that included one or more graphics. We wondered whether SuperBook would continue to have an advantage over printed books when the user might potentially be distracted by a figure

---

[8] The version of SuperBook used in this study was actually a "hybrid" containing features found in Version 1 and Version 2 of SuperBook tested in the formative design studies.

popping up next to the page of text containing the answer to a question. The answer is somewhat complicated. People using the SuperBook/Pop-up system answered a greater proportion of search questions correctly (64%) than did users of any other system (SuperBook/Binder = 55%; Print/Embedded = 50%; Print/Separated = 50%). However, users of the two SuperBook combinations (average search time 7.4 minutes) took significantly longer to answer questions than users of the two print-based combinations (5.7 minutes). Such speed–accuracy tradeoffs always make interpretation difficult, but some further evidence points to the possibility that the graphics used in the SuperBook systems may have interfered with finding text-based answers. In particular, the SuperBook systems did not have an advantage on questions that shared words with the target text but not the target heading. For these kinds of questions, SuperBook/Pop-up users probably had the irrelevant graphics pop-up automatically because they probably got to 'hits' in the text by scrolling or by jump searching within a section rather than by operating on the Table of Contents. SuperBook/Binder users may have taken time to examine the graphics in the notebook associated with the text near the target information.

The final set of search questions assessed how well information contained in the graphics themselves could be found. These questions required users to find the relevant graphic in order to answer the question. Words in the question overlapped words in the heading and nearby text as they had in the previously described questions. These questions were mixed together with those previously described so the users could not easily tell whether the information was to be found in the text or in a graphic. For the figure search questions, three combinations produced similar search accuracies (SuperBook/Pop-up — 66%; Print/Embedded — 68%; Print/Separated — 62%), but the SuperBook/Binder combination (50% correct) was clearly worse than the others. Both SuperBook hypertext systems (average search time 8.5 minutes) were slower to use than the print-based systems (average time 5.4 minutes).

We have only begun studying how graphics can best be utilised, and as the experience with the CORE project (described below) shows, our implementation of graphics in SuperBook is far from perfect at this point. These first results of analysing the use of graphics are complicated, but they suggest a few broad conclusions. For one, results of the earlier SuperBook design evaluation studies were replicated with different texts and questions. The agreement of the text search data in this study and the evaluation of SuperBook Version 1 is quite remarkable. Second, SuperBook with pop-up graphics produced search accuracies better than the other combinations when answers could be found in text, and at least as good as other combinations when answers were contained in a figure. On the other hand, the SuperBook/Pop-up combination must be improved: some evidence suggests that the pop-up graphics interfere with finding target text information, and finding information in a pop-up graphic is slower than finding information in the same graphic presented as part of a printed text.

Third, compared to the SuperBook/Pop-up combination, the SuperBook/ Binder combination appears to impede finding text-based information when graphics are present. It also was the worst combination for finding information contained in a graphic. This result suggests that simply supplementing a 'dumb' terminal text retrieval system with a notebook of printed graphics has some performance limitations. Finally, the performance of the two print/graphics combinations was nearly identical. As long as the graphics were presented in the same binder (and medium) as the text, it did not make much difference whether the graphics were actually embedded in the text or separated (in some cases by up to 100 pages) at the back of each section. While the contrast between this result and the poor showing for pop-up graphics is puzzling, it does hold out a ray of hope that we can find an efficient way to place graphics electronically within SuperBook.

OTHER APPLICATIONS AND TESTS

It was clear at this point that it is possible to deliver realistic texts electronically in a manner that makes them more efficient to use and more desirable than the original paper versions. Reports of our usability results began to generate interest among potential users of the SuperBook browser and among other electronic text researchers as well. This led to some further explorations and to the collection of new observations comparing SuperBook with other systems. The first test of its use for an actual practical application took the form of an acceptance test performed by Pacific Bell.[9] They wanted an electronic text delivery system for a large document — approximately 10,000 pages — for service representatives. Before adopting SuperBook, they loaded a sample of user text into SuperBook, and into an anonymous commercial text retrieval product for comparison. Supervisors devised a set of questions representative of the information retrieval problems for which the documentation is actually used. Experienced service representatives attempted to find answers in one of three conditions: the original paper document they used every day, the SuperBook version, or the comparison system. SuperBook users were given a brief self-administered instruction manual, which took about an average of half an hour to complete. (Users of the comparison system were given a much longer session of proprietary tutorial instruction.) All study participants then had a one-hour session in which they attempted to answer the set of questions, and were asked for their opinions about the system.

Search accuracy and time for those using the SuperBook browser and the printed text are shown in Table 4a. (We do not have access to data on the comparison system.) Although this is a rather small sample, the results are in accord with those for students using the statistics manual — in this case approximately a 20% improvement in search accuracy and speed

---

[9] Lorrie Hanke, project manager for the Pacific Bell text retrieval project, conducted these studies.

Table 4a: Pacific Bell Text Retrieval Study Results
Study 1 — 10,000 Page Manual

Form of Documentation	Proportion Correct	Time (minutes)
SuperBook	.61	3.6
Print	.49	4.4

Table 4b: Pacific Bell Text Retrieval Study Results
Study 2 — "Job Aid" Tables

Form of Documentation	Proportion Correct	Time (minutes)
SuperBook	.87	1.4
Print	.74	1.7

favouring SuperBook over the printed document. A second study was carried out to assess whether SuperBook might also be suitable for presenting certain job aids — mostly tabular material used for very rapid reference to check information in fields of forms filled out by service representatives processing telephone change orders. SuperBook again proved more efficient (see Table 4b) despite the fact that the three service representatives in this study were all veterans who were extremely efficient at using the printed job aids.

Pacific Bell has adopted a reimplemented version of SuperBook for the delivery of documentation, largely on the strength of these acceptance trials. Further follow-up trials of the system in actual use are planned. These will be of special interest. There are very few data available that allow comparison of results from controlled laboratory usability studies with observation of usability and productivity effects after deployment for any computer systems; we know of none for hypertext systems.

As of mid-1991, researchers at some forty universities and research labs had obtained research copies of the software and were engaged in a variety of explorations, some more formal than others. So far, preliminary results of actual experiments evaluating SuperBook with new materials, new kinds of students or users and tasks, and in comparison with other systems are few. Roy Rada and students at the University of Liverpool have reported some small-scale studies in which students used a book on hypertext either in a commercial hypertext system or in SuperBook. Text input was easier, information retrieval was more efficient and desirability ratings were higher for SuperBook. A group at Texas A and M University has begun a related effort. Other groups at the University of Maryland and Guelph University have begun systematic experiments on some of the individual features of the

SuperBook interface, notably the dynamic 'fisheye' Table of Contents. In other projects, SuperBook has been used to search biographical information about employees to locate subject matter experts in a large company, to analyse electronic bulletin board entries, to browse library card catalogues, search computer manuals, find items in a corporate assets database, and sift evidence to track down electronic toll fraud perpetrators.

Ports and filters

Many potential applications of SuperBook involve texts formatted in different ways, or require delivery on other hardware platforms than those of the initial implementation. As a consequence several small and large projects, ranging from research prototype studies to full-blown software system developments have been mounted to reimplement the SuperBook browser in various ways. The most ambitious of these was a reimplementation for large-scale use at Pacific Bell, done partly by a Bellcore software development organisation and partly by an organisation within Pacific Bell. In this implementation, a client–server model is used. The text database and search engine are kept on a central server machine which communicates over a network with separate front end programs that actually display text and manage interaction with the user. Databases of different 'books' can also be distributed over network nodes. Closely related client–server implementations with a UNIX server machine have been experimentally prototyped for Macintosh front ends, and for PC front ends. Versions capable of running on dumb terminal front ends have been created using both Emacs and the UNIX *curses* tools. An experimental prototype of a version in native Macintosh window manager language has been tried. Prototype ports have also been done for X-windows versions on both Sun and Macintosh workstations. The Mac and X versions have a very similar look and feel to the original — with some notable exceptions. The dumb terminal versions appear quite different. As mentioned previously, many new filters have been written to convert text in other tag and mark-up languages into the SuperBook reduced markup set. A variety of documents originally available in Interleaf, LaTex, several different PC-based word processing packages, SGML, as well as several printer tape formats have been converted successfully for use in SuperBook.

The interest, for the purposes of this chapter, of all of these ports and extensions is not just to advertise the availability of different platforms in which researchers might explore the technology. Implementing new versions always raises new usability and utility questions. What changes will alter utility and which will leave it unaffected? What characteristics of systems or interface styles are desirable or undesirable for SuperBook or for electronic text in general? In almost every port, one or more changes in interface or functionality had to be made to accommodate the new hardware or software base. Often substantial compromises were required. For example, in devising a version for a dumb terminal, the fancy windowing and mouse-screen interactions had to be largely forgone. Instead the display is a split screen with a Table of Contents on the left (or above, or alternating with) the page of text section. Search strings are entered in the command line, and movement between one window and the next is done by keys, as is moving down and opening sections of the Table of Contents. Does this degrade user performance? Are the oft-touted window, icon, mouse, graphic features merely window dressing or are they essential? Unfortunately, as of this writing, we have no formal evaluation studies from which to draw conclusions. Informal use of these variants, and reports from users suggest that the degradation may be much less than we originally feared. That is, people seem to be able to use these other interfaces quite effectively and with enthusiasm. Nonetheless, given what we have preached above and will preach below, we would want no one to conclude, yet, that they are superior to print!

New filters and the port to the X window system raised some interesting issues that will undoubtedly crop up again as we try to pursue the creation of intellectual tools for widespread use. Many formatting conventions and styles used in paper print (see e.g., Hartley, 1981, 1985; Wright, 1985; Freedle, 1987) are believed to be important for the communication of information. Designers of paper text believe that the way in which documents are laid out, the use of indentation, white space, and various forms of typographical emphasis are important tools. SuperBook supports almost none of this. When a filter is built to take text from a form that has been carefully engineered for such niceties, they are simply lost. We need to know what the effect of this drastic denuding is. While we have shown that in a few examples the resulting online text is easier and more pleasant to use than the fancy stuff on paper, we have by no means shown that the fanciness is useless. If some version of it could be used online, would things not be better still? This raises a whole host of research questions regarding what kinds of 'print' presentations are actually effective. Hark back to the suggestions made as a result of the essay test experiment in Version 1. We speculated there that the power of the computer to reformat the screen in response to the user's actions could be a powerful technique. But so far we know almost nothing about how to go about it.

In one experiment, the SuperBook front end was ported to an X windows environment. A serious attempt was made to conform to Motif style standards. Problems, not yet resolved, arose in doing this. For example the buttons used in the original SuperBook browser both invoke commands and open menus. This is not allowed in Motif, where all such selections must lead to menus from which commands are chosen. Doing so unavoidably requires a larger number of keystrokes and mouse clicks to execute some of the functions that had been systematically streamlined during SuperBook's evolution. Scrolling in Motif requires an elevator style scroll bar in which the top and bottom indicate the range available for scrolling. SuperBook, not being designed for the examination of a 'file' but rather for searching and browsing text of enormously variable length, does not naturally define such a range. The only permitted alternative in Motif is a paging button, a feature that was intentionally changed from an earlier version of SuperBook to improve usability.

How does one deal with these issues? One approach that we advocate is periodic return to a standard usability test. Using a standard text along with a standard set of questions that have been reasonably calibrated by prior use offers a benchmark test for any variant or intended improvement. Such a test, even with a relatively small number of subjects, will quickly reveal whether some of the advantages previously gained by iterative improvement have been surrendered, or whether significant further advances have been made. A power analysis[10] of our previous formative evaluation studies indicates that a 10% change in search accuracy and a 30% change in search time will be detected more than 95% of the time by repeating the experiment with as few as 10 subjects. It would obviously be even better to be able to do bench mark studies with more than one kind of material. For text browsers, this may become possible as more research is done and additional documents of different kinds with different kinds of questions are developed and standardised against a baseline print condition. If and when it becomes clear that SuperBook or some other technology is always and in every way superior to a comparable print presentation, it might be feasible to substitute a standard online interface for print as the benchmark. But for the time being the issue of whether to use the online versus traditional medium is likely to be of sufficient intrinsic importance to dictate using print as the baseline.

However, the use of a standard text as the only test vehicle is not always desirable. For example, in many applications, people will doubt whether the text and tasks for which the browser is to be used are sufficiently similar to those of an online statistics and graphics package to make a safe generalisation. Indeed, that has been our experience. The telephone company application needed to be tested with its own kind of documentation in both paper and SuperBook versions. The same kind of demands were felt in comparisons of the SuperBook browser with more radical hypertext systems, which are intended for documents created by a different style of authoring. In our studies of an online chemistry library, to be described next, journal publications in chemistry along with a whole variety of different kinds of tasks, are essential to an adequate evaluation.

Moreover, as we shall see, some of the features and functions that work well for one kind of text and task, may not be as effective for others. These considerations greatly complicate the problem of formative design evaluation. Nonetheless, two procedures seem attractive as regular components of such evaluation. One is to try each new system on some well-developed test that has been used previously. A good example is the

---

[10] In constructing an experiment to evaluate hypertext designs, the experimenter should weigh the implications of Type I and Type II errors against the cost of running a more or less powerful experiment. For example, in our studies a 30% change in response time can be detected with 95% confidence 80% of the time in an experiment with six subjects. We would require more than twice as many subjects to detect (with 95% confidence) a 20% change in response time 80% of the time.

statistics text and test. Only under rather unusual circumstances would one want a new system to do much worse on that test. The second procedure is to develop at least a small set of new text and relevant tasks.

THE CORE (CHEMISTRY ON LINE RETRIEVAL EXPERIMENT) PROJECT

One of the dreams of electronic document delivery and hypertext has been that scholars and students would have whole libraries of information available at their desks. The closest approximation that we have had to this so far has been dial-in services for collections of high-value professional or commercial documents, such as legal case summaries or large abstract collections, and recently the dissemination of some materials on CD-ROM. While there has been a great deal of publicity and excitement, especially among promoters of these techniques, there have been serious gaps in their end-user utility, and especially in their actual usability for reading text on-line. They require arcane and inconsistent access routes and user dialogues and almost always employ Boolean query languages that are too difficult for most end users. Consequently, 'intermediary', information specialists are typically needed to intercede between the actual user of the information and the database. Not only is this expensive and time-consuming, but it adds a difficult and error-prone translation process to an already difficult and error-prone search process. Although some professionals, such as lawyers, use these systems heavily, they are also often quite dissatisfied with them. An apparently consensus view is that of the US federal judge who recently told one of us, "those computer search systems are sometimes helpful, but you just can't rely on them to do the whole job." Empirical studies (Blair and Maron, 1985) have shown that in some circumstances, even with diligent intermediary-based search, recall rates (the proportion of actually relevant documents found) for legal searches may be less than 20%. Unfortunately, we have no comparable numbers for the traditional paper-library-clerk techniques but it is clear that the legal profession is not ready to abandon paper and read the documents off a screen.

Another aspect of the problem is that a very large portion of the use of online systems is merely for identification of the document, with the actual reading being done either by local printing of the document or by delivery in paper from a depository. There are probably economies to be realised by this delivery technique, since excess copy production and distribution may be avoided. But it is still obviously expensive compared to the possibilities for fully electronic distribution and use.

Another barrier to full electronic document delivery has been the unavailability of large collections of text in suitable forms. Several factors are involved. Firstly, although most publishers have been producing text by electronic means — word processors or automated printing — for many years now, most of them have been discarding the machine-readable form. Even the Association for Computing Machinery, which is a large publisher in its own right, has not retained its electronic files. Secondly, there are literally hundreds of different text tagging and formatting systems and conventions that greatly complicate any attempt to provide a collection of text from more than one source. For the most part, text that has been distributed on CD-ROM has come bundled with proprietary indexing and search software that makes it virtually impossible to integrate smoothly with other sources. Thirdly, until recently, the cost of electronic storage, especially in the more flexible and desirable magnetic media, of local distribution networks, and of high-quality terminal display equipment, has been too high to be attractive for general use with full text. Finally, delivery tools to make electronic text at least as usable as the paper counterpart have only recently been developed.

Currently, potential solutions to all of these problems exist for some kinds of document collections and some applications. Thus new experiments with electronic delivery of full text on a much larger scale than mere prototypes, but still much smaller than whole libraries, have become feasible. The CORE project is one such experiment (for additional proposals see Kahn and Cerf, 1988; Information Networking Institute, 1990). Its goal is to deliver a large majority of the journal literature needed by one academic speciality in electronic form to workstations in a library and terminals at the desks of professors and students. The project is a collaboration among five institutions. The Cornell University Albert Mann Library houses and administers the experiment. The American Chemical Society is providing ASCII and microfilm versions of the last 10 years of 20 journals. Chemical Abstracts Service provides electronic versions of their hierarchical indexing scheme tagged to all of these articles. The Online Computer Library Center (OCLC) is contributing expertise in large database storage, access and search techniques. Bellcore is contributing expertise on text and graphic conversion, and transmission as well as developing experimental prototype user interfaces. Bellcore is also responsible for the formative design evaluation studies for the delivery vehicles. It is these studies and their bearing on general problems in the design of electronic text delivery systems that we will discuss here.

A CORE sample study

We have conducted a preliminary study in the CORE project in which chemistry students used three different systems to perform tasks representative of scholarly usage of the scientific journal literature (see Egan *et al.*, 1991). We used a small sample of the ultimate CORE database, some 1,068 articles (4,100 journal pages or approximately 30 MB of ASCII text) from the *Journal of the American Chemical Society*, 1988. This set of articles is the first available instalment of the final CORE database.

This first study had several goals. One was to establish the baseline performance possible when using printed materials for typical purposes. There is a great deal of lore and opinion about the effectiveness of printed

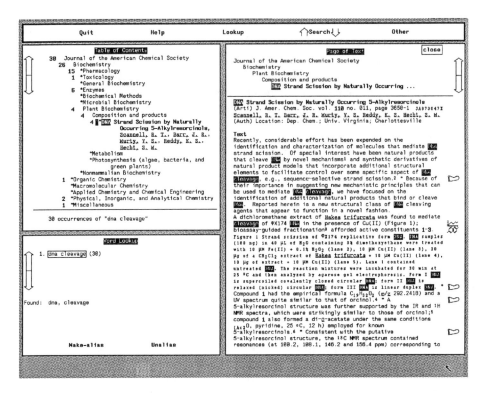

Figure 4: SuperBook browser with Table of Contents organised according to *Chemical Abstracts* subject hierarchy. Display shows results of expanding the Table of Contents, looking up the words "dna cleavage" and having frequency of occurrences posted.

journals in supporting scholarly tasks, but little quantitative empirical data. To obtain baseline performance, one group of students (N=12) participated in the study using printed materials. A second goal was to compare the performance obtained with printed materials to that obtained with either a hypertext system or a more traditional full text document retrieval system. For this purpose, a second group of subjects used the SuperBook system and a third group used the "Pixlook" system (described below). These systems differ in many ways, but it is clear that the SuperBook system embodies many hypertext-like features whereas Pixlook embodies many more standard document retrieval features. A third goal was to adduce information that would help us to improve the design of both the Pixlook and SuperBook systems.

The baseline retrieval and display condition in this study provided the material that chemistry researchers currently have available in printed form. The material consists of *Chemical Abstracts*, 1988, and 12 printed issues of the *Journal of the American Chemical Society*, 1988. The *Chemical Abstracts* includes bound volumes containing sequentially numbered

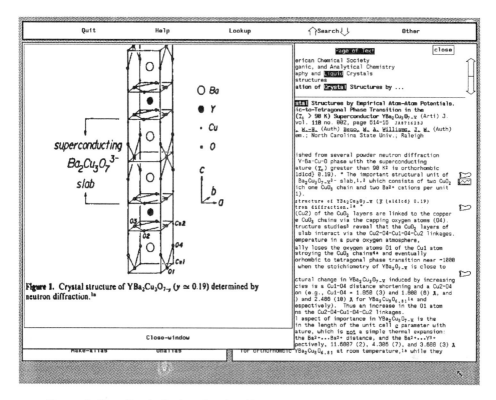

Figure 5: SuperBook display showing bitmap image of figure and associated page of text from the CORE database.

abstracts published weekly throughout each year, and Volume Indexes published every six months to index the abstracts. The abstracts are categorised into one of 80 hierarchically arranged sections according to the principal topic of the article. The 1988 Volume Indexes and Index Guide (that links names for chemical substances and subjects to a controlled indexing vocabulary used in the Volume Indexes) occupy approximately 15 linear feet of shelf space.

The version of the SuperBook browser used in this experiment supported a variety of pop-up bitmap graphics, user synonym creation, truncated term searching, and simulated fielded search for the author, title, and reference fields in the chemistry journals. For the SuperBook Table of Contents, we used the *Chemical Abstracts* section and subsection hierarchy. When a user typed a query, the frequency of hits was posted against this hierarchy, and users could expand the hierarchy down to the actual sections of individual articles (see Figure 4). Users could select pop-up bitmap images of figures, chemical scheme drawings, equations, etc. by clicking on special icons in the margin of the text (see Figure 5).

```
Which page next? Return: next page, dot: hits list, q: new query: q
new query? alkene epoxidation cytochrome p-450
Page Matches   Title
 158    4 Epoxidation of Alkenes by Cytochrome P-450 Models, Castellino, A. J., Bruice, T. C.
 239    4 Heme Imidazole H-Bonding, Traylor, T. G., Popovitz-Biro, R.
1313    4 Radical Intermediates in the Epoxidation of Alkenes by Cytochrome P-450 Model Systems. The Design of a Hypersensitive Radical
          Probe, Castellino, A. J., Bruice, T. C.
1953    4 Alkene Structure and Epoxide Formation Rates, Traylor, T. G., Xu, F.
1187    3 Biomimetic Oxidation with Molecular Oxygen, Okamoto, T., Sasaki, K., Oka, S.
1284    3 A Peroxide Model Reaction for Placental Aromatase, Cole, P. A., Robinson, C. H.
2465    3 [Tetrakis(dichlorophenyl)porphinato]iron-Oxene Adduct, Sugimoto, H., Tung, H.-C., Sawyer, D. T.
 546    2 Bromonium Ion Formation and Olefin Reactivity, Bellucci, G., Bianchini, R., Chiappe, C., Marioni, F., Spagna, R.
 897    2 x-Hydroxylase Oxyfunctionalization Capabilities, Katopodis, A. G., Smith, H. A., Jr., May, S. W.
1981    2 Stereoselective Synthesis of Spiroketals, DeShong, P., Waltermire, R. E., Ammon, H. L.
1978    2 Probing Ergot Alkaloid Biosynthesis: Identification of Advanced Intermediates along the Biosynthetic Pathway, Kozikowski, A.
          P., Wu, J.-P., Shibuya, M., Floss, H. G.
1979    2 Evidence for a Cytochrome P-450 Catalyzed Allylic Rearrangement with Double Bond Topomerization, McClanahan, R. H., Huitric,
          A. C., Pearson, P. G., Desper, J. C., Nelson, S. D.
2818    2 J. Am. Chem. Soc. 1986, 108, 7074-7078 Isotopically Sensitive Branching and Its Effect on the Observed Intramolecular Isotope
          Effects in Cytochrome P-450 Catalyzed Reactions: A New Method for the Estimation of Intrinsic Isotope Effects, Jones, J. P.,
          Korzekwa, K. R., Rettie, A. E., Trager, W. F.
2818    2 J. Am. Chem. Soc. 1987, 109, 2171-2173 The Separation of the Intramolecular Isotope Effect for the Cytochrome P-450 Catalyzed
          Hydroxylation of n-Octane into Its Primary and Secondary Components, Jones, J. P., Trager, W. F.
2826    2 Active Sites of Nonheme Iron Oxygenases, Cox, D. D., Benkovic, S. J., Bloom, L. M., Bradley, F. C., Nelson, M. J., Que, L.,
          Jr.,, Wallick, D. E.
2264    2 Heme d Prosthetic Group, Sotiriou, C., Chang, C. K.
2975    2 Highly Effective Mechanism-Based Inactivation of Dopamine b-Hydroxylase by a Novel Ketene Thioacetal, Bargar, T. M.,
          Broersma, R. J., Creemer, L. C., McCarthy, J. R., Hornsperger, J.-M., Attwood, P. V., Jung, M. J.
3284    2 S-[2-(N7-Guanyl)ethyl]glutathione Formation, Peterson, L. A., Harris, T. M., Guengerich, F. P.
3395    2 Anaerobic Reduction of Haloalkanes by Cytochrome P-450, Luke, B. T., Loew, G. H., McLean, A. D.
3477    2 ``Picnic-Basket'' Porphyrins, Collman, J. P., Brauman, J. I., Fitzgerald, J. P., Hampton, P. D., Naruta, Y., Sparapany, J.
          W., Ibers, J. A.
3585    2 Total Synthesis of (-)-Spacionin, Whitesell, J. K., Allen, D. E.
3622    2 Electrochemical Reduction of Ketones, Swartz, J. E., Mahachi, T. J., Kariv-Miller, E.
3784    2 Insertion of (g5-CSMe5)(PMe3)Ir into the C-H Bonds of Functionalized Organic Molecules: A C-H Activation Route to 2-Oxa- and
          2-Azametallacyclobutanes, Potential Models for Olefin Oxidation Intermediates, Klein, D. P., Hayes, J. C., Bergman, R. G.
4002    2 Oxygen Donation in the Reaction of 3CF2 with O2, Rahman, M., McKee, M. L., Shevlin, P. B., Sztyrbicka, R.
4023    2 Benzo[a]pyrene-Guanine Nucleoside Adducts, Rogan, E. G., Cavalieri, E. L., Tibbels, S. R., Cremonesi, P., Warner, C. D.,
          Nagel, D. L., Tomer, K. B., Cerny, R. L., Gross, M. L.
4038    2 Mo- and W-Substituted Hemoproteins, Shiro, Y., Takeda, M., Morishima, I.
4044    2 Formation of Nitridoiron(V) Porphyrins Detected by Resonance Raman Spectroscopy, Wagner, W.-D., Nakamoto, K.
4082    2 Selective Binding of One Enantioface of Monosubstituted Alkenes to the Chiral Transition Metal Lewis Acid
          [(g5-C5H5)Re(NO)(PPh3)]+, Bodner, G. S., Fern'andez, J. M., Arif, A. M., Gladysz, J. A.
4087    2 Catalysis of Alkene Oxidation by Nickel Salen Complexes Using NaOCl under Phase-Transfer Conditions, Yoon, H., Burrows, C.
          J.
   1    1 Reactions of Co+ and Ni+ with Alkanes, Hanratty, M. A., Beauchamp, J. L., Illies, A. J., van Koppen, P., Bowers, M. T.
  15    1 Interaction of Lanthanide Ions with Alkanes, Schilling, J. B., Beauchamp, J. L.
 209    1 Reaction of Dicarbomethoxycarbene with Acetaldehyde, L'Esperance, R. P., Ford, T. M., Jones, M., Jr.
 275    1 Pentene Hydrogenolysis and Homologation, Rodriguez, E., Leconte, M., Basset, J. M., Tanaka, K., Tanaka, K.-I.
 368    1 Transferability of Natural Bond Orbitals, Carpenter, J. E., Weinhold, F.
 423    1 The First Neutral Square Planar Cobalt(III) Complexes, Brewer, J. C., Collins, T. J., Smith, M. R., Santarsiero, B. D.
 429    1 Electron-Transfer Kinetics of Zn-Cyt c, Elias, H., Chou, M. H., Winkler, J. R.
 435    1 Zinc/Ruthenium-Modified Myoglobins, Axup, A. W., Albin, M., Mayo, S. L., Crutchley, R. J., Gray, H. B.
Which page to view? (+ for more titles)
```

Figure 6: PixLook display showing post-coordinated "hits list" as a result of typing
the search terms *alkene epoxidation cytochrome p-450*.

The Pixlook system has many features found in some of the more sophisticated document retrieval systems. These include full text indexing in which the unit of indexing is the entire article, fielded search in which search can be restricted to any combination of nine fields (title, author, abstract, references, etc.), Boolean searches, and post-coordinated hits list in which the title line of articles matching all n search words are presented first followed by articles matching n-1 search words, etc.

A typical Pixlook episode might begin with a user typing in one or more search terms using any of the nine special fields in various Boolean combinations. Pixlook then returns a post-coordinated 'hits list' of articles that match one or more of the user's search terms (see Figure 6). Alternatively, a user might browse the full-page images of the tables of contents of various journals. In either case, entry to the text is gained by typing in a page number (typically the first page of an article on the hits list or one listed in the Table of Contents). A bitmap image of that journal page is then presented, displayed first from an image scanned at 100 dpi (see Figure 7). The user can 'zoom' any page to get a magnified image (displayed from a 200 dpi scanned image), and can pan the image to bring any particular portion of the journal page into view on the screen. From that

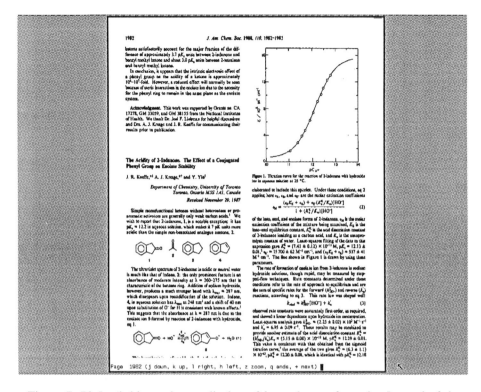

Figure 7: PixLook bitmap image display of journal page from the *Journal of the American Chemical Society*, 1988.

point, the user can visually search the article, reading and turning pages to find the desired information.

CORE tasks
In collaboration with chemistry faculty members at Cornell University, we designed five tasks representative of the work for which chemistry students, faculty, and researchers use chemistry journals. The chemistry professors then produced a number of task examples based on the *JACS*, 1988 articles.

The *Browsing Task* simulates browsing recent journals to 'keep up to date' in certain topics. In the experiment, subjects browsed an individual *JACS*, 1988 issue (approximately 100 articles) for information on eight prespecified topics. The topics served as a controlled 'interest profile' and were generated by the subject matter experts. When they found an article dealing substantively with one of the topics on the list, subjects jotted down its beginning page number.

The *Citation Task* simulates a situation in which a researcher has a very specific question whose answer is contained in a known reference. Subjects look up the reference — either in the printed journals or one of the electronic systems — and read the target article to find the answer. The *Search Task* is essentially the same as the Citation Task, except that the subject is given only the question and not the citation.

Two additional tasks, somewhat more open-ended than the Citation and Search, were also administered. The *Essay Task* simulates writing an introductory paragraph to a research paper that summarises the recent work done on a topic. For this task, subjects were given a topic that is dealt with by several articles in *JACS*, 1988. They had to find the sources and write an essay summarising the information and citing the references they found.

The final task, *Analogous Transformations*, is strongly graphically oriented and very difficult. Chemists often try to find information about transforming substance A into substance B, where A and B have never before been synthesised. When working on such a problem, the chemist will search for a transformation that takes a known substance C into another known substance D, where C is related to A, and D is related to B. The problem statement consists of a structure diagram for a proposed transformation, and chemists search for known chemical reactions involving structures that appear similar to those proposed.

CORE results

Chemistry graduates and undergraduates carried out each of the five tasks using one of the three systems over the course of three sessions lasting a total of more than seven hours. Browsing accuracy for SuperBook (84%) was significantly higher than that for Pixlook (77%) with Print having intermediate accuracy (80%). The detailed pattern of performance (see Table 5) showed that chemists browsing the printed journals found 80% of the articles relevant to the topics on their list, whereas those using the electronic systems found almost all the relevant articles (SuperBook 93%, Pixlook 95%), a highly significant difference (p<.001). On the other hand, presumed false alarms in browsing (i.e. indicating that a topic included as a 'foil' was covered substantively in an article) was significantly less frequent in Print (19%) and SuperBook (27%) than in Pixlook (43%). Browsing using Print and SuperBook averaged 18.1 and 19.8 minutes per issue respectively, marginally faster than Pixlook browsing time of 25.2 minutes per issue.

We think that the extra time spent on the browsing task by Pixlook users is attributable to reading the bitmap page images to find where search terms occur and determine whether a 'hit' within an article indicates that the article substantively deals with a topic. In Pixlook it is not possible to highlight users' search terms within an article, since the interface presents scanned images. Instead, a list of articles containing one or more hits is presented and users must read through the text of an article to rule out tangential references to topics. In the SuperBook system, hits are highlighted within the text; users can easily jump from one hit to the next and read the surrounding context. This explanation is consistent with a finding from the log files that SuperBook users browsed approximately 50% more articles for

Table 5: Browsing Results

	Proportion Correct	Proportion of Hits	Proportion of False Alarms
Print	.80	.80	.19
SuperBook	.84	.93	.27
Pixlook	.77	.95	.43

20 seconds or more than Pixlook users did, and with the lower false alarm rates for SuperBook users compared to Pixlook users (Table 5).

When the chemists were asked to answer a specific question given a complete citation to the article containing the answer, their accuracy was nearly identical across the three systems (approximately 76%). However, the systems did differ reliably in the time taken to complete the citation task. SuperBook subjects took longer (average completion time was 7.6 minutes) than subjects using either Print (5.4 minutes) or Pixlook (5.5 minutes). By analysing the log files, we were able to isolate the time difference between SuperBook and Pixlook users. Approximately 40% of the time difference is due to extra time taken by SuperBook users to get to the target article. Both Print[11] and Pixlook can be accessed by page number, and when a complete citation is given subjects simply open a printed journal to the correct page or type in the page number in Pixlook. A similar method was available to subjects using SuperBook but, because of a flaw in user training, was never used. Instead, SuperBook subjects found the cited article by searching for its author, or sometimes they even conducted an unrestricted topic search. This strategy problem should be easy to remedy without any changes to the SuperBook interface.

A more interesting challenge is posed by the fact that once SuperBook subjects arrive at the target article, they still take longer to answer the question compared to subjects using Pixlook or the printed journals. Analyses of the log files show that SuperBook users are more likely to 'wander' from the target article and spend more time off the target than Pixlook users. This aspect of using SuperBook is due to its hypertext-like nature. Users can very easily jump unintentionally across the boundary of the target article by jump searching, scrolling or operating on the Table of Contents. Changes to the SuperBook interface are being prototyped to address this issue.

For the Search Task where chemists had to find out very specific information without a citation to the target article, accuracies for SuperBook (76%) and Pixlook (72%) were substantially higher than that obtained with

---

[11] The situation for Print is not entirely realistic here, because the users had the pile of journals available at hand. Normally, users of printed materials would have to spend time going to another place (elsewhere in the library or another library with the appropriate collection) to find the relevant articles even if they had a complete citation to the articles.

the Print system (23%). Similarly, search times were much faster with SuperBook (average completion time was 9.5 minutes) and Pixlook (11.2 minutes) than with Print (19.5 minutes). Analyses of the log files showed that SuperBook users took significantly less time to find a relevant target article compared to Pixlook users (1.8 minutes vs. 3.0 minutes), but again tended to spend more time wandering away from the target article once they had located it. Note that this phenomenon appears to be a direct consequence of a feature sometimes claimed to be a major advantage of hypertext, the reduction of the importance of document boundaries (cf. Nelson, 1967).

The essays written in the experiment were scored blind by a graduate student who developed several methods of scoring. Although users of the electronic systems tended to score higher on all measures, the one significant difference was that essays written by chemists using either electronic system summarised more relevant articles than those written by chemists using the printed index system. The chemists, irrespective of the system used, averaged a little more than half an hour to complete each essay. Productivity scores (sum of all essay scores/time spent) of SuperBook and Pixlook users were significantly better than the scores of those using the print system.

As expected, most users had great difficulty finding analogous transformations. While there were no reliable differences among conditions, subjects using Pixlook (35% correct) tended to score higher than those using the printed journals and index (27%), while the SuperBook subjects (15%) scored lowest. Analyses of log files shows that the majority of subjects using SuperBook and Pixlook never got to any target article containing information about an analogous transformation. In many cases, subjects simply did not use appropriate search words. They coded the pictorial representation of the problem incorrectly and looked up words that, while having hits in the journal database, led them away from the target information. SuperBook subjects encountered an additional problem, however. Of the seven SuperBook subjects who got to an appropriate target article, three failed to access the pop-up graphics critical to solving the problem. The performance of those three subjects looks just like the performance of those who never even got to a target article. Note that this is not a problem with Pixlook or Print, since getting to a target article is tantamount to seeing the graphics; the graphics are continually displayed, and the articles are typically only three or four pages long.

This analysis pinpoints a common issue in designing hypertext systems. Given that information linked to a text is displayed only at the option of the user, how should that information 'make itself known' to the user? Should the user be told only that 'something' is available, what that 'something' is, either cryptically by an icon or 'type' label, or in detail? Should some links at least sometimes be obligatory, others sometimes hidden? In the present case, the linked information consisted of graphics critical to solving a problem. The linked information also might consist of additional text, or, in the future, other text adjuncts such as sound, animations, and video. Having linked information call attention to itself at appropriate times is an unsolved and difficult problem. Tradeoffs involving display space and the user's time are involved. A segment of linked information that demands attention inappropriately might be worse than no information at all. We have not solved this problem, but we are working on heuristics for deciding when and where graphical information linked to a text ought to be exposed automatically.

It is interesting to contrast the experience and results so far with the CORE experiments with those of earlier studies of SuperBook applications. There are three striking differences in the materials being delivered. First, the chemistry journal articles are a large and diverse set of individual documents. They were authored by many different people, contain information on a wide variety of topics within chemistry, and are presented in many styles and organisational formats. Thus they do not have the single overall hierarchical structure on which some of the important search and navigation tools of SuperBook were originally predicated. In some ways the body of information they represent is more like the loosely connected collection of modules often imagined to be the target of hypertext systems. How the SuperBook approach fares with such materials is one of the interesting questions to be answered.

The availability of the *Chemical Abstracts* section and subsection categories as an organising scheme for these articles provided a source of structure that SuperBook could exploit. This scheme juxtaposes articles classified under the same categories. Using this scheme it is possible, for example, to search or browse easily all articles classified as dealing primarily with "Cyclohexanes" or "Electronic Spectra", etc. This structure is, however, imposed on the 'modules' after they are collected, rather than acting as an active organising principle in their composition. Thus, it is interesting that the chemists used the SuperBook Table of Contents "expand" function an average of more than seven times per Search Task. This figure compares to an average of about three 'expands' per problem in the second formative design study employing the statistics text. It is noteworthy that success rates for finding answers were very similar in the two cases, both being around 80% correct.

A second set of potentially significant contrasts is in the total quantity of material and in the length of individual documents. While the S manual was a single document of 550 pages, our first CORE experiment delivered slightly more than 1,000 separate documents averaging about four pages in length. While SuperBook generally retained its advantage over print for the chemistry materials, there were some particular tasks that were better supported by print or by the Pixlook equivalent of print. In particular, once having found a short document in which a particular fact is known to be set forth, the page image display systems made it easier to keep from 'wandering away' from the target, and virtually assured that users would notice important graphical adjuncts. Certain hypertext features of the SuperBook system enabled users to stray unintentionally from a target article, and required a positive user action to access graphics linked to the text.

For what size document and for which tasks will a page image display system produce better performance than a hypertext system? Will page image display systems have an advantage for five-page documents, or ten? For what proportion of realistic tasks can users be sure that an answer they are looking for is definitely contained in a particular document, section or node? Are there simple changes in SuperBook's features that will overcome this deficiency, and, if so, will the alterations be good or bad for its use with other kinds of materials? These questions will be addressed in later experiments. Meanwhile, the reader should note that while these issues may seem minor, even picayune, they make the difference between the electronic form being better or worse than what it replaces. And similar 'trivia' undoubtedly have equally dominant effects in other forms of hypertext.

A third special characteristic of the chemistry journal literature is its high dependence on graphical presentations. Chemists, especially organic chemists, had warned us that access to pictures was critical. (In fact, a prototype search tool, locally referred to as "ComicBook", had been informally explored — and rejected — in which the primary navigation was through successive pages of miniatures of all of the graphics appearing in articles, with the text accessed only by clicking first on a picture). The results of the evaluation studies seemed to indicate that leaving it up to the user to follow a link to a picture, rather than making it appear automatically embedded in the text, was a disadvantage for this literature. It seems doubtful that this feature was disadvantageous for the earlier uses of SuperBook in which there were many fewer graphics, and in which their use was comparatively more illustrative than informative. Indeed, as noted previously, an early pilot study for our experiment on text/graphics combinations began with the automatic picture display default, but that interfered too much with the use of the TOC. It is plausible that the eventual solution here will be technological, the availability of much larger high-resolution screen space so that pictures can always be displayed without interfering with simultaneous display of text and search tools. However, in the meanwhile, there are interesting research questions raised about what kinds of text and graphics are best served by what kinds of interface techniques.

FUTURE CHALLENGES

Contrasts between CORE and previous SuperBook evaluations have served to emphasise some research issues for the future. For one thing it seems clear that different kinds of text browsers, or information delivery tools in general, may be required for different kinds of materials and tasks. Full text search and structured navigation make users very much better at finding text segments that answer well-specified questions. But support for incidental learning and discovery by browsing does not yet offer an improvement over (fairly ineffective) traditional methods. The specialised task of analogous transformation search with the chemistry journals was poorly accomplished with any of the tools. It is not clear that the fault here lies with the text delivery system rather than the intrinsic intellectual difficulty of the task. But the latter possibility is actually the more exciting challenge. Should we not set our sights on providing information access tools to make the most difficult jobs easy? More modestly, there is still the challenge to do better for this particular task, and a suggestion that there may be many other specialised tasks not yet encountered with which we should be concerned. Thinking about general methodological approaches to customisation for special tasks is yet another appealing research direction.

Graphics
The presentation of graphics is a particular challenge. As we have seen, the handling of graphics in paper print, or in electronic emulations of paper, seems to be as good as we can do currently. The present superior resolution of paper printing technology is one barrier to substituting the electronic medium. But surely there must be some ways in which computer power can augment the use of graphics. One, of course, is the use of motion and animation, techniques that are not available in paper, but not yet well developed as components of electronic documents either. Still another intriguing challenge is to find new ways to help users search for pictorial information. One approach we plan to pursue is to index the graphics using words that are part of or surrounding the graphical items. Our Text/Graphics combination experiment suggests that popping up a graphical item that has a hit might be the best way to call attention to a potentially relevant figure. Another approach suggested by our first CORE study is to categorise the graphics and automatically pop up a subset of them. The chemists, for example, claim that the chemical structure drawings are far more important to see than other graphics items, especially when searching for an analogous transformation.

Search
Better, and more general search techniques are still needed even for textual materials. SuperBook's techniques are extremely effective for structured text. (Even here, however we believe improvement is still possible, e.g., by the addition of true adaptive indexing.) But search in large unstructured collections is still a very uncertain matter. The articles of encyclopædias, large databases of news stories, and the like, not only often come without well-constructed hierarchical organisations, but often are not susceptible to such structuring. It is often simply impossible to relate all of the items in a meaningful and useful way. Under these circumstances, users have had to rely on search methods that are known to produce at best low recall and low precision.

     We, and others, have been chipping away at improving traditional information retrieval methods. The latent semantic indexing (LSI) approach, which uses a powerful statistical analysis of large quantities of similar text to induce usage relations among terms, alleviates somewhat the synonymy problem. It improves retrieval accuracy by roughly 25%. Here is an intuitive example of the small gain this represents. Like other state-of-the-art retrieval schemes, LSI ranks all the text segments in order of predicted relevance. If a user looks far enough down the list to find six out of ten actually relevant items in a collection, only six junk items will have been examined, instead of eight with the previously best systems. While this is a useful improvement, it obviously has not solved the problem. Our view, and that of many others in the information retrieval field, is that the essential problem is that users do not know enough about what they are looking for and are unable to frame queries well enough to match relevant documents. Lest the reader be erroneously tempted, there are no other known methods for retrieval in unstructured domains that work better. For example, humanly constructed indices and thesauri, even when used by highly trained 'intermediaries', do not materially improve matters. In particular, note that hypertext links partake of the same underlying problems and have, when used alone, so far proven to be woefully inadequate retrieval devices.

A promising possibility for reducing the 'bad query' problem is a technique called "relevance feedback" (see Salton and McGill, 1983). In relevance feedback, a first attempt returns a number of items, the user chooses one or more of them, and the next search is for similar ones. The information retrieval scheme used by Thinking Machines Inc. in its retrieval product uses this approach coupled with a traditional word-matching technique. Dumais (1991) has recently been exploring a version in which latent semantic indexing is used to establish the similarity between queries and text items, and between one text item and another. The prototype of this system called "infosearch", uses a SuperBook like interface to help the user judge the relevance of items by bringing full text of abstracts up in a page-of-text window. Early tests show this to be another significant step forward, but still far short of perfection. Possibly the similarity rankings can be used to form automatic links in the traditional hypertext sense between one segment of text, or between one article, and another. These, as well as manually, i.e. intellectually, created links by authors or users may offer improvement if combined with automatic search capabilities. All in all, there is still much work to be done and considerable opportunity to improve search capabilities, especially for the unstructured collection case, and to make the electronic form of access in this case also superior to traditional paper methods.

A final area of challenge, virtually untouched so far, is doing something to increase the actual comprehension of segments of text. The intriguing suggestion from essays written with the help of SuperBook, that reformatting can cause users to pick up information they would otherwise miss, needs extension. It is plausible that the better knowledge of the text structure on the part of SuperBook users, as indicated by superior recollection of the heading structure, could lead to better comprehension. No measurements have been done to assess this possibility. But what really needs doing, is research to understand more clearly the obstacles to better comprehension of text and thence to suggestions for ways in which computer methods could be of benefit. An often made suggestion is that hypertext facilities be used to offer definitions, and other accessory explanation and development. The instruction manual constructed by Watt (1988) seems to have accomplished this goal (see also Todres and Teibel, 1990). Other experiments (e.g., Gordon *et al.*, 1988) call into question the generality of this idea. The history of computer-aided instruction is a particular caution. Many of the early systems such as Plato and TICCIT offered tools for extensive cross-referencing and branching. Our impression of the history of use of these systems is that the generation of good branching text was extremely hard for authors, and demonstrations of its actual utility and popularity with students and other readers were not impressive (e.g., Alderman, Appel and Murphy, 1978).

SOME REFLECTIONS

We will close this long account by reflecting briefly on where we stand and offering some opinions based on what we think we have learned from the SuperBook project (see also Egan, 1989).

Different kinds of books and different kinds of tasks and different kinds of users will pose different problems and opportunities for machine-mediated text use. The kinds of texts and tasks so far supported by or even experimented with by computer delivery are a severely restricted sample. They include citation records and abstracts for finding articles and papers, a small number of reference and instruction manuals and a few textbooks, plus online access to some small sets of classical literature. But real text includes: poetry and fiction designed to be read for entertainment, journalistic reporting and historical accounts, text books and treatises on an enormous variety of highly specialised topics, ritual documents like the Bible, the Koran and the Torah, enormous quantities of overlaid commentary and commentary on commentary, and volumes of art and photography of almost purely graphic content. Along with the vast proliferation of content has come a matching profusion of specialised communicative conventions and techniques.

We opine on options

Simply multiplying the number of available features in online systems will hardly solve problems posed by differences among tasks, texts, and users. There is much loose talk about providing user customisability of interfaces, rich feature sets to allow users greater flexibility, and the creation of different options for different kinds of users. In our opinion, these are marketing slogans and strategies designed to appeal to the 'feature checklist approach' to evaluating products. There is little empirical justification for most proposals to increase the number of options and features; in fact there are good reasons to fear such proposals. Most features invented without test are no better than what existed before, and a plethora of features defeats simplicity and ease of use. Indeed as the SuperBook evaluation studies and others (see Barnard, 1987) have shown, when given a large number of possible operations and features by which the same tasks can be accomplished, users will not uniformly choose the best means either in general or for themselves.

Research on designing interfaces to accommodate the huge variation in background, aptitudes, age, and other characteristics of potential users is instructive here (see Egan, 1988). Perhaps the best approach found so far is to evolve very simple interfaces that are robust with respect to variations in important user characteristics. For example, Egan and Gomez (1985) found that user's age correlated .50 or higher with measures of difficulty in using a typical text editing system. One practical implication was that users who could finish training within the prescribed period of time averaged 10 years younger than users who did not finish the training! Egan and Gomez were able to isolate much of the difficulty encountered by older users to the process of generating syntactically complicated command strings. When a new editor design was tried with which users could accomplish the editing task without complicated command strings, older users were no longer penalised. A similar pattern of results was found by Greene, Gomez and Devlin (1986) in their study showing how effective use of a database query language was limited to people scoring in the upper echelons of reasoning aptitude. Dumais (1991) reported a similar result in her study relating associative fluency aptitude to performance with a text retrieval system. In all these cases, simplifying the interface design in specific ways enabled a greater range of people (including older people, those not scoring extremely high in reasoning and associative fluency) to use the interface effectively. Furthermore, people who already were good performers with the earlier designs were not impeded by the simpler design. Thus, in all these studies the robust design appeared to be as good or better for all users.

While the 'robust interface' approach has worked, the approach of creating different interfaces or different sets of options for different groups of users has not been as productive. Except for tailoring interfaces to some very obvious characteristics (e.g., if a user speaks Spanish, the interface should use Spanish), it is usually not clear how one design might optimise performance for one group of people while a different design optimises performance for a different group. The extensive instructional research literature on the 'aptitude-treatment interaction' (ATI) hypothesis reinforces this conclusion. Briefly the ATI hypothesis is the notion that the best way to present materials for people to understand or learn differs dramatically depending on the aptitudes of the student. There have been literally hundreds of experiments trying to demonstrate the reality of such phenomena (e.g., that 'high spatial' students learn better from diagrams whereas 'high verbal' students learn better from texts). This hypothesis seems to appeal to strong intuitive beliefs, so it has been tested in a wide spectrum of different fields and topics (see Cronbach and Snow, 1977). The bottom line is that such interactions have been extremely hard to show anywhere. There are indeed some examples (e.g., Egan and Greeno, 1973), but they usually depend on the partial orderings of needed prior information before the introduction of a new topic, that is experience with the subject matter itself, rather than with the kinds of individual differences often imagined.

Attempts at trying to find ways to lead users through text bases optimally are not necessarily doomed to failure, but trying to improve text delivery by allowing different options, modes, and techniques for different people has been tried before and is not an easy golden road to success. And, as we have emphasised before, the provision of more than the minimal number of options slows decision time and adds to confusion, and the provision of anything but the generally best strategic sequence of actions seems likely to lead, on average, to less optimal method choice rather than more.

About links
Hypertext designers, users and advocates who read this chapter will have been struck by the rather cautious use of links in the SuperBook system. There are lots of linking mechanisms there, but they are not so prominently displayed or so much relied upon as in more frankly hyper systems. In a sense every word is automatically linked to every other occurrence of itself or a truncated version of itself, through a sort of typing mechanism in which its semantics are explained by showing where it occurs in the structured view of the document. But no particular words are selected from the text for highlighting or 'anchoring' functions. Unique anchor and target strings can be inserted in the text, which will similarly become automatically linked. There are also links from marginal icons to a variety of different diversions, user added annotations, footnotes, graphics of different kinds (in the CORE version there are different icons for ordinary figures and graphs and for chemical schemes), and for tables. There are links between headings and between words embedded in headings in the Table of Contents and the text to which they are labels. In fact, diversion is implemented in a fairly general way as object references, and thus could be used as a link to various other information in other media, video, animations, audio files and the like. How is this different from the links which form the main feature of systems explicitly designed as hypertext? The main difference seems to be primarily a matter of emphasis. We have not explicitly encouraged the creation of new forms of information structures compounded of isolated segments of text linked together with explicitly created pointers, as others have. We have avoided this partly because our driving interest was in the better delivery of existing text. But it would be less than full disclosure if we did not also confess that we have considerable misgivings about the more traditional hypertext goal. We are concerned with the question of whether authors can in fact provide good link structures, or whether users can and will provide structures which prove helpful to them on later occasions. We are concerned

with whether people can author and construct text that allows rich multiple paths that are sufficiently well ordered and comprehensible. We are concerned about whether the protocol of reading from a text that tempts users to go off in many diverse directions at multiple points will be a well functioning cognitive tool. We note that diversions such as references, "see also" and footnotes in paper text are very often muted so that the ordinary reader will not be tempted to interrupt the flow of ideas, and will not have to make frequent conscious decisions about where to go next. But, what we are most concerned about, is that these popular ideas for reconstituting the way information is delivered have not very often actually been tried, and in so far as they have, have not proved superior. Thus, since we are rather practical folk, constrained in the last instance to produce text delivery systems that will improve the productivity of telephone company employees, we have moved much more slowly in these directions, preferring to construct our system of components with some demonstrated prior advantage. It has, as we have shown, been hard enough to make successful systems with such building blocks.

Details, details
Our experience with the iterative design and test of interfaces leads us to the conclusion that details are extremely important. The actual implementation of any interface and associated dialogue protocols between user and system requires a very large number of petty design decisions. For most of these there are no strong principles or even guidelines. Moreover the effects of any one decision usually depend on many other decisions. For a trivial example, the decision of where to locate a 'search for next occurrence' button does not matter in the abstract, but only in conjunction with where the text will occur from which users will move their eyes and the cursor. In early implementations of SuperBook, automatically displayed graphics reduced search effectiveness by covering the TOC. But icon-selected graphics caused some users to miss needed pictures in the CORE experiment. Other examples already mentioned are the failure to tell SuperBook subjects in the instructions that there was 'fielded' citation search available, which cost them an average of two minutes per search in the relevant condition, and the added clicks needed on every operation as a result of conformance with Motif style standards. Because of the complexity of humans and of interface design we are even more convinced than ever of the utter necessity of formative evaluation in design.

To move forward from here, more knowledge is needed about the deficiencies of print, and of the nonprint mechanisms so far used to replace print. We want, of course, to relax some of the unnecessary constraints of paper and print technology, and to exploit some of the opportunities of computers. But this is not to say that everything that is done in print is bad, or that everything you could do with a computer is good. It is the problem of finding out which is which that is critical to solve. Because humans are so complex and variable, because the competing traditional technology is so well evolved, because there are as yet so few computer systems to aid human cognition that are of proven benefit, intuition is a rather poor guide in the design of such systems. If we slavishly design new systems merely to try to mimic as well as possible, but necessarily imperfectly, what can be done already in print, we will surely not succeed well. On the other hand, attempts to build new and better computer-based cognitive tools on the foundation of intuitive hunches and clever ideas has not been impressive. There is another way.

ACKNOWLEDGEMENTS

Many people have contributed to the work reported here. Those listed as authors are distinguishable from the others primarily by the fact that they played larger rôles in the formative design evaluation of the hypertext systems described, the main focus of this paper. But the design process was greatly influenced by ongoing research in information retrieval and display, as recounted above, and implementations of the many experimental systems was an equally important and difficult component.

For the foundational work on design principles and techniques we acknowledge especially Susan Dumais, for her work on menu and spatial filing schemes, George Furnas, for his work on fisheye views, unlimited and adaptive indexing, and Louis Gomez for his work on logical query languages and contributions to the initial SuperBook design.

With respect to implementation of experimental systems and test vehicles, we acknowledge especially Jordan Perel for the X-windows version, Michael Littman for the two dumb terminal versions as well as experiments with LSI and other interface variants, and members of the Bellcore software development team who built the client–server version of SuperBook. We also acknowledge the important contributions of our collaborators at Pacific Bell and Cornell University who made the evaluations in 'field' settings effective.

REFERENCES

Alderman, D. L., Appel, L. R. and Murphy, R. T. (1978) PLATO and TICCIT: An evaluation of CAI in the community college. *Educational Technology*, 18, 40–45.

Ausubel, D. P., Novak, J. D. and Hanesian, H. (1978) *Educational Psychology: A Cognitive View* (2nd edition). New York: Holt, Rinehart and Winston.

Barnard, P. (1987) Cognitive resources and the learning of human-computer dialogues. In J. M. Carroll (ed.) *Interfacing Thought: Cognitive Aspects of Human-Computer Interaction*. Cambridge, MA: MIT Press.

Becker, R. A. and Chambers, J. M. (1984) *S: An Interactive Environment for Data Analysis and Graphics*. Belmont, CA: Wadsworth.

Blair, D. C. and Maron, M. E. (1985) An evaluation of retrieval effectiveness for a full-text document-retrieval system. *Communications of the ACM*, 28, 280–299.

Bush, V. (1945) As we may think. *Atlantic Monthly*, 76, 101–108.

Clark, H. H. (1969) Linguistic processes in deductive reasoning. *Psychological Review*, 76, 387–404.

Cleverdon, C. (1984) Optimizing convenient online access to bibliographic databases. *Information Services and Use*, 4, 37–47.

Coke, E. U. (1982) Computer aids for writing text. In D. H. Jonassen (ed.) *The Technology of Text: Principles for Structuring, Designing and Displaying Text*. Englewood Cliffs, NJ: Educational Technology Publications. 383–399.

Cronbach, L. J. and Snow, R. E. (1977) *Aptitudes and Instructional Methods*. New York: Irvington.

Deerwester, S., Dumais, S. T., Furnas, G. W., Landauer, T. K. and Harshman, R. A. (1990) Indexing by latent semantic analysis. *Journal of the American Society for Information Science*, 41, 391–407.

Dumais, S. T. (1988) Textual information retrieval. In M. Helander (ed.) *Handbook of Human-Computer Interaction*. Amsterdam: Elsevier. 673–700.

Dumais, S. T. (1991) Iterative searching in an online database. *Proceedings of the Human Factors Society Annual Meeting*. Santa Monica, CA: Human Factors Society.

Dumais, S. T. and Landauer, T. K. (1984) Describing categories of objects for menu retrieval systems. *Behavior Research, Methods, Instruments and Computers*, 16, 242–248.

Dumais, S. T. and Wright, A. L. (1986) Reference by name vs. location in a computer filing system. *Proceedings of the Human Factors Society 30th Annual Meeting*. Santa Monica, CA: Human Factors Society. 824–828.

Dwyer, F. M. (1972) *A Guide for Improving Visualized Instruction*. State College, PA: Learning Services.

Egan, D. E. (1988) Individual difference in human-computer interaction. In M. Helander (ed.) *Handbook of Human-Computer Interaction*. New York: Elsevier Science Publishers (North Holland). 543–568.

Egan, D. E. (1989) What can we learn from electronic text browsing systems? *Machine Mediated Learning*, 3, 207–210.

Egan, D. E. and Greeno, J. G. (1973) Acquiring cognitive structure by discovery and rule learning. *Journal of Educational Psychology*, 64, 85–97.

Egan, D. E. and Gomez, L. M. (1985) Assaying, isolating, and accommodating individual differences in learning a complex skill. In R. Dillon (ed.) *Individual Differences in Cognition, Volume 2*. New York: Academic Press. 173–217.

Egan, D. E., Lesk, M. E., Ketchum, R. D., Lochbaum, C. C., Remde, J. R., Littman, M. and Landauer, T. K. (1991) Hypertext for the electronic library? CORE sample results. In *Proceedings of Hypertext '91*. New York: ACM. 299–312.

Egan, D. E., Remde, J. R., Gomez, L. M., Landauer, T. K., Eberhardt, J. and Lochbaum, C. C. (1989) Formative design-evaluation of SuperBook. *ACM Transactions on Information Systems*, 7, 30–57.

Egan, D. E., Remde, J. R., Landauer, T. K., Lochbaum, C. C. and Gomez, L. M. (1989) Acquiring information in books and SuperBooks. *Machine Mediated Learning*, 3, 259–277.

Fairchild, K. F., Poltrock, S. E. and Furnas, G. W. (1988) SEMNET: Three-dimensional graphic representations of large knowledge bases. In R. Guindon (ed.) *Cognitive Science and its Applications for Human-Computer Interaction*. Hillsdale, NJ: Lawrence Erlbaum Associates. 201–233.

Frase, L. T. and Kreitzberg, V. S. (1975) Effects of topical and indirect learning directions on prose recall. *Journal of Educational Psychology*, 67, 320–324.

Freedle, R. O. (1987)(ed.) *Discourse, Production and Comprehension*. Norwood, NJ: Ablex.

Furnas, G. W. (1982) The FISHEYE view: A new look at structured files. Bell Laboratories Technical Memorandum.

Furnas, G. W. (1985) Experience with an adaptive indexing scheme. In *Proceedings of CHI '85 Human Factors in Computing Systems*. New York: ACM. 131–135.

Furnas, G. W. (1986) Generalized fisheye views. In *Proceedings of CHI '86 Human Factors in Computing Systems*. New York: ACM. 16–23.

Furnas, G. W., Landauer, T. K., Gomez, L. M. and Dumais, S. T. (1983) Statistical semantics: Analysis of the potential performance of keyword information systems. *Bell System Technical Journal*, 62, 1753–1806.

Furnas, G. W., Landauer, T. K., Gomez, L. M. and Dumais, S. T. (1987) The vocabulary problem in human system communication. *Communications of the ACM*, 30, 964–971.

Gagné, R. M. and Briggs, L. J. (1981) *Principles of Instructional Design*. New York: Holt, Rinehart and Winston.

Gomez, L. M., Egan, D. E. and Bowers, C. (1985) Learning to use a text editor: some learner characteristics that predict success. *Human-Computer Interaction*, 2, 1–23.

Gomez, L. M., Lochbaum, C. C. and Landauer, T. K. (1990) All the right words: Finding what you want as a function of richness of indexing vocabulary. *Journal of the American Society for Information Science*, 41, 547–559.

Gordon, S., Gustavel, J., Moore, J. and Hankey, J. (1988) The effects of hypertext on reader knowledge representation. In *Proceedings of the Human Factors Society 32nd Annual Meeting*. Santa Monica, CA: Human Factors Society. 296–300.

Gould, J., Alfaro, L., Finn, R., Haupt, B., Minuto, A., and Salaun, J. (1987) Why reading was slower from CRT displays than from paper. In *Proceedings of CHI+GI '87 Human Factors in Computing Systems and Graphics Interface*. New York: ACM. 7–11.

Greene, S. L., Gomez, L. M. and Devlin, S. J. (1986) A cognitive analysis of database query production. In *Proceedings of the Human Factors Society*. Santa Monica, CA: Human Factors Society. 9–13.

Harman, D. (1991) How effective is suffixing? *Journal of the American Society for Information Science*, 42, 7–15.

Hartley, J. (1981) Eighty ways of improving instructional text. *IEEE Transactions on Professional Communication*, PC-24, 17–27.

Hartley, J. (1985) *Designing Instructional Text* (2nd edition). London: Kogan Page.

Hauptmann, A. G. and Green, B. F. (1983) A comparison of command, menu-selection, and natural language programs. *Behaviour and Information Technology*, 2, 163–178.

Information Networking Institute (1990) Development Plan for an Electronic Library System. Final Report. INI Technical Report 1990-1. Pittsburgh, PA: Carnegie Mellon University.

Jones, W. P. and Dumais, S. T. (1986) The spatial metaphor for user interfaces: experimental tests of reference by name versus location. *ACM Transactions on Office Information Systems*, 4, 42–63.

Kahn, R. E. and Cerf, V. G. (1988) *The Digital Library Project Volume 1: The World of Knowbots* (Draft). Reston, VA: Corporation for National Research Initiatives.

Kintsch, W. and van Dijk, T. A. (1978) Toward a model of text comprehension and production. *Psychological Review*, 85, 363–394.

Klare, G. R. (1977) How does technical documentation get done? Some observations. Technical Memorandum TM 77-1222-6, Bell Laboratories.

Landauer, T. K. and Nachbar, D. W. (1985) Selection from alphabetic and numeric menu trees using a touch screen: breadth, depth, and width. In *Proceedings of CHI '85 Human Factors in Computing Systems*. New York: ACM. 73–78.

Lee, E., MacGregor, J., Lam, N. and Chao, G. (1986) Keyword-menu retrieval: an effective alternative to menu indexes. *Ergonomics*, 29, 115–130.

Lenat, D. B. and Guha, R. V. (1990) *Building Large Knowledge-Based Systems: Representation and Inference in the Cyc Project*. Reading, MA: Addison-Wesley.

MacLean, A., Barnard, P. and Wilson, M. (1985) Evaluating the interface of a data entry system: Performance and preference measures yield different trade-off functions. In P. Johnson and S. Cook (eds.) *People and Computers: Designing the Interface*. Cambridge: Cambridge University Press.

Mantei, M. M. (1982) A study of disorientation behavior in ZOG. Unpublished PhD dissertation, University of Southern California, Los Angeles.

Marchionini, G. and Shneiderman, B. (1988) Finding facts vs. browsing knowledge in hypertext systems. *IEEE Computer*, 21, 70–80.

McConkie, G. W., and Raynor, K. (1975) The span of the effective stimulus during a fixation in reading. *Perception and Psychophysics*, 17, 578–586.

McKnight, C., Dillon, A. and Richardson, J. (1990) A comparison of linear and hypertext formats in information retrieval. In R. McAleese and C. Green (eds.) *Hypertext: State of the Art*. Oxford: Intellect.

Nielsen, J. (1990) *Hypertext and Hypermedia*. San Diego, CA: Academic Press.

Nielsen, J. (1992) *Usability Engineering*. San Diego, CA: Academic Press.

Nelson, T. H. (1967) Getting it out of our system. In G. Schechter (ed.) *Information Retrieval: A Critical Review*. Washington, DC: Thompson Books.

Paap, K. R. and Roske-Hofstrand, R. J. (1988) Design of menus. In M. Helander (ed.) *Handbook of Human-Computer Interaction*. Amsterdam: Elsevier. 205–235.

Pruzansky, S., Tversky, A. and Carroll, J. D. (1982) Spatial versus tree representations of proximity data. *Psychometrica*, 47, 3–24.

Remde, J. R., Gomez, L. M. and Landauer, T. K. (1987) SuperBook: An automatic tool for information exploration — hypertext? In *Proceedings of Hypertext '87*. Chapel Hill, NC. 175–188.

van Rijsbergen, C. J. (1981) *Information Retrieval* (2nd edition). London: Butterworth.

Rothkopf, E. Z. (1972) Structural text features and the control of processes in learning from written materials. In R. O. Freedle and J. B. Carroll (eds.) *Language Comprehension and the Acquisition of Knowledge*. Washington, DC: Winston. 315–335.

Rouse, S. H. and Rouse, W. B. (1980) Computer-based manuals for procedural information. *IEEE Transactions on Systems, Man and Cybernetics*, SMC–10, 506–510.

Salton, G. (1971) *The SMART Retrieval System — Experiments in Automatic Document Processing*. Englewood Cliffs, NJ: Prentice-Hall.

Salton, G. (1989) *Automatic Text Processing*. Reading, MA: Addison-Wesley.

Salton, G. and McGill, M. (1983) *Introduction to Modern Information Retrieval*. New York: McGraw-Hill.

Schallert, D. L. (1980) The role of illustrations in reading comprehension. In R. J. Spiro, B. C. Bruce and W. F. Brewer (eds.) *Theoretical Issues in Reading Comprehension*. Hillsdale, NJ: Lawrence Erlbaum Associates. 503–524.

Smith, E. E. and Medin, D. L. (1981) *Categories and Concepts*. Cambridge, MA: Harvard University Press.

Spärck Jones, K. (1971) *Automatic Keyword Classification for Information Retrieval*. London: Butterworth.

Sternberg, R. J. (1980) Representation and process in linear syllogistic reasoning. *Journal of Experimental Psychology: General*, 109, 119–159.

Todres, A. and Teibel, D. A. (1990) Issues in document usability: quality procedures, individual differences, and non-linear texts. Bellcore Technical Memorandum.

Todres, A. and Wilson, C. (1989) Bellcore format standards: An empirical assessment of quality and usability. Bellcore Technical Memorandum.

Tullis, T. (1988) Screen design. In M. Helander (ed.) *Handbook of Human-Computer Interaction*. Amsterdam: Elsevier. 377–411.

Watt, J. H. (1988) Level of abstraction structured text. *IEEE Transactions on Systems, Man and Cybernetics*, SMC–18, 497–505.

Weyer, S. A. (1982a) Searching for information in a dynamic book. Unpublished PhD dissertation, Stanford University, Palo Alto, CA.

Weyer, S. A. (1982b) The design of a dynamic book for information search. *International Journal of Man-Machine Studies*, 17, 87–107.

Wright, P. (1978) Feeding the information eaters: suggestions for integrating pure and appli.d research on language comprehension. *Instructional Science*, 7, 249–312.

Wright, P. (1985) Editing: Policies and processes. In D. H. Jonassen (ed.) *The Technology of Text, Volume 2: Principles for Structuring, Designing, and Displaying Text*. Englewood Cliffs, NJ: Educational Technology Publications.

6

To Jump or Not to Jump : Strategy Selection While Reading Electronic Texts

Patricia Wright
MRC Applied Psychology Unit, Cambridge, UK

INTRODUCTION

This chapter will suggest that hypertext design would benefit from a richer appreciation of the variety of reading strategies that people can adopt, coupled with a deeper understanding of the factors that influence people's selection among these strategies. Fortunately, hypertexts offer a reading environment in which studying readers' strategic choices is easily done. So hypertexts have drawn attention to reading activities that have received relatively little study by researchers concerned with printed materials. Browsing is one kind of reading activity that may be facilitated by hypertexts; deliberate searching is another (e.g., Marchionini and Shneiderman, 1988). Both activities are obviously different from linear reading but, like more conventional reading, they can make heavy demands upon readers' knowledge of the content area and understanding of the document structure. There is evidence that individuals vary widely in the manner and in the success with which they apply search activities to texts. Students who are good searchers spend a considerable time deciding how they will search. They take pains to organise their search activities. In contrast less able students spend more time engaged in the activities of searching and moving around in a document (Dreher and Guthrie, 1991). It is possible that similar differences exist for other reading activities such as using adjunct materials (e.g., dictionaries) while reading. Studies examining such reading activities will be discussed later in this chapter.

Although information-seeking while working with printed materials has received relatively little attention, the problems of retrieving information have been central to many research projects on electronic documents (e.g., Lucarella, 1990; Marchionini, 1989). Indeed the ease of retrieving information is sometimes thought to be a major advantage of having documents in electronic form rather than on paper, even for documents that are conventional linear structures. Much of this advantage comes from the assistance that readers can be given through computer-based tools. Simple tools enable searches to be based on matching strings of alphanumeric characters. With sophisticated tools readers can create complex definitions of the search target in order that only highly relevant information will be retrieved (e.g., Fischer, Henninger and Redmiles, 1991). Another way of helping readers refine their search target is by offering feedback on the distribution of the search target within the document (e.g., Lesk, 1989). This feedback enables the search to be refined to take account of the characteristics of the document being read. It may be satisfactory to search for 'hypertext' in a dictionary or encyclopædia but this will not be a useful search target for a document that contains the proceedings of a conference on hypermedia. This contrast between the encyclopædia and the conference proceedings is such that most readers would appreciate the need for the search terms to be different. However, in many texts the appropriateness of a particular target can be much less obvious, and feedback concerning the context (e.g., chapter or section) in which the target occurs can be very helpful. It will certainly save searchers finding themselves at one of the target locations and only then recognising they have overlooked that 'book' is not only a printed document but also a verb for making an arrest or a theatre reservation and can relate to certain gambling activities.

Because hypertexts are often non-linear information structures within which readers can move about relatively easily, they have brought to the fore several issues about readers' activities of seeking additional information while reading. In paper texts the author may use footnotes, endnotes or appendices to provide ancillary material. There have been studies of how readers choose to integrate some categories of ancillary material with the main text during the course of reading. Usually these studies have examined how readers combine examples or illustrations with the main text (e.g., Chi et al., 1989; Mandl and Levin, 1989) but generalisable conclusions are difficult to attain. It is a pervasive problem for research in this area that the way readers integrate text and graphics may vary with reading purpose. Readers who are studying a text to pass an exam may focus on the main text and give little attention to the ancillary material, whereas people who are reading a document in order to carry out the procedures described may be happy to follow the steps of a worked example and pay scant regard to the main text (LeFevre and Dixon, 1986). So generalisations about how readers deal with ancillary materials, such as examples and illustrations, can only be made with caution. Readers have strategies among which they select but the determinants of that selection are only slowly being uncovered.

It may be helpful to outline three factors that have contributed to the relative lack of interest shown by researchers in the problems of reading strategies in spite of the sizeable research literature on the psychology of reading processes. One factor has been the logistic difficulty of unobtrusively monitoring readers' interaction with a printed text. This is no longer a difficulty for studies based on electronic documents such as hypertexts, although evidence that a page has been displayed is not necessarily evidence that it has been read. The second factor has been the absence of strategy selection as a component in models of the reading process. Most models of reading confine themselves to the processes of construing meaning from an orthographic input. Certainly this is a difficult enough task. Nevertheless, there are several issues relating to the strategies readers can adopt that are of great importance for generating hypertexts. Authors need to make a judgement about whether readers are going to be willing to undertake this process of construal at all. People will often deliberately ignore information the author had hoped they would read (Wright, 1988a). Even when people are willing to read the text they may set themselves a particular level of understanding that seems adequate. Sometimes a quick skim through the text will suffice. At other times detailed analysis and comparison of different parts of the text will be undertaken. Indeed studies of the readers of academic journals have shown that both kinds of reading may be combined in the same overall task as readers hop and skip around the publication (Dillon, Richardson and McKnight, 1989). Because researchers tend to explore a particular reading task, they implicitly set the appropriate level of understanding, and so have not needed to be concerned with deliberate strategic variation in the level of understanding sought by readers. Perhaps if the variety of reading activities were seen as constituents of the broader category of information-seeking skills, the need for models of strategy selection would be more evident.

The third factor contributing to the neglect of reading strategy as an important component of models of reading has been that most research studies are concerned with similar reading purposes. The reader, often a school child or university student, is asked to read a text in order to recall it or to answer questions about it. This is a highly valid task in an educational context but it does not capture many of the kinds of literacy skills needed in daily life where texts may be short (e.g., wall notices, cooking instructions — cf. Wright, 1988b) and where the visual display features of the message may change its interpretation (e.g., "*SLOW children crossing*" — Nickerson, 1981). In the broader context of the many kinds of reading that people engage in, particularly reading done as part of some decision-making or problem-solving activity, the importance of understanding the factors influencing readers' selection of reading strategies becomes salient. The examples discussed below illustrate how research studies using hypertexts have shed light on the contribution that information design factors make in determining people's reading strategies.

This chapter will discuss readers' information-seeking strategies when the information being sought can be jumped to from the current text location. The studies reported will start with fairly conventional linear texts.

These afford an opportunity to see whether readers will avail themselves of the chance to access information that is only a click away from the main text. Then some of the special features that hypertexts offer will be considered together with their implications for the strategic reading skills that people may need for using electronic documents effectively. Finally some of the implications of hypertexts for psychological research on reading and working with written materials will be discussed, particularly in relation to strategic decisions that extend beyond reading to other cognitive activities such as attending and perceiving.

JUMPING TO A GLOSSARY

It has already been mentioned that one of the major advantages of electronic documents is that from the text page displayed on screen, readers can jump to additional information such as explanations, cross-references, etc. What is not known is whether readers who see it as their main objective to understand the gist of an author's message will bother to make use of such functionality. Ancillary material which provides explanatory detail is a particularly interesting case because readers are able to exercise considerable discretion over when these explanations are read. The kinds of information that glossaries give about technical terms offer a useful subdomain in which to explore this aspect of readers' information-seeking strategies because there are a wide range of interface and display variants possible. If readers' behaviour is not influenced by design factors, this suggests that the information-seeking activity is driven by internal criteria, such as readers' awareness of their current level of comprehension (Guthrie and Mosenthal, 1987). On the other hand, if display or interface factors influence readers' willingness to check on vocabulary items, this suggests that readers may be computing some 'cognitive cost' of accessing the extra information. Whether that cost relates solely to the information-seeking activity itself or whether it reflects some increased difficulty in the primary task of building a representation of the author's gist, would be a subsequent question to be resolved once it was known that the behaviour was not entirely governed by the constituents of the processes of reading, understanding and remembering the text.

In order to examine the effects of design factors it is obviously helpful to start by establishing a baseline. Consider readers presented with a series of short narrative texts (200 words) that they could read and re-read if they wished. They know that they will have to answer multiple choice questions about the content immediately after reading each story. Into such a text an author can introduce novel words and tell readers that whenever they encounter a word whose meaning they are unsure of they can click on it and a definition will be given in the margin. Such a study was done by Black *et al.* (1992). The novel words they used (e.g., *hoadle*) followed the orthographic rules of English, were not essential to the main flow of the text, but nor could the meanings of these words be guessed from the surrounding context (e.g., *"As the clown moved toward the hoadle the guard joined in the entertainment and, with a sweeping bow, ushered her onto the platform. From now on travelling by train was going to be fun."* Readers who clicked on *hoadle* would be shown *"HOADLE: A hinged panel closing a narrow opening in a wall or fence."*). Black *et al.* reported that readers clicked on over 90% of these unknown words. The definitions were given in the margin alongside the text and varied in length from a short phrase (e.g., *Hoadle: a door*) to a longer sentence but length had no effect on people's willingness to access the explanations nor did replacing the quiz with the instruction to retell the story into a tape recorder. So readers appear very willing to look at glossary information when they know that they do not know a word encountered while reading. In further studies by Black *et al.* the definitions were presented as auditory rather than visual information. Readers were still very willing to click on the unknown words but there was a tendency (non-significant) for people to re-read the text more often than before (with visual definitions a quarter of the group re-read three or more of the six texts, with auditory definitions half the group re-read at least three texts before going on to the quiz). This effect of the change in modality suggests that readers may experience a cognitive cost for multimedia integration, a cost which impacts on the discourse processing of the main text.

Support for this suggestion that the cognitive costs of jumping may increase if a modality change is involved came from another series of studies reported by Black *et al.* in which for half the readers the definition was accompanied by a picture. The results suggested that more people re-read at least three stories if the glossary definition included pictures (40% re-read) than if it did not (10% re-read). Again these differences were not statistically significant, so the data can only be considered as suggestive of a line of enquiry that needs closer investigation. But it appears possible that the reading of a prose text (as distinct from reading a table, graph or diagram) may suffer if there are interruptions involving *other* processing resources.

Some psychological theorists have argued that cognition is accomplished by a series of interacting but relatively independent subsystems (e.g., Allport, 1980; Barnard, 1985). From this perspective, performance might be expected to show greater degradation when the same interpretative processes are being used for different tasks (i.e. understanding the main discourse and also the glossary information). Other psychological models could point to the potential of a common processing bottleneck such as working memory (e.g., Baddeley, 1986). From neither theoretical approach would the disruption of the modality changes have been expected. It is possible that a critical determinant of the ease of information integration while reading is the nested relation between these two reading subtasks. That is to say, if the reader's verbal processes are already activated, then this may expedite processing glossary information that is in a similar verbal form (visual/auditory), and may facilitate the integration of that information with an understanding of the main text. Although this discussion cannot be conclusive it illustrates the potential of hypertexts for challenging and sharpening psychological theories.

The pictures used in the second series of studies by Black *et al.* were line drawings of architectural terms such as *cornice, architrave*, etc. These words were chosen because they would be familiar to many people although their meaning might not be known precisely. It was found that readers clicked on significantly fewer architectural terms (62% available definitions) than on the previous novel words (where 96% definitions were clicked). Many of these architectural terms could not be correctly defined at the end of the study although the meanings of the words had not been checked while reading. In order to see whether this decline in glossary access arose from readers confusing familiarity with understanding, the texts were modified so that the clickable items in the text were visually cued by the addition of a superscript black spot. For a new group of readers the frequency of accessing the glossary returned to a high level (93% definitions were clicked) comparable to that occurring for completely novel words. These data show that there are contexts where display factors can become important determinants of readers' willingness to jump. Whether the visual cue challenged readers to assess if they fully understood the words, or whether the cue reassured readers that the author had provided an explanation, is not yet clear. So further research is needed before it will be possible to specify the critical features of the contexts where visual cues to glossary information are desirable, but at least it is now known that design features of hypertexts can have an important influence on readers' willingness to jump.

In both these series of studies exploring readers' use of glossary information, the glossary was accessed by clicking on a word within the main text. It is a convention in printed materials to present glossary information separate from the main text. In an electronic document this can be done in several ways. The second series of studies by Black *et al.* (the texts with architectural terms) included a condition where all the technical terms that would be used in the text were presented in a list on the left-hand side of the screen. Any item in this list could be clicked to display the verbal definition together with a picture in the lower part of the screen below the text, as in the previous experiments. Items in the glossary list were highlighted if they were also in the text currently displayed on screen. It was found that when readers' access to the definitions was physically separated from the body of the text, even though still on the same page, this reduced people's willingness to access definitions. Now 76% definitions were clicked, compared with 93% definitions when accompanied by black spots in the text. Nevertheless, people were more willing to use the glossary list than they were to click on these architectural terms when the words were within the text but had no visual cues to show that they were clickable items (62% definitions clicked). These findings show that people's information-seeking strategies are not determined solely by the reading processes that generate text comprehension. There are such process-driven strategies (evidence from studies with novel words), but they occur with textual items that readers are certain they do not know and which they believe the author will have catered for. In other circumstances, perhaps if readers are uncertain whether they know enough about a technical term, hypertext design factors can be critical and readers' willingness to jump can be influenced by how the jumping opportunities are presented at the interface. If this is true for highly localised information within a text (such as definitions), it may also be true for global information such as overviews and summaries.

JUMPING TO ACCESS AN OVERVIEW DIAGRAM
One of the common functions of a diagram in a text is to reiterate the message of the text, expressing the information in a different way. The design may focus on selective aspects of the text, e.g., in order to show how items mentioned in the text are linked or related. There are a variety of options open to readers in how they choose to integrate this information with the development of their understanding of the text. People may choose to study an overview diagram before reading the text, seeking to create some form of mental model into which the author's information can be fitted. This would seem a reasonable strategy given the evidence that prose overviews studied before reading are often found helpful in interpreting and remembering text (Hartley and Davies, 1976).

On the other hand, readers may prefer to use such overview diagrams as summaries after they have finished reading. Again it is known that verbal summaries are helpful to readers (Hartley, Goldie and Stein, 1979). Diagrams, because of their change in representational form, may offer readers an opportunity to test their understanding of the relations expressed in the text. For this reason some diagrams may have advantages over verbal summaries if the verbal listing elicits recognition by the reader rather than a reinterpretation or new synthesis of the material. It is also possible that for complex texts, involving many links and relationships, readers may avail themselves of this summary view as an aid to developing their understanding during the course of reading the text. Readers' choices among these alternative strategies are by no means mutually exclusive and may well vary with factors such as reading purpose and familiarity with the domain. Fortunately, these choices can be explored using electronic documents which enable readers' selection of information to be monitored unobtrusively. The following series of studies used an unfamiliar content domain, so that people would need to read the text, and the single purpose of reading for a subsequent quiz. Even within these limits, several insights into readers' strategic information-seeking choices were obtained.

Wright, Hull and Black (1990) offered readers access to an overview diagram that summarised relations among people and their commercial interests. These links were described in more detail in a 650-word prose text that purported to be the background to a commercial fraud. On every screen page there was a button labelled "Diagram" which readers could click whenever they wished. Once on the diagram page there was a single button that took readers back to their point of departure in the text. It was found that readers studied the diagram before and after reading but not during their reading of the prose. However, readers more often looked at the diagram during the course of reading if the author specifically suggested within the text that readers should do this. This raises the possibility of a difference between electronic and paper-based documents in the strategies readers adopt. Whalley and Flemming (1975) reproduced a two-column page from a published journal article and reported that many of their students were reluctant to follow an author's advice to look at a diagram on the same page as the main text. Of course the difference between the findings of these two studies may not lie in the communication medium (paper or screen) but in the nature of the readers (students versus paid volunteers) or the character of the diagram (an electronic circuit diagram versus a box diagram of links between people and companies) or even the experimental techniques used (Whalley and Flemming used a pen torch that readers shone on the dimly lit page, so enabling the researchers to monitor readers' progress through the text). It is hoped that further work with hypertexts will shed light on the contribution of these alternative possibilities. Given the wide range of design options that exist for hypertexts, the need to understand how reading strategies are influenced by an author's design decisions becomes ever more urgent.

Wright *et al.* found that a highly successful way of increasing readers' understanding was to remove the diagram button and instead have the author intermittently include the diagram as the next screen page. Readers did not need to pause on this page, they could go on to the next page. But many readers did pause to study the diagram and their understanding of the text was significantly better than those who had a choice about accessing the diagram. This improvement was evident both in readers' scores on a subsequent quiz and in the numbers of people who were happy to read the text only once rather than re-reading it before taking the quiz. Such data suggest that readers' strategies for integrating text and diagrams may not be well-honed. For the materials used in this study, the diagrams were a source of valuable information which readers knew how to use, but they did not fully appreciate when to access and integrate the convergent sources.

In electronic documents total space is usually less restricted than in printed materials. As a consequence there are fewer limitations on the numbers of diagrams that can be made available to readers than usually apply to printed documents. Instead of just a single illustration, hypertexts could provide a series of diagrams which gradually built up the complex picture as new items of information were introduced in the text. Wright *et al.* examined such a 'growing' diagram and again contrasted giving readers free access to it or having it encountered as people read the text. Here too it was found that the forced encounter produced better performance. People having the growing diagram spent significantly less time reading the material than did people who encountered the full diagram. So encouraging hypertext authors to take charge of readers' encounter with diagrams may be an efficient and effective way by which authors can supplement an apparent deficit in reading strategy. Of course, in time with increasing exposure to hypertexts, readers may learn new strategies for integrating information. Whether this will influence the reading strategies they apply to printed documents cannot be predicted.

A different question about readers' integration of text and diagrams is, "What would happen if the diagram were made the primary information source, and the text accessed from it instead of the other way round?" In technical documentation (e.g., manuals or handbooks) it is common to find that a diagram is the organising theme for a section of the material. It could therefore be a powerful substitute for a conventional access structure such as a table of contents. But the non-linearity inherent in most diagrams could cause problems for readers who use it to access more than one or two sections of the text. For example, it may be difficult for readers to keep track of which parts of the text have been read and which have been overlooked. Some of the questions relating to how adequately a diagram can be used for accessing a text were explored by Wright and Ummelen (1990). Using essentially the same text and diagram as the earlier Wright *et al.* studies, but with the diagram showing small tick marks alongside elements where the associated text had been read, it was found that readers were as able to cope with this style of reading as with the more conventional text. Readers neither took longer nor scored less on the quiz than did readers who jumped in the other direction and accessed the diagram from the text. This is another aspect of hypertext functionality that suggests it may be possible for some electronic documents to meet readers' needs with a facility that has no ready counterpart in printed materials.

No strong claims can be made from any of these studies which are small-scale both in terms of the population of readers and the nature of the texts used. Nevertheless the findings from these studies illustrate that electronic documents not only offer ways of exploring readers' strategies but also increase the range of reading strategies that readers may need to develop when working with computer-based information, particularly hypertexts. These studies also show that there is an increased onus on writers and information providers to ensure that material is presented in a form that can be easily used. It cannot be assumed that readers will have the necessary skills in information integration or will know which actions are most appropriate when jumps can be made across representational forms (i.e. pictures and words).

MODELS OF READING STRATEGIES

The issues raised by the design of electronic multimedia documents such as hypertexts draw attention to how little we understand the range of cognitive processes recruited when people are working with written materials. Indeed they highlight how little we seem to know about reading for information-use as distinct from reading in order to learn or reading for pleasure. The psychology of decision making or problem solving is not easily applied to predict what people will do as readers when they are seeking to find and act upon written information. Little is known about the range of strategies that people will use, and even less about the factors influencing their selection among these strategies. There have been innovative attempts to develop an understanding of the cognitive processes of authoring from a problem-solving perspective (e.g., Flower and Hayes, 1980). However, when problem-solving has been applied to skilled reading it has usually been in the context of understanding word meanings, including pronominal reference and metaphor, rather than as a determinant of reading strategy for a task involving information use.

To account for the way people use written materials as part of some larger task, it has been necessary to create completely novel models of reader's behaviour. For example, Guthrie (1988) has outlined a significant new approach to understanding readers' information-seeking skills which does not rely on existing models of problem solving. The model specifies five subtasks that readers engage in that together constitute the activity of finding relevant information in a text:

(a) specifying the target information to be acquired by the search, together with all its constraints and parameters;
(b) deciding which structural features (e.g., chapters or sections) of the text being searched will be relevant search destinations for this target information;
(c) extracting the appropriate details from each relevant destination;
(d) integrating the details extracted and evaluating whether they meet the target specification set earlier;
(e) recycling from (a) if the evaluation at (d) is negative.

This model was put forward to account for the behaviour of readers working with printed texts but there is no obvious reason why it should not apply to electronic documents, even non-linear materials such as hypertexts. The major difference will be that readers of electronic documents may have access to computer support which changes the way some of the subtasks are carried out. For example, the availability of text string searching and of combinatorial searching may influence how readers use the structural features of the text (subtask (b) in Guthrie's model). Indeed it might be argued that hypertexts can involve an extra subtask between (b) and (c) since readers not only decide where to go but also how to get there. So new information genres such as hypertexts afford a valuable environment within which predictions from the model can be examined and the model itself can be extended.

Hypertexts are also important for the development of psychological theory because they illustrate how much more we need to know about the integration of a range of cognitive processes (attention, comprehension, memory) within any single reading strategy. These processes are often examined by researchers as topics in their own right but there seems to be a missing layer of psychological theorising. The past 50 years has seen major developments in psychologists' understanding of the cognitive constituents of the human information processing system but there is not yet a detailed account of how these processes will combine during the performance of a particular task. The existing psychological models are models of the competencies that the cognitive system has, descriptions of its potential and limitations. What is needed in addition are models of how these competencies are combined in specific performances. For example, the current models of perception and attention find no need to address questions such as why readers choose to ignore information, either before or after reading it; nor why, having read an author's advice about what they should look at next, people choose not to comply. Yet this non-compliance may be the most significant determinant of people's performance on a reading task and so becomes of major importance in the context of hypertext design. For an author to know that people could have understood the information if they had read it is of little moment if they choose not to read it at all.

Similarly, the current models of memory do not lend themselves to predicting how readers cope with the diverse memory requirements of information-seeking tasks. There is a need to understand how people remember what they are looking for as they search for information, as well as keeping track of where they are going, what they have already found and where they have already looked in a text. It is known that hypertexts with navigation styles offering similar functionality but differing in their implementation can influence the ease of some of these categories of remembering during information-seeking tasks. It has yet to be established whether this is because the interface requirements force a reconfiguration of the reader's processing resources or because readers make strategic changes in the allocation of their cognitive resources. The answers to such questions will have implications for hypertext design.

Some theorists have appreciated this problem of moving from cognitive constituents to cognitive integration. Newell (1990) has made a very eloquent plea concerning the need for a unified theory of cognition and has shown how this can be derived from a particular cognitive architecture (viz., SOAR). It remains to be seen whether the essentially reductionist approach that he espouses, decomposing goals into subgoals until all actions can be represented as IF... THEN... procedural rules, is a means of achieving this.

Some theorists have departed from traditional approaches in other directions in order to talk about the ways in which the availability of information in one cognitive subsystem will determine the output of other subsystems (e.g., the model of interacting cognitive subsystems proposed by Barnard, 1985). Barnard has found it convenient to approach design decisions by examining issues relating to the uncertainty associated with the actions being performed. If users do not know what to do this is classed as item uncertainty; if users do not know in what order to do things this is classed as order uncertainty (Barnard, 1987). He has demonstrated that this approach can yield valuable insights into some issues of interface and dialogue design — issues as diverse as command naming in text editing and making appropriate menu selections in an email task. In both studies it was found that reducing the classes of uncertainty improved performance. It remains to be seen whether this classification will be powerful enough to address the wide range of interface issues to which hypertexts are drawing attention. For example, in the studies of an overview diagram and glossaries discussed earlier it was seen that readers may know where information is and how to access it but choose not to, perhaps for reasons of anticipated cognitive costs rather than 'uncertainty' relating to the activity itself. Nevertheless, attempts such as Barnard's at coming to grips with the need for models that integrate cognitive processes are to be applauded, both for their recognition of the gap in other psychological approaches and for the breadth of the design issues they seek to address (Barnard, 1991).

There are several difficulties facing all integrationist models. One is that they need to be very powerful and that power risks giving them the ability to predict all performance outcomes. Setting appropriate limitations to the models can be a problem. Here lies the second difficulty. These limitations will often appear related to environmental factors, as when the display features of a hypertext change the reader's behaviour, rather than being the limits of cognitive resources. Psychologists have traditionally confined their models to cognitive constituents and have chosen to incorporate environmental features only in a rudimentary, sometimes almost perfunctory, way. If a worthwhile cognitive ergonomics is to be achieved this traditional bias may need to be set aside. A better understanding of how cognitive activities are influenced by environmental factors would seem to be a prerequisite to knowing how readers' information-seeking will be influenced by design decisions. In broader contexts than the reading of texts it has been pointed out that the display characteristics of the environment will facilitate some actions rather than others (Norman, 1988). For hypertexts these environmental affordances can be quite subtle. Two pieces of information may be the same number of clicks away from the current reading location but, for reasons not yet well understood, the psychological distances of a pop-up window and a replacement window may feel very different to readers (Stark, 1990). Perhaps seeing the old information concurrently with the new is a critical feature that perceptually shortens the distance of a jump. Sophisticated psychological theories will be needed to incorporate the affordances of such environments because what is being encouraged or discouraged is not so much a specific activity such as jumping but rather the creation of a subgoal by the reader, the subgoal of information-seeking, a subgoal that might be realised in a variety of activities.

The importance of readers being free to generate and select among their subgoals contrasts with a characteristic of much contemporary research in cognitive psychology, where tasks are carefully chosen to ensure that the processing operations of interest to the researcher dominate the performance being measured. This is sensible. Unfortunately it precludes evidence that would be helpful for the creation of integrationist theories; evidence relating to the way people choose among their cognitive resources and seek to circumvent their cognitive limitations. Yet this is the kind of information that becomes readily apparent and easily monitored when people are working with hypertexts. Readers can be invited to undertake complex tasks which are capable of being done in a variety of ways and which are cognitively rich in the range of processing options they involve. People's selection among these options are likely to offer valuable insights which will promote the development of theories in that missing layer concerned with the integration of cognitive processes.

Of course the benefits are not all one way. Hypertexts are a significant challenge to psychologists for the reasons outlined above. In turn, a better understanding of how cognitive processes are integrated could assist those who are developing hypertexts. Such an understanding could inform and enhance the design decisions made by writers and by information providers. It could sensitise the decision making by software engineers who create the architectures underlying hypertexts. For example, one consequence of an appreciation of the need for supporting readers and writers of hypertexts could be the provision of many more kinds of tools for finding, collecting and manipulating information. In time, the transparent integration of these tools with the display of the text content may be common place. If there are going to be tools then readers need to become skilful tool users. Understanding the variety of reading strategies that people can adopt provides a basis for recognising the range of information handling skills that the readers of electronic documents will need. It may also suggest ways of helping people acquire these new skills. As the amount of electronic documentation increases, so does the urgency of acquiring these new ways of reading for problem solving and decision making. Hypertexts not only bring a spotlight to bear on the problems, they also offer a research tool for finding solutions.

SYNOPSIS

This chapter started by explaining why the answer to the title question was not readily available from the sizeable research literature that exists on reading, because that literature has little to say about many of the document related activities that readers engage in, such as browsing and searching. So as a preliminary to answering the question about whether readers wish to jump around in a hypertext, several empirical studies were reported. It was found that people would jump from the main text to use a glossary if they were certain the word was unknown or if the word was visually cued as having a definition available. However, this willingness to jump could be influenced by design features at the point of departure from the text (e.g., the way that accessing the glossary was integrated with the main body of text), and also by the form in which the definitions were provided, e.g., their modality (visual/auditory) and their representational form (verbal/pictorial). Another series of studies gave readers optional access to overview diagrams and found that readers did not necessarily adopt those information-seeking strategies that would have yielded best comprehension of the text. However, the data also showed that any hypertext authors aware of these problems would have a range of design solutions available. Finally the discussion returned to the issue of a need for a theory of reading strategies, but suggested that rather than seeking to extend models of the reading process it might be more appropriate to look towards psychological models that integrate a diversity of cognitive resources (perception, attention, language, memory, motor skills and so forth). As yet it is not obvious that these models can accommodate what is known about the strategic choices made by hypertext readers, but hypertexts clearly offer several interesting challenges to this class of psychological theory.

ACKNOWLEDGEMENT

The many helpful comments from Ann Hill Duin and the editors on an earlier draft of this chapter were much appreciated.

REFERENCES

Allport, D. A. (1980) Patterns and actions: cognitive mechanisms are content specific. In G. Claxton (ed.) *Cognitive Psychology: New Directions.* London: Routledge and Kegan Paul. 26–64.

Baddeley, A. D. (1986) *Working Memory.* Oxford: Clarendon Press.

Barnard, P. J. (1985) Interacting cognitive subsystems: a psycholinguistic approach to short-term memory. In A. Ellis (ed.) *Progress in the Psychology of Language, Vol 2.* London: Lawrence Erlbaum Associates. 197–258.

Barnard, P. J. (1987) Cognitive resources and the learning of human-computer dialogues. In J. M. Carroll (ed.) *Interfacing Thought: Cognitive Aspects of Human-Computer Interaction.* Cambridge, MA: MIT Press. 112–158.

Barnard, P. J. (1991) Bridging between basic theories and the artefacts of human-computer interaction. In J. M. Carroll (ed.) *Designing Interaction: Psychology at the Human–Computer Interface.* Cambridge: Cambridge University Press. 103–127.

Black, A., Wright, P., Black, D. and Norman, K. (1992) Using dictionary information: some factors influencing whether readers will check the meanings of unknown words in a text. *Hypermedia*, 4, in press.

Chi, M. T. H., Bassok, M., Lewis, M. W., Reiman, P. and Glaser, R. (1989) Self explanations: how students study and use examples in learning to solve problems. *Cognitive Science*, 13, 145–182.

Dillon, A., Richardson, J. and McKnight, C. (1989) The human factors of journal usage and the design of electronic text. *Interacting with Computers*, 1, 183–189.

Dreher, M. J. and Guthrie, J. T. (1991) Cognitive processes in textbook chapter search tasks. *Reading Research Quarterly*, 25, 322–339.

Fischer, G., Henninger, S. and Redmiles, D. (1991) Intertwining query construction and relevance evaluation. In S. Robertson, G. M. Olson and J. S. Olson (eds.) *Reaching Through Technology*. Proceedings of CHI'91. Reading, MA: Addison-Wesley. 55–62.

Flower L. S. and Hayes, J. R. (1980) The dynamics of composing: making plans and juggling constraints. In L. W. Gregg and E. R. Steinberg (eds.) *Cognitive Processes in Writing*. Hillsdale, NJ: Lawrence Erlbaum Associates. 31–50.

Guthrie, J. T. (1988) Locating information in documents: examination of a cognitive model. *Reading Research Quarterly*, 23, 178–199.

Guthrie, J. T. and Mosenthal, P. (1987) Literacy as multidimensional: locating information in text. *Journal of Educational Psychology*, 79, 220–228.

Hartley, J. and Davies, I. (1976) Preinstructional strategies: the role of pretests, behavioural objectives, overviews and advance organisers. *Review of Educational Research*, 46, 239–265.

Hartley, J., Goldie, M. and Stein, L. (1979) The role and position of summaries: some issues and data. *Educational Review*, 31, 59–65.

LeFevre, J. and Dixon, P. (1986) Do written instructions need examples? *Cognition and Instruction*, 3, 1–30.

Lesk, M., (1989) What to do when there is too much information. *Proceedings of Hypertext '89*. New York: ACM. 305–318.

Lucarella, D., (1990) A model for hypertext based information retrieval. In A. Rizk, N. Streitz and J. André (eds.) *Hypertext: Concepts, Systems and Applications*. Cambridge: Cambridge University Press. 80–94.

Mandl, H. and Levin, J. L. (eds.) (1989) *Knowledge Acquisition from Text and Pictures*. Amsterdam: North-Holland.

Marchionini, G. (1989) Information seeking strategies of novices using a full text electronic encyclopedia. *Journal of the American Society for Information Science*, 40, 54–66.

Marchionini, G. and Shneiderman, B. (1988) Finding facts versus browsing knowledge in hypertext systems. *IEEE Computer*, 21, 70–80.

Newell, A. (1990) *Unified Theories of Cognition*. Cambridge, MA: Harvard University Press.

Nickerson, R. (1981) Understanding signs: some examples of knowledge dependent language processing. *Information Design Journal*, 2, 2–16.

Norman, D. A. (1988) *The Psychology of Everyday Things*. New York: Basic Books.

Stark, H. (1990) What do readers do to pop-ups and pop-ups do to readers? In R. McAleese and C. Green (eds.) *Hypertext: State of the Art*. Oxford: Intellect. 2–9.

Whalley, P. and Flemming, R. W. (1975) An experiment with a simple recorder of reading behaviour. *Programmed Learning and Educational Technology,* 12, 120–124.

Wright, P. (1988a) The need for theories of NOT reading: some psychological aspects of the human-computer interface. In B. A. G. Elsendoorn and H. Bouma (eds.) *Working Models of Human Perception.* London: Academic Press. 319–340.

Wright, P. (1988b) Functional literacy: reading and writing at work. *Ergonomics,* 31, 265–290.

Wright, P., Hull, A. J. and Black, D. (1990) Integrating diagrams and text. *The Technical Writing Teacher,* 17, 244–254.

Wright, P. and Ummelen, N. (1990) Given a diagram, when do readers read text? Forum 90 Postharvest. Box 38, S-124 21 Bandhagen, Sweden.

7

Effects Of Semantically Structured Hypertext Knowledge Bases on Users' Knowledge Structures

David H. Jonassen
University of Colorado, USA

OVERVIEW

Some hypertext researchers and designers believe that hypertext information structures should reflect the structures of human memory and that by empirically deriving and then mapping the semantic structure of information onto hypertext and explicitly illustrating that structure in the hypertext interface will result in greater changes in the knowledge structures of the users (Jonassen, 1990, 1991b; Lambiotte *et al.*, 1989; McAleese, 1990; McDonald, Paap, and McDonald, 1990). This chapter introduces techniques for ascertaining an expert's knowledge structure and mapping it onto hypertext. It then reviews the results of an ongoing series of studies that test these ideas. The studies show that merely illustrating content structures in the interface is not sufficient for helping learners acquire that structure. Rather, it is the nature of the processing task and goals for learning whilst interacting with a hypertext that determines the effects of its use on learners' knowledge structures.

ASSOCIATIVE NETWORKS

Some hypertext researchers have asserted that hypertext mimics the associative networks of human memory (Fiderio, 1988; Jonassen, 1990, 1991a, 1991b; McAleese, 1990; McDonald, Paap, and McDonald, 1990). Schema theory and active structural networks have provided the major theoretical rationales for developing associatively structured hypertext (Jonassen, 1989b). Schema theory (Rumelhart and Ortony, 1977) contends that knowledge is stored in information packets or schemas that comprise our mental constructs for ideas. Schemas have attributes, which most often consist of other schemas. Each schema that we construct represents a mini-framework in which to interrelate information about a topic into a single conceptual unit. These schemas are organised into a network of interrelated concepts known as a semantic network. These network structures are composed of nodes or ideas and ordered labelled relationships that connect them (Norman, Gentner and Stevens, 1976). The nodes are representations of concepts or schemas, and the links define the propositional relationships between them. Semantic structures in hypertext represent schemas as nodes and the relationships between schemas as the hypertext links. The rationale for doing so is that by explicitly mapping the semantic network of an expert onto the hypertext, learners may come to think like an expert more readily. This rationale will be explained in greater depth in subsequent sections.

Associative hypertext engine
Bush (1945) observed that ideas result from "the association of thoughts, in accordance with some intricate web of trails carried by cells of the brain". This observation and the continued development of associative network theory have provided a conceptual foundation for the development of hypertexts. Hypertext, like other technologies such as databases and expert systems, is a knowledge-based system. That is, subject content is stored in a knowledge base which is structured by a particular data model. The data model defines the organisation of the information. This organisation, in turn, defines the logical relationships between the information in the knowledge base. The logic in each type of data model varies with the kinds of relationships that comprise it. The logic implied by the data model provides the engine for accessing and using the information in the knowledge base. Most expert systems, for instance, use a rule-based engine, with rules that state relationships between conditions and consequents (e.g., IF speed < V1 AND runway position > 7 AND power is => 95%, THEN abort take-off).

A hypertext engine, on the other hand, is associative. That is, it is based upon an associative network of ideas. An associative data model, because of the range of relationships possible, does not constrain the relationships or links as much as rule-based engines. Links may be defined by an open set of associations, so hypertext structures may take on a variety of forms. Therefore, hypertext structures are malleable and the logical structure of any hypertext may emulate the logical structures of a variety of instructional designs or functions (Jonassen, 1991b). If hypertext mimics human associative networks, then the hypertext engine should mirror the semantic network of an experienced performer or expert. That is, we can map the associative knowledge structure of an expert or knowledgeable person onto the structure of a hypertext. In the next section, I will explain how hypertexts can emulate expert knowledge structures and how to assess the changes in learners' knowledge structures as a result of interacting with such hypertexts.

MAPPING KNOWLEDGE ONTO HYPERTEXT

Learning and semantic networks

As pointed out above, our semantic networks are conceptual representations of what we know. The interrelated knowledge within semantic memory enables humans to combine ideas, infer, extrapolate or otherwise reason with the information. Learning consists of building new structures by assimilating environmental information and constructing new nodes that describe and interrelate them with existing nodes and with each other (Norman, 1976). It requires forming links between existing knowledge and new knowledge in order to comprehend information from the environment. Learning therefore may be conceived of as a reorganisation of the learner's knowledge structure that results from the learner's interactions with the environment. This hypothesis has been empirically demonstrated. As a result of teaching, the learner's knowledge structure closely resembles the instructor's (Shavelson, 1974; Thro, 1978). Learning, according to this conceptualisation, is the mapping of subject matter knowledge (usually that possessed by the teacher or expert) onto the learner's knowledge structure.

Hypertext engines or structures may be designed to reflect the semantic structure of a subject matter expert. The research question that is implied by these assumptions is, "if the node-link structure of the hypertext reflects the semantic structure of the expert, will the expert's knowledge structure be more effectively mapped onto the novice browser?" This is the question that has been investigated in the studies described below.

Investigating this question requires the definition of new research tools and procedures. If we accept the previously stated premise that learning is the reorganisation of knowledge structures, then we need tools for depicting knowledge representations and displaying those representations during instruction. If we want to design hypertexts that reflect the semantic structure of an expert, then we need means for assessing the knowledge structure of the expert and later conveying it to the learner. Jonassen (1990) reviewed three methods for assessing knowledge structures. The best established and most accurate method is scaling of free word association lists (Preece, 1976). When provided with a blank list, the learner generates a list of free associations to that word. The words that are first recalled are the strongest associates. A semantic map (a spatial map that reflects the semantic distances between ideas) can be calculated from these associates by calculating relatedness coefficients and multi-dimensionally scaling those coefficients (Jonassen, 1987; Shavelson, 1974) which produces an n-dimensional map illustrating the semantic associations in a content domain. This map becomes the browsing interface.

Another, simpler method for mapping knowledge structures is a notetaking technique known as pattern noting (Buzan, 1974; Fields, 1982). The pattern noter begins by noting the central idea in the middle of the page and using a free association technique to add related concepts which radiate out from those lines to create a map of a content domain. This method has

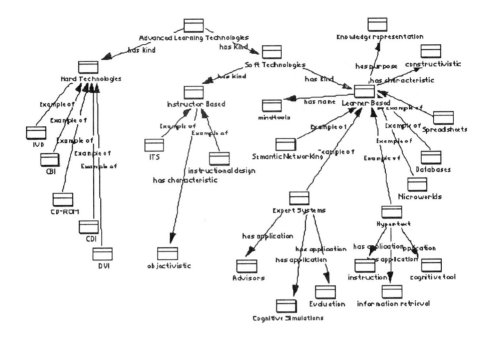

Figure 1: Part of a semantic map produced with Learning Tool.

been shown to replicate accurately the same structures as those produced by free word associations (Jonassen, 1987).

The semantic maps that are produced by both word association and pattern noting have now been implemented in computer environments. Programs such as Learning Tool (Kozma, 1987), SemNet (Fisher *et al.*, 1988), and Pathfinder Nets (McDonald, Paap, and McDonald, 1990) facilitate the production of semantic maps. Figure 1 illustrates part of a semantic map produced with Learning Tool. Learners may use this software as a cognitive strategy to increase the meaningfulness of information and facilitate knowledge acquisition. The software may also be used to assess the knowledge reorganisation effects of learning.

SEMANTIC NETWORKS FOR DESIGNING HYPERTEXT

If we accept the suggestion that hypertext should mirror the semantic structure of an experienced performer or expert, then we need methods for mapping that semantic networks onto the hypertext. This may be accomplished by having an expert or group of experienced individuals or experts generate semantic maps using any of the techniques described above. The maps provide a node-link structure which may be mapped directly onto the hypertext interface. The concepts in the semantic maps comprise hypertext nodes and the relationships are in effect hypertext links. Being able to work interactively and iteratively with an expert or group of knowledgeable individuals to refine, clarify, and correct these structures should provide more meaningful and useful maps. The assumption of this method, that using semantic maps to define the structural model of a hypertext by directly mapping the expert's organisation of ideas onto the hypertext, has been the subject of considerable debate (Jonassen and Mandl, 1990) and is the subject of a series of studies described below.

Developing graphical browsers from semantic maps
The most direct way to map the expert's semantic structure onto a hypertext is to use the semantic map as a graphical browser in the hypertext. Graphical browsers are maps or graphical listings of available nodes in a hypertext. They represent a graphical interface between the user and a hypertext that is designed to reduce navigation problems within the hypertext (Jonassen, 1988). Getting lost in a large web of hypertext nodes and links is a common problem among hypertext users, so graphical browsers are developed to provide a spatial map of the organisation of nodes in a hypertext. Most often, however, the arrangement or structure of nodes that are illustrated in a graphical browser is arbitrary (e.g., rows and columns of nodes). The hypothesis of our recent research (Jonassen and Wang, 1990; 1991) is that by arranging the nodes in a graphical browser according to an expert's semantic map, you are explicitly conveying the organisation of ideas in the expert's knowledge structure. That is, you are showing the user how the expert thinks. So, while navigating through a hypertext, the user is in effect navigating through the expert's knowledge structure. The research questions that we have pursued focus on the extent to which the semantic structure illustrated in graphical browsers actually maps onto the user's knowledge structure. To what extent will the user model or replicate that structure in their own knowledge representations?

RESEARCH
We have pursued a series of empirical studies to assess the effects of explicit semantic structuring of hypertext on the knowledge structures of learners. We wanted to know the extent to which a semantically structured hypertext affects the acquisition of structural knowledge. I will briefly describe the methodology and assessment issues common to each of the studies and then briefly review the methods and results specific to each study, followed by a discussion of conclusions and implications of this research.

Methods
In order to assess the effects of semantically structured hypertext on learner's knowledge structures, it was necessary to develop instruments that assessed the learners' structural knowledge. Structural knowledge is the knowledge of how concepts within a domain are interrelated (Diekhoff, 1983). Structural knowledge enables learners to form the connections that

they need to describe and use scripts or complex schemas. It is a form of conceptual knowledge that mediates the translation of declarative knowledge into procedural knowledge. Procedural knowledge is predicated upon structural knowledge in order to fulfil the functional relationships between ideas.

In order to assess structural knowledge acquisition following various treatments, we developed three subscales of ten questions each to measure different aspects of structural knowledge: a) relationship proximity judgements, b) semantic relationships, and c) analogies. All of the structural knowledge test questions were developed to focus on relationships between important concepts contained in the hypertext. The relationship proximity judgements required that students assign a number between 1 and 9 to each of several pairs of concepts to indicate how strong a relationship they thought existed between the concepts in each pair (Diekhoff, 1983). For example:

____ information retrieval systems and online documentation

____ hypertext processing strategies and database

The semantic relationships subscale consisted of multiple choice questions that required students to identify the nature of the relationship between two concepts. These relationships were paraphrased from the hypertext knowledge base. For example:

____ unstructured hypertext ...... navigating hypertext

    a. produces problems in
    b. defines the functions of
    c. counteracts the effects of
    d. enabled by

Finally, the analogies subscale required students to complete 10 analogies consisting of four of the concepts from the hypertext. For example:

____ accessing information : index :: integrating information : ......

    a. links
    b. hypermaps
    c. idea generator
    d. multi-user access

These questions were used to assess structural knowledge acquisition. In order to provide standards for assessment, three authors and researchers in the hypertext field agreed on the answers to each of these questions. In addition to assessing structural knowledge, 10 lower-order information-recall questions were developed.

The hypertext that was used for all of these studies was the HyperCard version (Jonassen, Roebuck and Wang, 1990) of the book

Hypertext/Hypermedia (Jonassen, 1989a). This hypertext is a browsing system consisting of 240 cards and 1167 links in three stacks supported by bookmarking and limited annotation capabilities. All treatments in all studies contained embedded referential links in the cards. Terms in the text were highlighted, enabling learners to immediately traverse the links. The treatments varied in terms of the types of browsers that learners used and the ways that they depicted structural information. Each of the 75 major concept nodes contained a main 'related terms' card, which was the first card accessed when traversing a link to that node. In the control group, this card provided a list of terms that are related to the concept being currently examined. This list provided links to those nodes but no structural information about the nodes or links. The experimental treatments (described in more detail below) replaced these lists with graphical browsers or retained the lists but overtly communicated the nature of each link when it was being traversed. They were designed to provide or require the learner to generate explicit structural information about the nodes and links in the hypertext.

The studies involved undergraduate pre-service teachers in a teacher education program, who were assigned to learn about an important new instructional technology, hypertext, as an assignment in a pre-service instructional technology course. Students individually interacted with and studied the hypertext for one to two hours in order to acquire as much information about this new technology as possible. A monitoring program was added to the stacks to audit the learner interactions.

Study 1: List vs map vs link window
Issues
In the first study, we compared the extent to which users acquire structural knowledge by using a graphical browser vs a pop-up window mediating each link. Each graphical browser showed the current node and all nodes linked directly to it and depicted the nature of the link between each of those nodes (see Figure 2 for an example). Each of the boxes in the graphical browsers were hot buttons. In order to navigate the hypertext, users would click on any box to traverse the link to that topic.

In the second experimental treatment, the nodes related to the current node were presented in list form (showing no structural information). In order to traverse a link, users simply clicked on a term. Whenever the user clicked on a term to select it, that is to navigate that link, a window filling 70% of the screen area would pop up. The text in this pop-up window explicitly stated the nature of the relationship between the node the learner was leaving and the node to which the learner was going. So, whenever the student traversed a link between the existing and the target node, the window explicitly stated the relationship between the node they were leaving and the one they had selected, providing an explicit statement of structural knowledge.

Both experimental conditions provided structural information to the student. The graphical browser treatment illustrated the organisation of

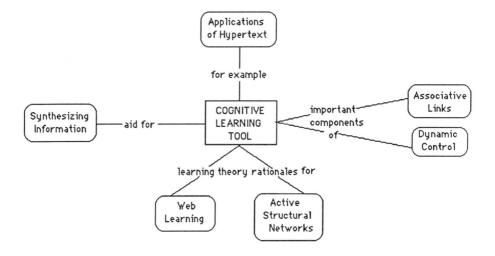

Figure 2: Graphical browser used in the study.

information in the hypertext knowledge base, while the pop-up treatment explicitly stated relationships on a node-by-node basis. The control group interface provided lists of related terms without any explicit structural information.

Results
The dependent variables in this study included recall, relationship, proximity, and analogy subscales of the post-test. The recall (15 items), relationship (10 items), and analogy (10 items) subscales were summed for each subject. The proximity ratings were compared with experts' ratings. For the proximity scores, correlation coefficients were calculated for each subject, in which the proximity ratings of the subject were correlated to the proximity ratings of a panel of three experts.

ANOVAs were calculated for each of the four dependent variables. The only dependent variable with even a marginally significant difference was the recall variable ($F(2,93)=2.75$, $p<.07$). A *post hoc* analysis showed that the control and the map versions differed significantly, with the control group (M=7.8) outperforming the map version (M=6.6), the lowest scores overall.

Scores on the structural knowledge tasks were essentially equivalent. The highest relationship scores (M=5.6) and proximity scores (M=.62) were posted by the pop-up treatment, however this difference was not significant. Analogy scores for all three groups were barely higher than chance (overall M=2.9). The processing difficulty of a higher-order reasoning task like analogies was very problematic for these students.

There was some evidence, however, that learners were processing some of the structural information. The total number of structurally related cards accessed by students was also calculated. Structural cards were the maps (map group) or the lists in the pop-up treatment group and the control group. These cards contained the structural information that defined the relationships between the nodes on the knowledge base. The number of structural cards accessed was different between groups (F(2,93)=3.75, p<.05) while the total number of cards accessed and the total time spent viewing structural cards did not differ significantly. The control group accessed 106 cards while the pop-up and map groups accessed 85 and 92 cards respectively.

The absence of main effects for structural knowledge outcomes did not necessarily mean that no structural coding occurred. When the number of structural information cards accessed during study was regressed on the dependent variables, significant differences occurred. The number of high-level structural cards (main map and eight first-level maps, e.g., Characteristics of Hypertext) that were accessed by students significantly predicted the relationship scores (F=3.7, p=.05). The number of structural cards accessed also significantly predicted the time spent (F=5.37, p<.05). So, accessing structural information in the hypertext did predict the amount of structural knowledge acquired. Total time spent interacting with structural cards was also calculated by group. The time spent on structural cards did not significantly predict any of the dependent variables.

Study 2: Generative processing of structural information
Issues

One of the weaknesses of the first study was the lack of instructional support provided to the learner. Hypertext is a technology that supports information retrieval and search tasks. However, these tasks are not necessarily correlated with instruction. One of the most significant potential problems in learning from hypertext is integration of the presented information into knowledge structures (Jonassen, 1989a). Learning requires that users not only access information but also interpret it by relating it to prior knowledge.

Therefore, in the second study, we attempted to provide additional instructional support by including a more generative form of treatment. Generative learning occurs when learners relate information meaningfully to prior knowledge (Wittrock, 1974). The control treatment was compared with the pop-up treatment (same as in Study 1) and the generative processing treatment. The generative treatment was similar in appearance to the pop-up window version of the same hypertext used in Study 1. However, rather than being told what the nature of the relationship was between the nodes being linked, the learners were required to classify the nature of each link themselves. The pop-up window presented 12 different link types and required the learner to determine which of the link types most accurately depicted the nature of the relationship implied by the link that they were traversing. The user had the option of returning to the previous node or moving forward to see the node they had selected as many times as necessary. Knowledge of results was provided for each selection by the user until the user selected the correct link type.

Results
As in the first study, no significant main effects were found at the .05 level. As in the first study, recall scores differed ($F=2.87$, $p=.06$). A *post hoc* test showed that the control group ($M=5.38$) scores were significantly higher than the generative group scores (4.42). As in Study 1, control group subjects were better able to recall information, as they were less distracted by the structural knowledge activities. Relationship scores were slightly higher for both experimental treatments ($M=5.75$) than for the control group ($M=5.1$) though this difference was not significant. Analogy scores for all three groups barely exceeded chance ($M=2.8$ overall) and were not significant. As in the first study, these students found the analogy questions quite difficult. As anticipated, recall scores were higher in the control group, but neither structural strategy produced any increase in structural knowledge acquisition.

Study 3

Issues
While instructional tasks are normally thought to be an important predictor of integration of information into knowledge structures (although this was not supported by Studies 1 and 2), probably the most important determinant of learning is the awareness and understanding of the required task or learning outcome. In the previous two studies, it became clear that learners were not certain how to 'learn from hypertext' or how to process structural information. Students in these studies were most familiar with performing specific, convergent, recall-oriented learning tasks. The uncertainty involved in trying to integrate knowledge when the task was not clear and the form of learning material was so different became obvious throughout the course of experimentation. So, the third study provided a more deliberate structural knowledge focus by using semantic networking as a practice and evaluation strategy. That is, this study required learners to create a semantic network as an embedded learning strategy, a task which required the acquisition and manifestation of structural knowledge.

Semantic networking as an integrative strategy
Semantic networking software may be used as a cognitive learning strategy to help learners integrate information from hypertext (Jonassen, 1989b). The process of browsing a hypertext models the accretion process in learning (Rumelhart and Norman, 1978). However, a significant problem in learning from hypertext is the integration of what is acquired while browsing into the learner's knowledge structure (Jonassen, 1989b). Adding a semantic networking program to a hypertext browser provides learners with a tool

for integrating information into their knowledge structure. This process of semantic networking elicits the process of restructuring as defined by Rumelhart and Norman.

Methods

The third study assigned half of the students the responsibility of constructing a semantic network about the topic of the hypertext following the study period. The other half were told only to study the hypertext to acquire knowledge during the study period. In the experimental treatment, we provided learners with the semantic networking program, Learning Tool (see Figure 1 for example) and informed the learners that after browsing through the hypertext, they would be responsible for producing a semantic network about the topic of the hypertext. These learners had acquired competence with the semantic networking program earlier. Learning effects were assessed, as in the other studies, immediately following treatment and before any semantic nets were created, so time-on-task did not differ for the groups. Our purpose was to focus their attention on the structural information with the understanding that they would be required to produce a semantic net.

This third study included a second factor, the type of structural knowledge support in the interface. The control treatment were provided with the list interface (as in Studies 1 and 2) which provided no structural cues. The experimental group were provided with the graphical browser treatment, as in the first study.

Results

In the third study, learners who were given the task of creating a semantic network performed significantly better (M=6.6) on the relationship task than the two groups instructed only to study the materials (M=5.2) according to the two-factor ANOVA, F=7.82, p<.01. This result indicates that by focusing the learner's attention on structural aspects of the information in the hypertext, structural knowledge acquisition improved significantly. The graphical browser assisted this process. Students provided with graphical browsers scored slightly though not significantly higher than the control group.

No differences in recall scores were found. However, a one factor ANOVA comparing scores between the four treatment groups indicated that the graphical browser/semantic networking group performed significantly better on the analogy subscale, F=2.77, p<.05. It appears that the visual support of the graphical browser in addition to focusing on structural relationships enhanced the comparisons necessary for completing analogies.

CONCLUSIONS

Attention to structural information

To the extent that learners attended to the structural cues provided in the hypertexts, they did acquire some structural knowledge. The *post hoc* regression analyses showed that students were in fact attending to some of the structural information. The number of structural cards accessed appeared to predict structural knowledge acquisition in the form of relationship judgements in two different forms. The time spent with the structural cards suggested a relationship between accessing those cards and the level of structural knowledge acquisition. These are weak effects at best, though with longer exposure to the hypertext, these findings may be substantiated.

We can only conclude from the results, however, that merely providing structural cues in the user interface of a hypertext will not result in significant increases in structural knowledge acquisition. The fact that control treatment subjects recalled more information is consistent with the reading research that shows that without cueing or practice, learners tend to recall micropropositions more readily than macropropositions. However, it appears that the structural information in the interface clearly impeded the recall information by the students in the structural knowledge treatments. It did not result in commensurately greater structural knowledge acquisition however. An explanation for the lack of structural knowledge acquisition from structural cueing in the interface is the "mistaken notion concerning hypertext... that the arbitrary 'webs' of facts in hypertext systems have much semantic significance" (Whalley, 1990, p.63), at least to the learners. What matters most in learning is the construction of personally relevant knowledge structures. It appears that arbitrarily imposed semantic nets may not be adequate to overcome personal ones or at least not directly map onto learners' knowledge structures. So, merely showing learners structural relationships, without a purpose for doing so, is probably not sufficient to result in meaningful encoding of that information. When structural knowledge outcomes are required, learners apparently do attend to the structural information and encode it into memory.

Cognitive limitations of browsing behaviour

According to Whalley (1990), the most natural mode of studying hypertext is browsing. The question is the extent to which unconstrained browsing can support instructional goals, especially without a clearly established purpose for studying. The data and the comments from students in the first two studies showed that they lacked a clear purpose for studying the hypertext. That lack of clear purpose manifested itself in consistent performance across groups, especially with the structural knowledge tasks. Learning from hypertext must rely on externally imposed or mediated learning tasks — that merely browsing through a knowledge base does not engender deep enough processing to result in meaningful learning.

Hypertexts are obvious information retrieval technologies. However, retrieval of information is not sufficient by itself to result in meaningful learning. When the goals of accessing information require deeper processing, then deeper processing is more likely to occur. However, simply browsing hypertext is not engaging enough to result in more meaningful learning. It may well be that hypertext is not be very appropriate for highly structured learning tasks, as Duchastel (1990) suggests.

Hypertext processing strategies

Students in these studies appeared, as expected, to lack hypertext processing strategies (Jonassen, 1989a), which likely precluded the most effective use of the technology. Hypertext, and the greater learner control of instruction that it entails, is a novel form of instruction for these learners. The more novel the appearance of the hypertext (i.e. graphical browser version), the more negatively the students reacted to it. A fair evaluation of learning from hypertext can only come from hypertext-literate learners who have developed a useful set of strategies for navigating and integrating information form hypertext.

Structural knowledge acquisition

The novel form of instruction, hypertext, was only exacerbated by the novel structural cues and structural learning outcomes. The explicit provision of structural information was unusual to these students. The requirement to process that information and integrate it into their own knowledge structures was even more novel to them, which negatively affected their performance on the tasks. The poor performance of learners on higher-order, structural knowledge tasks, especially the analogies, washed out most of the treatment effects. This calls into question the ability of learners to engage in meaningful learning rather than information retrieval from hypertext, especially in the context of a learning assignment.

ACKNOWLEDGEMENTS

I wish to thank Sherwood Wang for the contributions that he has made to the research reported in this chapter. He is the other half of the "we" that I refer to so often in the discussion of the research in this paper. He would have co-authored this chapter had I not been living 5,000 miles from home when it was written. Thanks also to Barbara Grabowski for reviewing an earlier draft of this chapter. I would also like to acknowledge that this chapter was written while I was a visiting professor on the Instructional Technology faculty at the University of Twente in the Netherlands. My sincere thanks go to them for their support.

REFERENCES

Bush, V. (1945) As we may think. *Atlantic Monthly*, 176(1), 101–108.

Buzan, T. (1974) *Use Both Sides of Your Brain*. New York: Dutton.

Diekhoff, G. M. (1983) Testing through relationship judgements. *Journal of Educational Psychology*, 75, 227–233.

Duchastel, P. (1990) Formal and informal learning with hypermedia. In D. Jonassen and H. Mandl (eds.) *Designing Hypermedia for Learning*. Berlin: Springer-Verlag.

Fiderio, J. (1988) A grand vision. *Byte*, October, 237–243.

Fields, A. (1982) Pattern notes: How to get started. In D. H. Jonassen (ed.) *The Technology of Text: Principles for Structuring, Designing, and Displaying Text, Volume 1*. Englewood Cliffs, NJ: Educational Technology Publications.

Fisher, K. M., Faletti, J., Thronton, R. Patterson, H., Lipson, J., and Spring, C. (1988) Computer-based knowledge representation as a tool for students and teachers. Paper presented at the annual meeting of the American Educational Research Association, New Orleans, LA, April.

Jonassen, D. H. (1987) Assessing cognitive structure: Verifying a method using pattern notes. *Journal of Research and Development in Education*, 20(3), 1–14.

Jonassen, D. H. (1988) Designing structured hypertext and structuring access to hypertext. *Educational Technology*, 28(10), 13–16.

Jonassen, D. H. (1989a) *Hypertext/Hypermedia*. Englewood Cliffs, NJ: Educational Technology Publications.

Jonassen, D. H. (1989b) Mapping the structure of content in instructional systems technology. *Educational Technology*, 29(4).

Jonassen, D. H. (1990) Semantic network elicitation: tools for structuring hypertext. In C. Green and R. McAleese (eds.) *Hypertext: State of the Art*. Oxford: Intellect.

Jonassen, D. H. (1991a) Hypertext as instructional design. *Educational Technology: Research and Development*, 39(1), 83–92.

Jonassen, D. H. (1991b) Representing the expert's knowledge in hypertext. *Impact Assessment Bulletin*, 9(1), 1–13.

Jonassen, D. H. and Mandl, H. (1990)(eds.) *Designing Hypermedia for Learning*. Berlin: Springer-Verlag.

Jonassen, D. H., Roebuck, N. and Wang, S. (1990) *Hypertext/Hypermedia* (HyperCard Version). Englewood Cliffs, NJ: Educational Technology Publications.

Jonassen, D. H. and Wang, S. (1990) Conveying structural knowledge in hypertext knowledge bases. Paper presented at the annual meeting of the Association for the Development of Computer-based Instructional Systems, San Diego, CA, October 30–31.

Jonassen, D. H. and Wang, S. (1991) Conveying structural knowledge in hypertext knowledge bases. Paper presented at the annual meeting of the Association for Educational Communications and Technology, Orlando, FL, February 14–17.

Kozma, R. B. (1987) The implications of cognitive psychology for computer-based learning tools. *Educational Technology*, 28(11), 20–25.

Lambiotte, J. G., Dansereau, D. F., Cross, D. R., and Reynolds, S. B. (1989) Multi-relational semantic maps. *Educational Psychology Review*, 1(4), 331–347.

McAleese, R. (1990) Concepts as hypertext nodes: The ability to learn while navigating through hypertext nets. In D. Jonassen and H. Mandl (eds.) *Designing Hypermedia for Learning*. Berlin: Springer-Verlag.

McDonald, J. E., Paap, K. R., and McDonald, D. R. (1990) Hypertext perspectives: Using Pathfinder to build hypertext systems. In R. W. Schvanenveldt (ed.) *Pathfinder Associative Networks: Studies in Knowledge Organisation*. Norwood, NJ: Ablex.

Norman, D. A. (1976) Studies in learning and self-contained education systems, 1973–1976. Tech Report N°. 7601. Washington, DC: Office of Naval Research, Advanced Research Projects Agency. (ED 121 786)

Norman, D. A., Gentner, S. and Stevens, A. L. (1976) Comments on learning schemata and memory representation. In D. Klahr (ed.) *Cognition and Instruction*. Hillsdale, NJ: Lawrence Erlbaum Associates.

Preece, F. F. W. (1976) Mapping cognitive structure: A comparison of methods. *Journal of Educational Psychology*, 68, 1–8.

Rumelhart, D. E. and Norman, D. A. (1978) Accretion, tuning and restructuring: Three modes of learning. In J. W. Cotton and R. Klatzky (eds.) *Semantic Factors in Cognition*. Hillsdale, NJ: Lawrence Erlbaum Associates.

Rumelhart, D. and Ortony, A. (1977) The representation of knowledge in memory. In R. C. Anderson, R. J. Spiro and W. E. Montague (eds.) *Schooling and the Acquisition of Knowledge*. Hillsdale, NJ: Lawrence Erlbaum Associates.

Shavelson, R. (1974) Methods for examining representations of subject matter structure in students' memory. *Journal of Research in Science Teaching*, 11, 231–249.

Thro, M. P. (1978) Individual differences among college students in cognitive structure and physics performance. Paper presented at the annual meeting of the American Educational Research Association, Toronto, Canada.

Whalley, P. (1990) Models of hypertext structure and learning. In D. Jonassen and H. Mandl (eds.) *Designing Hypermedia for Learning*. Berlin: Springer-Verlag.

Wittrock, M. C. (1974) Learning as a generative activity. *Educational Psychologist*, 11, 87–95.

8

Space — the Final Chapter
or Why Physical Representations are not Semantic Intentions

Andrew Dillon, Cliff McKnight
and John Richardson
HUSAT Research Institute, Loughborough University, UK

INTRODUCTION

The term 'hypertext' evokes many images (e.g., nodes and links, semantic webs, non-linear access and so forth) but perhaps one of the most common is that of users struggling to find their way around a complex information space. As a result, navigation has become a subject of great interest to many researchers in the field. In this chapter we will discuss navigation through hypertext in terms of its relevance as a concept as much as its presence as an issue and try to draw lessons for design and research from the psychological work that has been carried out on navigation in physical space. We will attempt to show that while relevant to hypertext, discussion of navigation is prone to difficulty when researchers and designers misapply arguments and evidence from the physical domain to the semantic domain.

THE EXTENT OF NAVIGATION DIFFICULTIES IN HYPERTEXT

Although there is a striking consensus that navigation is a difficulty for users of hypertext and frequent reference is made to "getting lost in hyperspace" (e.g., Conklin, 1987), empirical demonstrations of the problem are less than clear cut. As Bernstein (1991) put it:

> while the so-called 'navigation problem' has come to dominate hypertext research, evidence for its existence and nature is distressingly thin. (p. 365)

However, much of the difficulty results from the traditional methodological problems in reading research of adequately measuring the reading process as opposed to the reading outcome (Dillon, 1992). In the absence of a suitable measure of process activities, researchers tend to infer from outcomes so, for example, the impact of information structure on reading speed, accuracy or comprehension is often explained in terms of process difficulties such as navigation (e.g., Monk, Walsh and Dix, 1988).

If by the expression 'navigation difficulty' we accept the Elm and Woods (1985) definition of users not knowing how the information is organised, how to find the information they seek or even if that information is available then we can appreciate how such an approach may be justified. With paper documents there tend to be at least some standards in terms of organisation. With books, for example, contents pages are usually at the front, indices at the back and both offer some information on where items are located in the body of the text. Concepts of relative position in the text such as 'before' and 'after' have tangible physical correlates. No such correlation holds with hypertext. If users perform slower or less accurately with a hypertext than with paper and claim to have had problems finding material then a conclusion of navigation difficulty may appear justified.

There is some direct empirical evidence in the literature to support the view that navigation in hypertext can be a problem. Edwards and Hardman (1989), for example, describe a study which required subjects to search through a specially designed hypertext. In total, half the subjects reported feeling lost at some stage (this proportion is deduced from the data reported). Such feelings were mainly due to "not knowing where to go next" or "not knowing where they were in relation to the overall structure of the document" (descriptors provided by the authors). Unfortunately, without direct comparison of ratings from subjects reading a paper equivalent we cannot be sure such proportions are solely due to using hypertext. However it is unlikely that many readers of paper texts do not know where they are in relation to the rest of the text.

McKnight, Dillon and Richardson (1990) proposed time spent browsing contents and indices as a suitable metric for navigation problems in a study of users retrieving information from a document on winemaking presented as hypertext, word processor file or paper. Their results also suggested that navigation is a difficulty for hypertext users, since users of both the word processor and paper versions spent significantly less time in these sections.

Indirect evidence comes from the numerous studies which have indicated that users have difficulties with a hypertext (e.g., Gordon *et al.*, 1988; Monk, Walsh and Dix, 1988). Hammond and Allinson (1989) speak for many when they say:

> Experience with using hypertext systems has revealed a number of problems for users... First, users get lost... Second, users may find it difficult to gain an overview of the material... Third, even if

users know specific information is present they may have difficulty finding it. (p. 294)

There are a few dissenting voices. Landow (1990, 1991), for example, describes the navigation problem in hypertext as a fallacy or pseudo-problem and claims that even discussing navigation can lead to false assumptions about hypertext usage. Brown (1988) argues that:

> although getting lost is often claimed to be a great problem, the evidence is largely circumstantial and conflicting. In some smallish applications it is not a major problem at all. (p. 2)

This quote is telling in several ways. The evidence for navigational difficulties is often circumstantial or at least inferential, as noted above. The applications in which Brown claims it is not a problem at all are, to use his word, "smallish" and this raises a crucial issue with respect to hypertext. When we speak of documents being so small that a reader cannot 'get lost' in them or so large that navigation aids are required to use them effectively, the implication is that information occupies 'space' through which readers 'travel' or 'move'. Hammond and Allinson (1987) talk of the "travel metaphor" as a way of moving through a hypertext. Canter, Rivers and Storrs (1985) speak of "routes through" a database. Even the dissenters believe that the reader or user navigates through the document, the only disagreement being the extent to which getting lost is a regular and/or serious occurrence.

PSYCHOLOGICAL MODELS OF NAVIGATION

Navigation as an activity in itself is rarely seen as central to psychology and this is reflected in the subject matter and coverage of most textbooks. As Gould (1973) put it:

> psychologists, in their concern with 'perception', have barely touched upon the investigation of mental images of geographic space, for many of their efforts have concentrated upon the physics and physiology of the senses, often within highly controlled laboratory conditions. (p. 185)

While it might be tempting to dismiss those comments as the product of their time, it is only justifiable to do so if we can point out significant developments in psychology's understanding of navigation in the last twenty years. Yet these have not emerged. However, although the activity of navigation may have been given short shrift by the discipline it is not hard to see how aspects relevant to the study of navigation are dealt with in work on spatial imagery, orientation, distance judgement, environmental perception and so forth. Furthermore, as Neisser (1976) remarks, geographers, planners and other professionals have always been interested in navigation and if, as Downs and Stea (1973) claim, "each writer ultimately turns to psychology for the answer" the activity cannot be said to have been overlooked (even if the answers have not been forthcoming).

The disparity of approaches to navigation render it difficult to draw together a cohesive theory but general agreements do exist. Tolman's (1948) paper on cognitive maps is frequently cited as seminal as it postulates the existence of a cognitive map, internalised in the human mind which is the analogue to the physical layout of the environment — a view that is taken as axiomatic by most researchers despite its inherent presumptions about human cognition. According to Tolman, information impinging on the brain is:

> worked over and elaborated... into a tentative cognitive-like map of the environment indicating routes and paths and environmental relationships... (p. 192)

Recent experimental work takes the notion of some form of mental representation of the environment for granted, concerning itself more with how such maps are formed and manipulated. We have proposed elsewhere (Dillon, McKnight and Richardson, 1990; McKnight, Dillon and Richardson, 1991) that navigation in general can be conceptualised in psychological terms as involving four levels of representation: schemata, landmarks, routes and surveys and that several of these levels are of direct relevance to hypertext design. In the following section we review this approach which draws heavily on schema theory and consider how alternative views on navigation might shed further light on the concept.

Schema theory as an explanatory framework
Schema theory provides a convenient explanatory framework for the general knowledge humans seem to possess of activities, objects, events and environments. Regardless of its actual truth or explanatory power over alternative views of cognition such as prototype or feature-count theories (see e.g., Anderson, 1980), we can convincingly postulate the existence of some form of general knowledge of the world that aids humans in navigation tasks.

It seems obvious, for example, that we must possess schemata of the physical environment we find ourselves in if we are not to be overwhelmed by every new place we encounter. Presumably acquired from exposure to the world around us, schemata can be conceptualised as affording a basic orienting frame of reference to the individual. Thus, we soon acquire schemata of towns and cities so that we know what to expect when we find ourselves in one: busy roads, numerous buildings, shopping areas, people, etc. According to Downs and Stea (1977) such frames of reference exist at all levels of scale from looking at the world in terms of east and west or First and Third Worlds, to national distinctions between north and south, urban and rural and so on down to local entities like buildings and neighbourhoods.

In employing schema theory as our explanatory framework it is worth making a distinction between what Brewer (1987) terms "global" and "instantiated" schemata. The global schema is the basic or raw knowledge structure. Highly general, it does not reflect the specific details of any object or event (or whatever knowledge type is involved). The instantiated schema however is the product of adding specific details to a global schema and thereby reducing its generality. An example will make this clearer. In orienting ourselves in a new environment we call on one or more global schemata (e.g., the schema for city or office building). As we proceed to relate specific details of our new environment to this schema we can be said to develop an instantiated schema which is no longer general but is not sufficiently complete to be a model or map of the particular environment in which we find ourselves.

Global schemata remain to be used again as necessary. Instantiated schemata presumably develop in detail until they cease to be accurately described as schematic or are discarded when they serve no further purpose. In the above example, if we leave this environment after a short visit we are likely to discard the instantiated schema we formed, but if we stay or regularly return we are likely to build on this until we have a model of the environment. This is a very simple sketch and leaves many questions unanswered, such as what details are required to make a global schema become an instantiated one or if we always recall a specific detail about a place we visited but nothing else does this memory constitute an instantiated schema? We will not attempt answers to these questions here but recognise them as typical theoretical issues for schema theory to address.

While schemata are effective orienting guides, in themselves they are limited. In particular they fail to reflect specific instances of any one environment and provide no knowledge of what exists outside of our field of vision. As such, they provide the basic knowledge needed to interact with an environment but must be supplanted by other representations if we are to plan routes, avoid becoming lost or identify short cuts — activities in which humans seem frequently to engage.

Levels of schema instantiation: landmarks, routes and surveys
The second level of representation (but first stage of instantiation for the schema) proposed for navigation is knowledge of landmarks, a term used to describe any features of the environment which are relatively stable and conspicuous. Thus we recognise our position in terms relative to these landmarks, e.g., our destination is near building X or if we see statue Y then we must be near the railway station and so forth. This knowledge provides us with the skeletal framework on which we build our cognitive map.

The third level of representation is route knowledge which is characterised by the ability to navigate from point A to point B, using whatever landmark knowledge we have acquired to make decisions about when to turn left or right. With such knowledge we can provide others with effective route guidance, e.g., "Turn left at the traffic lights and continue on that road until you see the large church on your left and take the next right there..." and so forth. Though possessing route knowledge a person may still not really know much about her environment. A route might be non-optimal or even totally wasteful.

The fourth level of representation is survey (or map) knowledge. This allows us to give directions or plan journeys along routes we have not directly travelled as well as describe relative locations of landmarks within an environment. It allows us to know the general direction of places, e.g., "westward" or "over there" rather than "left of the main road" or "to the right of the church". In other words it is based on a world frame of reference rather than an egocentric one.

Navigational knowledge development

By navigational knowledge development we do not mean the acquisition of spatial knowledge and world views as they are discussed in developmental psychology but rather how adults become familiar with their environments. However there exists an interesting literature on childrens' spatial knowledge development that has parallels with this work (see e.g., Hart and Moore, 1973), some of which will be alluded to in this discussion.

Current thinking is dominated by the view that the last three levels of representation: landmark, route and survey knowledge are points on a continuum rather than discrete forms. The assumption is that each successive stage represents a developmental advance towards an increasingly accurate or sophisticated world view. Certainly this is an intuitively appealing account of our own experiences when coming to terms with a new environment or comparing our knowledge of one place with another and has obvious parallels with the psychological literature which often assumes invariant stages in cognitive development but it might not be so straightforward.

Obviously landmark knowledge on its own is of little use for complex navigation and both route and survey knowledge emerge from it as a means of coping with the complexity of the environment. However it does not necessarily follow that given two landmarks the next stage of knowledge development is acquiring the route between them or that once enough route knowledge is acquired it is replaced by or can be formed into survey knowledge. Experimental investigations have demonstrated that each form of representation is optimally suited for different kinds of tasks (see e.g., Thorndyke and Hayes-Roth, 1982; Wetherell, 1979). Route knowledge is cognitively simpler than survey knowledge but suffers the drawback of being virtually useless once a wrong step is taken (Wickens, 1984). Route knowledge, because of its predominantly verbal form, might suit individuals with higher verbal than spatial abilities, while the opposite might be the case for survey knowledge. Furthermore, age differences in navigational knowledge have been demonstrated which show older males relying more on landmark rather than route knowledge (Francescato and Mebane, 1973), a complete reversal of what we would expect if the invariant stage development model was true.

Thus while the knowledge forms outlined here are best seen as points on a continuum and a general trend to move from landmark to survey knowledge via route knowledge may exist, task dependencies and cognitive ability factors mediate such developments and suggest that an invariant stage model may not be the best conceptualisation of the findings.

Other issues

While this approach might be seen as a useful condensation of current thinking it is by no means indisputable and leaves several issues unresolved. We have made little reference to knowledge of how to behave in certain environments which must be tied at some level to our navigational schemata. Roads must be crossed in certain ways, e.g., at pedestrian crossings or when there is no traffic, or you must pay if you want to use public transport. It may be slightly artificial (not to mention dangerous) to separate such knowledge from our schemata for places. In this sense the frame of reference is close to the concept of script (Schank and Abelson, 1976).

Furthermore, as Shum (1990) noted when describing the likely content of cognitive maps, most human factors work has addressed only the descriptive attributes such maps possess and said little or nothing about their evaluative attributes such as "is this place worth visiting?" We could extend this to say that such value judgements are only part of what seems to be missing from the standard treatment of cognitive maps. We could consider affective issues to be associated with places such that when we enter an environment or even think about entering it, associated emotional responses might come into play. Too little is known about these aspects of human response to environments and their impact on navigation.

Cohen (1989) proposes that three variables are important to consider in understanding memory for places: scale, complexity and familiarity. Her argument is that essentially, variation in these factors alters the nature of the navigation task being performed. If this is the case, the nature of the representation employed by the human navigator may well alter and simple classifications such as "routes are represented procedurally and maps are represented propositionally" (see e.g., Bartram and Smith, 1984) are unlikely to tell the full story. Cohen argues that mental models (as used by Johnson-Laird, 1983) or analogues could also provide representational formats for navigational information, to which we could add representational formats such as episodic memory if we want to account for some other possible phenomena.

Our view is that the precise nature of the representation is less important to workers in the field of interactive technology than the insights any theory or model of navigation provides. To this extent we propose that a model based on schema theory and including landmarks, routes and surveys as instantiations of basic knowledge is of some utility in considering the design of electronic information spaces. In the following sections we develop this argument.

NAVIGATION IN THE PAPER DOMAIN

Documents as structures

If we are seriously to consider hypertext documents as navigable spaces there is no logical reason for denying paper texts the same status. There is evidence to suggest that from a reader's perspective at least, such a view is meaningful. For example, studies of regular readers' perceptions of journal articles (Dillon, Richardson and McKnight, 1989) and software manuals (Dillon, 1991a) have shown that such readers conceptualise documents as possessing a prototypical form or structure that aids location of material, suggesting at least that the idea of navigating through such structures is a valid notion.

Unfortunately, the term 'structure' is used in at least three distinct ways by different researchers and writers in this field. Conklin (1987) talks of structure being imposed on what is browsed by the reader, i.e. the reader builds a structure to gain knowledge from the document. Trigg and Suchman (1989) refer to structure as a representation of convention, i.e. it occurs in a text form according to the expected rules a writer follows during document production. Hammond and Allinson (1989) offer a third perspective, that of the structure as a conveyer of context. For them, there is a naturally occurring structure to any subject matter that holds together the 'raw data' of that domain.

In reality, there is a common theme to all these uses. They are not distinct concepts sharing the same name but different aspects or manifestations of the same concept. The main rôle of structure seems to differ according to the perspective from which it is being discussed: the writer's or the reader's, and the particular part of the reading/writing task being considered. Thus the structure of a document can be a convention to both the writer, so that he conforms to expectations of format, and to the reader, so he knows what to expect. It can be a conveyer of context mainly to the reader so he can infer from, and elaborate on, the information provided, but it might be employed by a skilled writer with the intention of provoking a particular response in the reader. Finally, it can be a means of mentally representing the contents to both the reader so he grasps the organisation of the text and to the author so that he can appropriately order his delivery.

It can be seen from the comments of subjects (as readers) in the journal and manual usage studies cited above that structure is a concept for which the meanings described seem to apply with varying degrees of relevance. Certainly the notion of structure as convention seems to be perceived by readers of journal articles, while the idea of structure supporting contextual inference seems pertinent to users of software manuals. Beyond these manifestations, research in the domain of linguistics and discourse comprehension lends strong support to the concept of structure as a basic component in the reader's mental representation of a text.

The theory of discourse comprehension proposed by van Dijk and Kintsch (1983) places great emphasis on text structure. According to this theory, readers acquire (through experience) schemata, which van Dijk and Kintsch term 'superstructures', that facilitate comprehension of material by allowing readers to predict the likely ordering and grouping of constituent elements of a body of text. To quote van Dijk (1980):

> a superstructure is the schematic form that organises the global meaning of a text. We assume that such a superstructure consists of functional categories... [and]... rules that specify which category may follow or combine with what other categories. (p. 108)

In addition to categories and functional rules, van Dijk adds that a superstructure must be socioculturally accepted, learned, used and commented upon by most adult members of a speech community.[1]

They have applied this theory to several text types. For example, with respect to newspaper articles they describe a schema consisting of headlines and leads (which together provide a summary), major event categories each of which is placed within a context (actual or historical), and consequences. Depending on the type of newspaper (e.g., weekly as opposed to daily, tabloid as opposed to quality, etc.) one might expect elaborated commentaries and evaluations. Experiments by Kintsch and Yarborough (1982) showed that articles written in a way that adhered to this schema resulted in better grasp of the main ideas and subject matter (as assessed by written question answering) than ones which were re-organised to make them less schema conforming.

The van Dijk and Kintsch theory has been the subject of criticism from some cognitive scientists. Johnson-Laird (1983), for example, takes exception to the idea of any propositional analysis providing the reader with both the basic meaning of the words in the text and the significance of its full contents. For him, at least two types of representational format are required to do this. He provides evidence from studies of people's recall of text passages that it is not enough to read a text correctly (i.e. perform an accurate propositional analysis) to appreciate the significance of that material. He proposes what he terms mental models as a further level of representation that facilitates such understanding. Subsequent work by Garnham (1987) lends further support to the insufficiency-of-propositions argument in comprehension of text.

---

[1] In reality the idea of superstructure appears to be more of a spin-off than a central tenet of van Dijk and Kintsch's theory. They postulate three general levels of text unit: microstructures, macrostructures and superstructures but prefer to concentrate on the first two, at this time having developed their ideas on these to a greater extent than they have on the third. However, experimental work seems to confirm the relevance of the third level of structure even if its exact relationship to their comprehension theory is not yet precisely specified. As van Dijk (1980) put it when describing superstructures: "It cannot possibly be the aim of this chapter to provide a theory of superstructures. A separate book would be needed... and we would even need separate studies for the different main kinds of superstructures" (p. 109). As yet, that book is unwritten.

The differences between Johnson-Laird and van Dijk are mainly a reflection of the differences between the psychologist's and the linguist's views of how people comprehend discourse. From the perspective of the human factors practitioner it is not clear that either theory of representation format is likely to lead to distinct (i.e. unique) predictions about electronic text. Both propose that some form of structural representation occurs — it is just the underlying cognitive form of this representation that is debated. The similarity of their views from the human factors perspective is conveyed in this quote from Johnson-Laird where he states that mental models:

> appear to be equally plausible candidates for representing the large-scale structure of discourse — the skeletal framework of events that corresponds to the 'plot of the narrative', the 'argument' of a non-fiction work and so on. Kintsch and van Dijk's proposal that there are macrorules for constructing high-level representations could apply *mutatis mutandis* to mental models. (p. 381)

In other words, the issue is not if, or even how, readers acquire a structural representation of texts they read (these are accepted as givens) but what form such structures take: propositions or mental models?[2] This is not an issue of direct concern to the designer of hypertexts, what is of importance is the provision and support of document structures that aid accurate structural representations (of whatever form) in the reader's mind.

Applying global schemata of documents
At a more global level Dillon (1991b) tested readers' ability to impose structure on randomly presented paragraphs and sentences of text. In the first of two experiments, subjects were given a selection of paragraphs from academic journal articles and asked to organise them into one article as fast as they could. To avoid referential continuity, every second paragraph was removed. In one condition headings were provided, in the other they were absent. The results indicated that readers had little difficulty piecing the article together into gross categories of Introduction, Method, Results and Discussion (over 80% accuracy at this level) but had difficulties distinguishing the precise order at the within-section level. When provided with headings, subjects formed the same major categories but were less accurate in placing second level headings in the correct section. This suggests that experienced journal readers are capable of distinguishing isolated paragraphs of text according to their likely location within a

---

2 van Dijk and Kintsch (1983) addressed some of Johnson-Laird's criticisms by incorporating a "situation model" of the text into their theory. This is a mental representation of the significance of the text in terms of its subject matter and the central figures/elements under discussion which facilitates the application of contextual knowledge stored in long-term memory (a major weakness of their original proposition based theory). However, they still retain the three levels of text structure (micro, macro and super) as the basic elements of their theory of comprehension, giving the situation model a relatively minor role.

complete article with respect to the major categories. Interestingly this could be done without resorting to reading every word or attempting to understand the subject matter of the paper.[3]

In the second study, subjects read a selection of paragraphs from two articles on both paper and screen and had to place each one in the general section to which they thought it belonged (Introduction, Method, Results or Discussion). Again subjects showed a high degree of accuracy (over 80%) with the only advantage to paper being speed (subjects were significantly faster at the 5% level in the paper condition) which is probably explicable in terms of image quality variables and manipulation differences. Taken together, these results suggest that readers do have a model of the typical journal article that allows them to gauge accurately where certain information is located. This model does not seem to be affected by presentation medium.

In this way the schema (superstructure) constitutes a set of expectancies about a text's usual contents and how they are grouped and positioned relative to each other. Obviously, in advance of actually reading the text we cannot have much insight into anything more specific than this, but the generality of organisation within the multitude of texts we read in everyday life affords stability and orientation in what is otherwise a complex information environment.

Cognitive maps of document spaces: instantiating the global schema

If picking up a new book can be compared to a stranger entering a new town (i.e. we know what each is like on the basis of previous experience and have expectancies of what we will find) how do we proceed to develop our map of the information space?

To use the analogy of the navigation in physical space we would expect that generic structures such as indices, contents, chapter headings and summaries can be seen as landmarks that provide readers with information on where they are in a text, just as signposts, buildings and street names aid navigation in physical environments. Thus when initially reading a text we might notice that there are numerous figures and diagrams in certain sections, none in others, or that a very important point or detail is raised in a section containing a table of numerical values. In fact, readers often claim to experience such a sense of knowing where an item of information occurred in the body of the text even if they cannot recall that item precisely and there is some empirical evidence to suggest that this is in fact the case.

Rothkopf (1971) carried out an experiment to test whether such occurrences had a basis in reality rather than resulting from popular myth supported by chance success. He asked people to read a 12-page extract from a book with the intention of answering questions on content afterwards. What subjects did not realise was that they would be asked to recall the

---

[3] Subjects were asked to note down what they thought each article was about after each condition but most had only vague notions based on keywords and phrases observed, even though the articles were in their general area of expertise.

location of information in the text in terms of its occurrence both within the page (divided into eighths) and the complete text (divided into quarters). The results showed that incidental memory for locations within any page and within the text as a whole were more accurate than chance, i.e. people could remember location information even though they were not asked to. There was also a positive correlation between location of information at the within-page level and accuracy of question answering.

There have been several follow-up studies by Rothkopf and by other investigators into this phenomenon. Zechmeister and McKillip (1972) had subjects read eight pages of text typed into blocks with four blocks per page. Subjects were asked to read the text before being tested on it. The test consisted of fill-in-the-blank questions, confidence ratings on their answers and location of the answer on the page. Again, an effect for knowledge of location was observed which was correlated to accuracy of answers, suggesting that memory for location and for content are independent attributes of memory that can be linked for mnemonic purposes. Interestingly no interaction of memory for location and confidence in answer was found. Further work by Zechmeister *et al.* (1975) and by Lovelace and Southall (1983) confirm the view that memory for spatial location within in body of text is reliable even if it is generally limited. Simpson (1990) has replicated this for electronic documents.

In the paper domain at least, the analogy with navigation in a physical environment is of limited applicability beyond the level of landmark knowledge. Given the fact that the information space is instantly accessible to the reader (i.e. she can open a text at any point) the necessity for route knowledge, for example, is lessened (if not eliminated). To get from point A to point B in a text is not dependent on taking the correct course in the same way that it is in a physical three-dimensional environment. The reader can jump ahead (or back), guess, use the index or contents or just page serially through. Readers rarely rely on just one route or get confused if they have to start from a different point in the text to go to the desired location, as would be the case if route knowledge was a formal stage in their development of navigational knowledge for texts. Once you know the page number of an item you can get there as you like. Making an error is not as costly as it is in the physical world either in terms of time or effort. Furthermore, few texts are used in such a way as to require that level or type of knowledge.

One notable exception to this might be the knowledge involved in navigating texts such as software manuals or encyclopædias which can consist of highly structured information chunks that are inter-referenced. If for example a procedure for performing a task references another part of the text it is conceivable that a reader may only be able to locate the referenced material by finding the section that references it first (perhaps because the index is poor or she cannot remember what it is called). In this instance one could interpret the navigation knowledge as being a form of route knowledge. However, such knowledge is presumably rare except where it is specifically designed into a document as a means of aiding navigation along a trouble-shooting path.

A similar case can be made with respect to survey knowledge. While it seems likely that readers experienced with a certain text can mentally envisage where information is in the body of the text, what cross-references are relevant to their purpose and so forth, we must be careful that we are still talking of navigation and not changing the level of discourse to how the argument is developed in the text or the ordering in which points are made. Without doubt, such knowledge exists, but often it is not purely navigational knowledge but an instantiation of several schemata such as domain knowledge of the subject matter, interpretation of the author's argument, and a sense of how this knowledge is organised that come into play now. This is not to say that readers cannot possess survey type knowledge of a text's contents, rather it is to highlight the limitations of directly mapping concepts from one domain to another on the basis of terminology alone. Just because we use the term navigation in both situations does not mean that they are identical activities with similar patterns of development. The simple differences in applying findings from a three-dimensional world (with visual, olfactory, auditory and powerful tactile stimuli) to a two-dimensional text (with visual and limited tactile stimuli only) and the varying purposes to which such knowledge is put in either domain are bound to have a limiting effect.

It might be that rather than route and survey knowledge, a reader develops a more elaborated analogue model of the text based on the skeletal framework of landmark knowledge outlined earlier. Thus, as familiarity with the text grows, the reader becomes more familiar with the various landmarks in the text and their inter-relationships. In effect the reader builds a representation of the text similar to the survey knowledge of physical environments without any intermediary route knowledge but in a form that is directly representative of the text rather than physical domain. This is an interesting empirical question and one that is far from being answered by current knowledge of the process of reading.

NAVIGATION IN ELECTRONIC SPACE

Schemata and models

The concept of a schema for an electronic information space is less clear-cut than for physical environments or paper documents. As we have stated elsewhere (see e.g., McKnight, Dillon and Richardson, 1991) computing technology's short history is one of the reasons for this but it is also the case that the medium's underlying structures do not have equivalent transparency. With paper, once the basic *modus operandi* of reading is acquired (e.g., page-turning, footnote identification, index usage and so forth) it retains utility for other texts produced by other publishers, other authors and for other domains. With computers, manipulation of information can differ from application to application within the same computer, from computer to computer and from this year's to last year's model. Thus using electronic information is often likely to involve the employment of schemata for systems in general (i.e. how to operate them) in a way that is not essential for paper-based information.

The qualitative differences between the schemata for paper and electronic documents can easily be appreciated by considering what you can tell about either at first glance. We have outlined the information available to paper text users in the section on paper schemata above. When we open a hypertext document, however, we do not have the same amount of information available to us. We are likely to be faced with a welcoming screen which might give us a rough idea of the contents (i.e. subject matter) and information about the authors/developers of the document but little else. It is two-dimensional, gives no indication of size, quality of contents, age (unless explicitly stated) or how frequently it has been used (i.e. there is no dust or signs of wear and tear on it such as grubby finger-marks or underlines and scribbled comments). At the electronic document level, there is usually no way of telling even the relative size without performing some 'query operation'. Such a query operation will usually return a size in kilobytes and will therefore convey little meaning to the average reader.

Performing the hypertext equivalent of opening up the text or turning the page offers no assurance that expectations will be met since many hypertext documents offer unique structures (intentionally or otherwise). At their current stage of development it is likely that users/readers familiar with hypertext will have a schema that includes such attributes as linked nodes of information, non-serial structures, and perhaps, potential navigational difficulties! The manipulation facilities and access mechanisms available in hypertext will probably occupy a more prominent rôle in their schema for hypertext documents than they will for readers' schemata of paper texts since they differ from application to application. As yet, empirical evidence for such schemata is lacking.

The fact that hypertext offers authors the chance to create numerous structures out of the same information is a further source of difficulty for users or readers. Since schemata are generic abstractions representing typicality in entities or events, the increased variance of hypertext implies that any similarities that are perceived must be at a higher level or must be more numerous than the schemata that exist for paper texts.

It seems therefore that users' schemata of hypertext environments are likely to be 'informationally leaner' than those for paper documents. This is attributable to the recent emergence of electronic documents and comparative lack of experience interacting with them as opposed to paper texts for even the most dedicated users. The current lack of standards in the electronic domain compared to the rather traditional structures of many paper documents is a further problem for schema development.

Acquiring a cognitive map of the electronic space

The roots of navigation problems in electronic space lie in the literature on users interacting with non-hypertext databases and documents as well as with menu-driven interfaces where it has been repeatedly shown that when users make an incorrect selection at a deep level they tend to return to the start rather than the menu at which they erred and that the actual-to-minimum ratio for screens of information accessed in a successful search is 2:1 (Lee *et al.*, 1984).

Research by Snowberry, Parkinson and Sisson (1985) indicates that the main source of difficulty in menu navigation is the relatively weak associations users have between category descriptors at the highest level of menu and the desired information at the lower. This is a fault of design where little attempt is made to identify the user's conceptualisation of the information space. Significantly enough, Lee *et al.*, (1984) discovered considerable variation among experts in terms of what they believe constitutes a 'good' or well-organised menu.

In terms of the model of navigational knowledge described above we should not be surprised by such findings. They seem to be classic manifestations of behaviour based on limited knowledge. For example, returning to the start upon making an error at a deep level in the menu suggests the absence of survey-type knowledge and a strong reliance on landmarks (e.g., the start screen) to guide navigation. It also lends support to the argument about route knowledge that it becomes useless once a wrong turn is made. Making 'journeys' twice as long as necessary is a further example of the type of behaviour expected from people lacking a mental map of an environment and relying on landmark and route knowledge only to find their way.

Jones and Dumais (1986) empirically tested spatial memory over symbolic memory for application in the electronic domain, citing the work of Rothkopf and others as indicators that such memory might be important. In a series of three experiments subjects simulated filing and retrieval operations using name, location or a combination of both stimuli as cues. Like the preceding work on texts they found that memory for location is above chance but modest compared to memory for names and concluded that it may be of limited utility for object reference in the electronic domain.

Therefore, we know that navigational difficulties exist where users need to make decisions about location in an electronic information space. There seems to be some evidence that the first stage of knowledge about navigation is of the landmark variety and that the organising principles on which the information structure is built are important. We now turn to the more specific evidence for hypertext.

Acquiring a cognitive map of a hypertext document

McKnight, Dillon and Richardson (1990) found that subjects reading hypertext spent significantly greater proportions of time in the index/contents sections of documents than readers using paper or word processor files, indicating a style of interaction based on jumping into parts of the text and returning to base for further guidance — a seemingly sub-optimal style for hypertext — and concluded from this that effective navigation was difficult for non-experienced users of a hypertext document.

Once more this is a classic example of using landmarks in the information space as guidance. Subjects in the linear conditions (paper and word processor versions) seemed much happier to browse through the document to find information, highlighting their confidence and familiarity with the structure presented to them. Similar support for the notion of landmarks as a first level of navigational knowledge development are provided by several of studies which have required subjects to draw or form maps of the information space after exposure to it (e.g., Simpson and McKnight, 1990). Typically, subjects can group certain sections together but often have no idea where other parts go or what they are connected to.

Unfortunately it is difficult to chart the development of navigational knowledge beyond this point. Detailed studies of users interacting with hypertext systems beyond single experimental tasks and gaining mastery over a hypertext document are thin on the ground. Edwards and Hardman (1989) claim that they found evidence for the development of survey-type navigational knowledge in users exposed to a strictly hierarchical database of 50 screens for a single experimental session lasting, on average, less than 20 minutes. Unfortunately the data are not reported in sufficient detail to critically assess such a claim but it is possible that given the document's highly organised structure, comparatively small size and the familiarity of the subject area (leisure facilities in Edinburgh), such knowledge might have been observed. Obviously this is an area that needs further empirical work.

While it is clear that empirical work on hypertext is limited, numerous designers and researchers have considered the navigation issues in less experimental ways, often without concerning themselves with the development of mental representations of the information space. In the following section we discuss the design of suitable maps, browsers and landmarks for users to aid navigation.

Providing navigational information: browsers, maps and structural cues
A graphical browser is a stylised representation of the structure of the database aimed at providing the user with an easy-to-understand map of what information is located where. According to Conklin (1987) graphical browsers are a feature of a "somewhat idealized hypertext system", recognising that not all existing systems utilise browsers but suggesting that they are desirable. The idea behind a browser is that the document can be represented graphically in terms of the nodes of information and the links between them, and in some instances, that selecting a node in the browser would cause its information to be displayed.

It is not difficult to see why this might be useful. Like a map of a physical environment, it shows the user what the overall information space is like, how it is linked together and consequently offers a means of moving from one information node to another. Indeed Monk, Walsh and Dix (1988) have shown that even a static, non-interactive graphical representation is useful. However, for richly interconnected material or documents of a reasonable size and complexity, it is not possible to include everything in a single browser without the problem of presenting 'visual spaghetti' to the user. In such cases it is necessary to represent the structure in terms of levels of browsers, and at this point there is a danger that the user gets lost in the navigational support system!

Some simple variations in the form of maps or browsers have been investigated empirically. In a non-hypertext environment Billingsley (1982) had subjects select information from a database aided by an alphabetical list of selection numbers, a map of the database structure or no aid. The map proved superior, the no aid group performing worst.

In the hypertext domain a number of studies by Simpson (1989) have experimentally manipulated several variables related to structural cues and position indicators. She had subjects perform a series of tasks on articles about houseplants and herbs. In one experiment she found that a hierarchical contents list was superior to an alphabetic index and concluded that users are able to use cues from the structural representation to form maps of the document. In a second study she reported that users provided with a graphical contents list showing the relationship between various parts of the text performed better than users who only had access to a textual list. Making the contents lists interactive (i.e. selectable by pointing) also increased navigational efficiency.

Manipulating 'last card seen' markers produced mixed results. It might be expected that such a cue would be advantageous to all users but Simpson reported that this cue seemed of benefit only during initial familiarisation periods and for users of non-interactive contents lists. Further experiments revealed that giving users a record of the items they had seen aided navigation, much as would be expected from the literature on physical navigation which assumes that knowledge of current position is built on knowledge of how you arrived there (Canter, 1984). In general, Simpson found that as accuracy of performance increased so did subjects' ability to construct accurate post-task maps of the information space using cards.

Such work is important to designers of hypertext systems. It represents a useful series of investigations into how 'contents pages' for hypertext documents should be designed. Admittedly, it concerned limited tasks in a small information space but such studies are building blocks for a fuller understanding of the important issues in designing hypertext systems. As always, more research needs to be done.

Several writers have suggested novel navigational tools for use in hypertext. However, such tools are rarely, if ever, evaluated but thrown into the designer's tool-box for future possible use. For example, Utting and Yankelovich (1989) provide a good review of various systems and a description of the rationale behind the "Web View" navigation aid but all is done in terms of a hypothetical scenario and there is no serious attempt at evaluation. Gloor (1991) offers us the "Cybermap", a form of hierarchical overview system constructed using automatic indexing and clustering techniques. The Cybermap has some potentially useful features such as dynamic links based on user profile and reading history. However, the algorithm used to generate the higher levels of the map (termed "hyperdrawers") imposes the restriction that all hyperdrawers should contain approximately the same number of nodes which seems extremely unrealistic and needs empirical justification before it can seriously be advocated as a design target.

Lai and Manber (1991) offer a means of "flying" through hypertext, a technique analogous to flipping the pages of a book. They stress that this is intended as an additional tool rather than as a replacement for other navigation or manipulation techniques. However, like the Cybermap, until flying is subjected to user evaluation its real usefulness cannot be known. Methods of navigation in a speech–only application have even been proposed (e.g., Arons, 1991) but such papers are probably most useful for the questions they raise rather than the answers they provide.

Navigating the semantic space
One aspect of the whole navigation issue that often appears overlooked in the hypertext literature is that of the semantic space of a text or electronic document. In other words, to what extent does a user or reader need to find his way about the argument that an author creates as opposed to, or distinct from, navigating through the structure of the information?

It is probably impossible to untangle these aspects completely. We noted earlier, in the section on readers' memory for spatial location on pages, that there was a correlation between memory for location and comprehension. This is attributed to the fact that they are independent aspects of memory which are capable of being linked for mnemonic purposes. In other words, memories may consist of a constellation of attributes in which the recall of any one attribute is facilitated by the recall of others.

One complication is that while we can easily compare how near ideas are in terms of location in a structure, i.e. how many links exist between two nodes or the number of selections/button presses need to be made to access node Z from node A, we cannot offer a similar measure of semantic distance. The extent to which two ideas are related may seem intuitively easy to assess but is unlikely to have a broadly agreed quantifiable metric (see e.g., the work of Osgood, Suci and Tannenbaum, 1957 and Kelly, 1955).

Ultimately, we believe the idea of directly navigating semantic space has to be spurious. Semantic space is an abstract psycholinguistic concept which cannot be directly observed, only represented by way of alternative instantiations. By definition, semantic space is n-dimensional and practically unbounded. In order to visualise the semantic space it needs to be given physical representation and in so doing, it becomes at most three-dimensional (though more often two-dimensional) and physically bounded. In this form it is easy to see how concepts such as navigation appear relevant and thus we may talk of moving through semantic space in a manner equivalent to navigating physical environments.

In effect we cannot navigate semantic space, at least not in the way we navigate physical environments, we can only navigate the physical instantiations that we develop of the semantic space. In this case, it is meaningful to utilise the concept of navigation in the manner outlined above (with all the inherent limitations) but we must be clear that here we are not navigating through, or on the basis of, semantics. Rather, we are imposing a physical structure on the semantics and expecting people to employ cues for distance, size and form in a manner based on physics that can have an effect on exposure to issues at the level of semantics.

Thus, any presentation medium offers its own physical limitations on the representations available and authors can impose further on these to provide an instantiation of semantic space in the form of an article or document. In navigating around the document the reader is exposed to the medium-constrained physical manifestation of the author's semantic space. The reader can never demonstrate absolute grasp of or conformity to the author's semantics. At best, a reader can replicate or demonstrate skill in constructing similar physical representations of that semantic space and it is this ability that is regularly tested in education, training and learning scenarios.

Perhaps to all intents and purposes such a distinction is unnecessarily fine, but it is important to avoid falling into the trap of viewing the structure of arguments and ideas as equivalent to their physical manifestation in the presentation medium. This is too simplistic. There is a relationship, but it is not so straightforward; and blurring the distinction leads to the false impression that navigation can be meaningfully talked about in semantic terms or that simply offering trails and backtracking facilities helps readers grasp the contents of an argument and thereby automatically improves reader comprehension levels. These are empirical issues and we emphasise again, it is important that such issues are investigated experimentally.

CONCLUSION

Navigation through hypertext documents is an issue worthy of attention from researchers and designers. The psychology of navigation, based as it is on studies of the human information processor interacting with a physical environment, offers some insights into how we acquire relevant information and develop knowledge of our environments, but does not provide a complete set of findings that are directly transferable to the electronic domain.

What is needed are well-controlled experiments which examine the best means of supporting navigation through large and complex information spaces. The field is replete with claims for wonderful interface styles and metaphors without the commensurate evaluation of such claims which is the hallmark of a true user-centred design process.

The issue is clouded by the confusion of terms such as information space and semantic space and the mistaken assumption that a document's physical instantiation through a presentation medium is equivalent to the semantic space an author intended to convey. Clearer definition of terms and an appreciation of the rôle of the medium in the message are not new recommendations, but then hypertext is nothing if not a new vehicle that raises old issues.

REFERENCES

Anderson, J. R. (1980) *Cognitive Psychology and its Implications*. San Francisco: W. H. Freeman.

Arons, B. (1991) Hyperspeech: navigating in speech-only hypermedia. In *Hypertext '91*, Proceedings of the Third ACM Conference on Hypertext. New York: The Association for Computing Machinery. 133–146.

Bartram, D. and Smith, P. (1984) Everyday memory for everyday places. In J. Harris and P. Morris (eds.) *Everyday Memory, Actions and Absentmindedness*. London: Academic Press.

Bernstein, M. (1991) Position statement for Panel on Structure, Navigation and Hypertext: The Status of the Navigation Problem. In *Hypertext '91*, Proceedings of the Third ACM Conference on Hypertext. New York: The Association for Computing Machinery. 365–366.

Billingsley, P. (1982) Navigation through hierarchical menu structures: does it help to have a map? *Proceedings of the Human Factors Society 26th Annual Meeting*. Santa Monica, CA: Human Factors Society. 103–107.

Brewer, W. (1987) Schemas versus mental models in human memory. In I. P. Morris (ed.) *Modelling Cognition*. Chichester: John Wiley and Sons. 187–197.

Brown, P. (1988) Hypertext — the way forward. In J. C. van Vliet (ed.) *Document Manipulation and Typography*. Cambridge: Cambridge University Press. 183–191.

Canter, D. (1984) Wayfinding and signposting: penance or prosthesis? In R. Easterby and H. Zuraga (eds.) *Information Design*. Chichester: Wiley and Sons. 245–264.

Canter, D., Rivers, R. and Storrs, G. (1985) Characterising user navigation through complex data structures. *Behaviour and Information Technology*, 4(2), 93–102.

Cohen, G. (1989) *Memory in the Real World*. London: Lawrence Erlbaum Associates.

Conklin, J. (1987) Hypertext: an introduction and survey. *Computer*, September, 17–41.

van Dijk, T. A. (1980) *Macrostructures*. Hillsdale, NJ: Lawrence Erlbaum Associates.

van Dijk, T. A. and Kintsch, W. (1983) *Strategies of Discourse Comprehension*. London: Academic Press.

Dillon, A. (1991a) Requirements analysis for hypertext applications: the why, what and how approach. *Applied Ergonomics*, 22(4), 458–462.

Dillon A. (1991b) Readers' models of text structures: the case of academic articles. *International Journal of Man-Machine Studies*, 35, 913–925.

Dillon, A. (1992) Reading from paper versus screens: a critical review of the empirical literature. *Ergonomics*: 3rd Special Issue on Cognitive Ergonomics, 35(10), 1297–1326.

Dillon, A., McKnight, C. and Richardson, J. (1990) Navigation in hypertext: a critical review of the concept. In D. Diaper, D. Gilmore, G. Cockton and B. Shackel (eds.) *Human-Computer Interaction: INTERACT '90*. Amsterdam: Elsevier. 587–592.

Dillon, A., Richardson, J. and McKnight, C. (1989) The human factors of journal usage and the design of electronic text. *Interacting with Computers*, 1(2), 183–189.

Downs, R. M. and Stea, D. (1973)(eds.) *Image and Environment: Cognitive Mapping and Spatial Behaviour*. London: Edward Arnold.

Downs, R. M. and Stea, D. (1977) *Maps in Minds: Reflections on Cognitive Mapping*. New York: Harper and Row.

Edwards, D. and Hardman, L. (1989) "Lost in hyperspace": cognitive mapping and navigation in a hypertext environment. In R. McAleese (ed.) *Hypertext: Theory into Practice*. Oxford: Intellect. 105–125.

Elm, W. and Woods, D. (1985) Getting lost: a case study in interface design. *Proceedings of the Human Factors Society 29th Annual Meeting*. Santa Monica, CA: Human Factors Society. 927–931.

Francescato, D. and Mebane, W. (1973) How citizens view two great cities: Milan and Rome. In R. M. Downs and D. Stea (eds.) *Image and Environment: Cognitive Mapping and Spatial Behaviour*. London: Edward Arnold. 131–147.

Garnham, A. (1987) *Mental Models as Representations of Text and Discourse*. Chichester: Ellis Horwood.

Gloor, P.A. (1991) CYBERMAP — yet another way of navigating in hyperspace. In *Hypertext '91*, Proceedings of the Third ACM Conference on Hypertext. New York: The Association for Computing Machinery. 107–121.

Gordon, S., Gustavel, J., Moore, J. and Hankey, J. (1988) The effects of hypertext on reader knowledge representation. *Proceedings of the Human Factors Society 32nd Annual Meeting*. Santa Monica, CA: Human Factors Society. 296–300.

Gould, P. (1973) On mental maps. In R. M. Downs and D. Stea (eds.) *Image and Environment: Cognitive Mapping and Spatial Behaviour*. London: Edward Arnold. 182–220.

Hammond, N. and Allinson, L. (1987) The travel metaphor as design principle and training aid for navigating around complex systems. In D. Diaper and R. Winder (eds.) *People and Computers III*. Cambridge: Cambridge University Press. 75–90.

Hammond, N. and Allinson, L. (1989) Extending hypertext for learning: an investigation of access and guidance tools. In A. Sutcliffe and L. Macaulay (eds.) *People and Computers V*. Cambridge: Cambridge University Press. 293–304.

Hart, R. A. and Moore, G. T. (1973) The development of spatial cognition: a review. In R. M. Downs and D. Stea (eds.) *Image and Environment: Cognitive Mapping and Spatial Behaviour*. London: Edward Arnold. 246–288.

Johnson-Laird, P. (1983) *Mental Models*. Cambridge: Cambridge University Press.

Jones, W. P. and Dumais, S. T. (1986) The spatial metaphor for user interfaces: experimental tests of reference by location versus name. *ACM Transactions on Office Information Systems*, 4(1), 42–63.

Kelly, G. A. (1955) *The Psychology of Personal Constructs*. New York: Norton.

Kintsch, W. and Yarborough, J. (1982) The rôle of rhetorical structure in text comprehension. *Journal of Educational Psychology*, 74, 828–834.

Lai, P. and Manber, U. (1991) Flying through hypertext. In *Hypertext '91*, Proceedings of the Third ACM Conference on Hypertext. New York: The Association for Computing Machinery. 123–132.

Landow, G. (1990) Popular fallacies about hypertext. In D. Jonassen and H. Mandl (eds.) *Designing Hypermedia for Learning*. Berlin: Springer-Verlag. 39–60.

Landow, G. (1991) Position statement for Panel on Structure, Navigation and Hypertext: The Status of the Navigation Problem. In *Hypertext '91*, Proceedings of the Third ACM Conference on Hypertext. New York: The Association for Computing Machinery. 364.

Lee, E., Whalen, T., McEwen, S. and Latrémouille, S. (1984) Optimising the design of menu pages for information retrieval. *Ergonomics*, 27(10), 1051–1069.

Lovelace, E. A. and Southall, S. D. (1983) Memory for words in prose and their locations on the page. *Memory and Cognition*, 11(5), 429–434.

McKnight, C., Dillon, A. and Richardson, J. (1990) A comparison of linear and hypertext formats in information retrieval. In R. McAleese and C. Green (eds.) *Hypertext: State of the Art*. Oxford: Intellect, 10–19.

McKnight, C., Dillon, A. and Richardson, J. (1991) *Hypertext in Context*. Cambridge: Cambridge University Press.

Monk, A., Walsh, P. and Dix, A. (1988) A comparison of hypertext, scrolling, and folding as mechanisms for program browsing. In D. Jones and R. Winder (eds.) *People and Computers IV*. Cambridge: Cambridge University Press, 421-436.

Neisser, U. (1976) *Cognition and Reality*. London: Freeman.

Osgood, C. E., Suci, G. J. and Tannenbaum, P. H. (1957) *The Measurement of Meaning*. Illinois: University of Illinois Press.

Rothkopf, E. Z. (1971) Incidental memory for location of information in text. *Journal of Verbal Learning and Verbal Behavior*, 10, 608–613.

Schank, R. and Abelson, R. (1976) *Scripts, Plans, Goals and Understanding*. Hillsdale, NJ: Lawrence Erlbaum Associates.

Shum, S. (1990) Real and virtual spaces: mapping from spatial cognition to hypertext. *Hypermedia*, 2(2), 133–158.

Simpson, A. (1989) Navigation in hypertext: design issues. Paper presented at *OnLine '89* Conference, London, December.

Simpson, A. (1990) Towards the design of an electronic journal. Unpublished PhD Thesis, Loughborough University of Technology.

Simpson, A. and McKnight, C. (1990) Navigation in hypertext: structural cues and mental maps. In R. McAleese and C. Green (eds.) *Hypertext: State of the Art*. Oxford: Intellect. 73–83.

Snowberry, K., Parkinson, S. and Sisson, N. (1985) Effects of help fields on navigating through hierarchical menu structures. *International Journal of Man-Machine Studies*, 22, 479–491.

Thorndyke, P. and Hayes-Roth, B. (1982) Differences in spatial knowledge acquired from maps and navigation. *Cognitive Psychology*, 14, 560–589.

Tolman, E. C. (1948) Cognitive maps in rats and men. *Psychological Review*, 55, 189–208.

Trigg, R. H. and Suchman, L. A. (1989) Collaborative writing in Notecards. In R. McAleese (ed.) *Hypertext: Theory into Practice*. Oxford: Intellect. 45–61.

Utting, K. and Yankelovich, N. (1989) Context and orientation in hypermedia networks. *ACM Transactions on Information Systems*, 7(1), 58–84.

Wetherell, A. (1979) Short-term memory for verbal and graphic route information. *Proceedings of the Human Factors Society 23rd Annual Meeting*. Santa Monica CA: Human Factors Society.

Wickens, C. (1984) *Engineering Psychology and Human Performance*. Columbus: Charles Merrill.

Zechmeister, E. and McKillip, J. (1972) Recall of place on a page. *Journal of Educational Psychology*, 63, 446–453.

Zechmeister, E., McKillip, J., Pasko, S. and Bespalec, D. (1975) Visual memory for place on the page. *Journal of General Psychology*, 92, 43–52.

Author Index

Subject Index